J. Alicia Dueck

Negotiating Sexual Identities

MASTERS OF PEACE

edited by the

UNESCO Chair for Peace Studies
of the University of Innsbruck / Austria

Volume 6

LIT

J. Alicia Dueck

Negotiating Sexual Identities

Lesbian, Gay, and Queer Perspectives on Being Mennonite

LIT

This publication has been founded with support from the Vice-Rector for Research of the University of Innsbruck, Prof. Dr. Dr. h.c. mult. Tilmann Märk.

Bibliographic information published by the Deutsche Nationalbibliothek
The Deutsche Nationalbibliothek lists this publication in the Deutsche Nationalbibliografie; detailed bibliographic data are available in the Internet at http://dnb.d-nb.de.

ISBN 978-3-643-90237-5

A catalogue record for this book is available from the British Library

Klosbachstr. 107
CH-8032 Zürich
Tel. +41 (0) 44-251 75 05
Fax +41 (0) 44-251 75 06
e-Mail: zuerich@lit-verlag.ch
http://www.lit-verlag.ch

LIT VERLAG Dr. W. Hopf
Berlin 2012
Fresnostr. 2
D-48159 Münster
Tel. +49 (0) 2 51-620 320
Fax +49 (0) 2 51-23 19 72
e-Mail: lit@lit-verlag.de
http://www.lit-verlag.de

Distribution:
In Germany: LIT Verlag Fresnostr. 2, D-48159 Münster
Tel. +49 (0) 2 51-620 32 22, Fax +49 (0) 2 51-922 60 99, e-mail: vertrieb@lit-verlag.de

In Austria: Medienlogistik Pichler-ÖBZ, e-mail: mlo@medien-logistik.at

In Switzerland: B + M Buch- und Medienvertrieb, e-mail: order@buch-medien.ch

In the UK: Global Book Marketing, e-mail: mo@centralbooks.com

TABLE OF CONTENTS

FOREWORD

Almost twenty years ago now, I was a member of a Mennonite church that chose to become a publicly Affirming congregation within the Supportive Communities Network of the Brethren Mennonite Council for Lesbian, Gay, Bisexual and Transgender Interests. After reaching agreement on that decision, we waited somewhat anxiously for the negative reaction that we expected from our regional and/or national Mennonite conference body. As far as I can recall, nothing happened, or if it did, I was blissfully unaware. Either the conference was already sufficiently if unofficially welcoming itself to avoid any censure, or our tiny unconventional congregational was already too 'fringe' to warrant much attention. Since then, as I've watched other such congregations disciplined and ostracized, my surprise and gratitude regarding the response to my own church has increased. While this particular congregation ceased to exist, for unrelated reasons, a number of years ago, it represented a pioneering voice for its time.

Sometimes the voices at the forefront of a social movement are scarcely heard, because they are so new and unexpected. But the insights and arguments they put forward are inevitably at the foundation of a later groundswell in that same movement. One hopes that the voice of Alicia Dueck is heard loud and clear even as it is forging new ground in the debates on the place of lesbian, gay, bisexual, transgendered, and queer (LGBTQ) individuals in Mennonite churches and communities. In the study that follows – in its initial form Dueck's master's thesis at the University of Innsbruck – we read highly personal stories of lesbian, gay, and queer Mennonite women and men combined with sophisticated theoretical analysis of issues related to individual and collective identity. This book is not easy reading, either intellectually or emotionally, but it is necessary reading.

At one level this is a deeply personal story, as Dueck situates her own life and exploration within the larger questions she is raising. But at another level, and more importantly, this is an incisive and insightful work of scholarship that begins to address the lacuna of academic inquiry on the topic of sexual identity within the denomination of Mennonites, a historic peace church. This book is a polemical challenge to Mennonites and their institutions with regard to their stance(s) towards LGBTQ persons, but it is also a philosophical challenge to the frameworks that Mennonite scholars and others have used to think about identity and community more broadly. Dueck challenges Mennonites to go beyond explanatory platitudes about the issue of sexual orientation and to centre "sex, gender, desire, and sexual practices" as an essential aspect of personal and community notions of 'being Mennonite.'

In order to think about identity in ways that move towards inclusivity, she deconstructs the normative categories of ethnicity and religiosity which themselves are today highly contested but yet exclusive. Being Mennonite is not something static or innate. Rather, Dueck proposes, it represents an identity that is "performatively constituted," that is, something that is performed in response to multiple idealized discourses about identification. As Dueck so aptly points out, identity(ies) and belonging are inextricably related, so that the process of exclusion of course shapes the identity of those both within and without the Mennonite fold. The exclusion of one part of a holistic entity thus defines the identity of the whole. The irony that results is felt keenly by LGBTQ individuals who claim a Mennonite identity as part of who they are, even while their sexuality is contrary to the dominant identity discourse put forward by most Mennonite institutions.

When I was pursuing my own research project on the history of Mennonite women, I became all too aware that, in their history and in their present, Mennonites tended to be reactive rather than proactive on social issues. That is, rather than drawing from their beliefs and history to take leadership on women's rights, Mennonites were pushed sometimes reluctantly to make changes in their churches, families, and communities. Indeed, without the wave of resistance to female subordination prompted by the secular feminist movement of the late twentieth century, it is unlikely that Mennonites on their own initiative would have made efforts to redress the inequality of men and women.

Now, in the twenty-first century, this pattern is regrettably also true regarding the rights of LGBTQ Mennonites. Mennonite church institutions, perhaps more so than individuals and families, remain in a quandary about what to do about LGBTQ persons in their midst, responding with condemnation at one end of the spectrum, to inclusion at the other, and in between a wide range of sometimes confusing and inconsistent positions. Alicia Dueck's voice provides a fresh new perspective to the dialogue and debate and will hopefully lead to a place where "difference is recognized and celebrated and all identifications, including that of LGBTQ Mennonite are recognized." In the end, Dueck calls us to re-think, not just what it means to be LGBTQ in the Mennonite church, but what it means to 'be Mennonite' itself.

Marlene Epp, Conrad Grebel University College
University of Waterloo; Waterloo, Ontario, Canada

ACRONYMS

ACOM-	Area Conference Only Member
AMBS-	Associated Mennonite Biblical Seminary
BC-	British Columbia
BFC3-	Being a Faithful Church 3
BMC-	Brethren Mennonite Council for Lesbian, Gay, Bisexual, and Transgender Interests
CCMBC-	Canadian Conference of Mennonite Brethren Churches
CIDA-	Canadian International Development Agency
CMBC-	Canadian Mennonite Bible College
CMU-	Canadian Mennonite University
EMC-	Evangelical Mennonite Conference
FASD-	Fetal Alcohol Spectrum Disorder
GWNN-	Group With No Name
Harmony-	Harmony: Mennonites for LGBT Inclusion
Hope-	Hope Mennonite Church
IJC-	Initiatives for Just Communities
LGBT-	Lesbian, Gay, Bisexual, Transgender
LGBTQ-	Lesbian, Gay, Bisexual, Transgender, Queer
LGQ-	Lesbian, Gay, Queer
MBCM-	Mennonite Brethren Church of Manitoba
MC British Columbia-	Mennonite Church British Columbia
MC Canada-	Mennonite Church Canada
MC Eastern Canada-	Mennonite Church Eastern Canada
MC Manitoba-	Mennonite Church Manitoba
MCC-	Mennonite Central Committee
MCC Canada-	Mennonite Central Committee Canada
MCC MB-	Mennonite Central Committee Manitoba
MCC USA-	Mennonite Central Committee United States of America
MEDA-	Mennonite Economic Development Associates
PFLAG-	Parents and Friends of Lesbians and Gays
SAMID-	Singleness and Marriedness in Dialogue
SCHS-	Steinbach Christian High School
SCN-	Supportive Communities Network
UW-	University of Winnipeg

PREFACE

This book comes forth out of a Masters thesis which received the Recognition Award for Women's and Gender-Specific Research of the University of Innsbruck, 2011. In the spirit of the program for which this thesis was completed[1], I bring together in the course of this study the personal and the academic, and indeed take my motivation for this research from my own search to understand my sexuality as it intersects with my identity as a Mennonite. I began this research from the particular vantage point of being a white, middle class, Canadian Mennonite woman in the process of examining her sexual identity. Through the course of this work, I also came to adopt the identifications of feminist and bisexual. And while not denying the lenses through which I approach my research, I also attempt to take into consideration the arguments which might challenge this perspective as well as offer it support.

The research and writing of the majority of this book took place over the course of 2010, although it is in reality the product of a much longer process of academic training and personal growth. I am concerned in this book with calling attention to the way in which sexuality and specifically lesbian, gay, bisexual, transgender and queer (LGBTQ) people are discursively framed in the Mennonite community and the way in which these idealizations of sexuality are encountered by lesbian, gay, and queer (LGQ) Mennonites in order to fashion a multiplicity of Mennonite identifications. I draw on the work of Judith Butler (1993, 2004a, 2004b, 2008) and Stuart Hall (1996) to argue for the contingent performativity of identifications and make use of a postmodern peace studies method (Dietrich, 2006) to point to the interconnection of identification with building many peaces in communities. I analyze historical and sociological studies on Mennonites, as well as primary source documents of Mennonite church conferences and community institutions, to understand the creation of the heterosexual marriage norm in the Manitoban Mennonite community. Furthermore, interviews with nine lesbian, gay, and queer Mennonites are presented in order to point to the way in which sexual processes of identification are made possible through the interaction of individuals with

1 This thesis was completed in partial fulfillment of the Masters Program in Peace, Development, Security, and International Conflict Transformation at the University of Innsbruck, Austria.

heteronormative discourses by which idealized codes of being Mennonite are challenged, invested in, and also re-imagined. The book concludes with a passionate call for re-approaching Mennonite studies scholarship, re-thinking the meaning of being Mennonite and of community itself. The second volume of this work, which contains many of the interview transcripts and institutional documents referenced in this book, is available at the website of the UNESCO Chair for Peace Studies at the University of Innsbruck (UNESCO Chair for Peace Studies, 2012).

Between the writing of this original work to its publication, a number of developments within the Mennonite community concerning sexuality have taken place. Significantly, the July 2011 Annual Assembly of Mennonite Church Canada (MC Canada) saw the presentation of a motion[2] from Harmony: Mennonites for LGBT Inclusion (Harmony) which was received with "a great deal of very positive, very encouraging dialogue" (W. Warkentin, 2011). The main aim of the motion was to call attention to the exclusion and hurt encountered by lesbian, gay, bisexual, and transgender (LGBT) people and their families in MC Canada churches and ask for a re-commitment to dialogue on matters concerning sexuality (Bergen, 2011). The motion was referred by Harmony, in discussion with MC Canada representatives, to the care of the General Board, to be incorporated in the Being a Faithful Church 3 (BFC3) process[3] for discerning matters of sexuality (Dyck, 2011a). Currently, in the BFC3 process, MC Canada is using a tool to collect responses from individuals, congregations, and scholars on how the conference should move forward in scriptural discernment as it relates to questions of sexuality. According to the timeline proposed by MC Canada, the entirety of the BFC3

---

2 An initial draft of the motion can be found in Appendix C, Volume 2 of this work at the website for the UNESCO Chair for Peace Studies (UNESCO Chair for Peace Studies, 2012). The motion which was presented at the July 2011 MC Canada Assembly can be found online (Harmony: Mennonites for LGBT Inclusion, 2011a). Those in support of the motion were asked prior to the Assembly to indicate their support by giving their name online at the Harmony website. A total of 243 individual names from across Canada were gathered including those from within and outside of MC Canada churches (Harmony: Mennonites for LGBT Inclusion, 2011b).

3 The BFC process first began in 2009 as a tool to help congregations, area churches, and the conference to discern matters of faith and practice which were causing tension and/or the attention of the church including: 1) unity and diversity in the life of the church; 2) being a peace church; 3) confessing and witnessing to Jesus Christ as Lord in a religiously pluralistic context; 4) human sexuality in the life of the church; 5) ecological concerns from a perspective of faith (Dyck, 2011b). The newest development of Being a Faithful Church is BFC3 which will focus on sexuality. From what it appears, BFC3 is the first BFC process which is going through a concentrated period of discerning foundations of scriptural interpretation.

process will take several years. September 2011-March 2012 is set aside for "discussions of criteria to guide interpretation of scripture", followed by the approval of this criteria at the July 2012 Assembly (Mennonite Church Canada, 2011: 1). From the period of September 2012 to March 2013, MC Canada will begin discussions on sexuality and as soon as July 2013 and as late as July 2014, the church "will speak into some matters of sexuality" (*Ibid.*). The specific topics of sexuality to be addressed include but are not limited to "common law marriage, same-sex relationships, extra marital sex, [and] pornography" (*Ibid.*).

Of course, there are issues with the BFC3 process. For example, the scholars who were specifically asked to feed into the process are biblical scholars from Mennonite educational institutions, none of which allow openly lesbian, gay, bisexual, transgender, and queer (LGBTQ) professors. Furthermore, those who will be compiling the online responses do not include LGBTQ people nor is there currently any plan to look at means of discernment beyond that of scripture. In terms of response, very few congregations and individuals had done so as of February 2011. Although Harmony was invited to feed into the BFC3 process through the online tool, this was without any promise of having any particular weight or role in the discussion. It is also not clear that MC Canada has taken initiative to specifically ask for the participation of other groups who are being looked at in the BFC3 process, such as cohabiting and unmarried couples, or sex positive people (Harmony: Mennonites for LGBT Inclusion, 2012a).

For me, the most fundamental problem with the BFC process is that it starts from the premise of recognizing all of the power and authority of existing statements of MC Canada on sexuality, including the *Confession of Faith* with its exclusionary Article 19 (Mennonite Church Canada, 1995a). The fact that the BFC process documents state, seemingly unproblematically, that the process is not about changing these statements but about treating each other in the church kindly and with love is disconcertingly and insultingly placating. For MC Canada

> What is at stake, fundamentally, is not whether a previous position will be restated (spiritual sufficiency) or whether a new road will be forged (spiritual surprise). What is at stake is our capacity to be the church in fulfilling our ongoing vocation of discerning the kairos of God for our time. In other words, the primary issue is not what exactly we will decide about the challenges that face us; the primary issue is whether we can be the church in doing so. It is very important not to lose sight of this fundamental focus. (Mennonite Church Canada, 2009)

These words grounding the BFC process are eerily reminiscent of the already existent *Agreeing and Disagreeing in Love* (Mennonite Church Canada, 1995c) document, which was coined in the mid-1990s as an attempt to bridge the divide between Mennonite peace convictions and exclusionary language and practices towards its LGBTQ population.

In a similar way, the BFC3 process says it is interested in dialogue but begins this based on current understandings of sexuality which are completely exclusionary. I am inclined to think that rather than bring any real dialogue or change, the BFC3 process will actually help to hide the inherent violence at work in the processes, statements, and practices of MC Canada. It is hardly any consolation to have a discussion using words like 'brothers and sisters in Christ' when the LGBTQ people in and outside the church are still deemed unethical by statements such as the *Resolution on the Issue of Homosexuality* (Mennonite Church Canada, 1998) and Article 19 of the *Confession of Faith* (Mennonite Church Canada, 1995a) which state clearly that homosexuality is a sin.

Also of note in 2011 is the increasing number of articles in the *Canadian Mennonite* on topics of sexuality. For many years, the *Canadian Mennonite* had an informal moratorium on publishing stories on sexuality which was lifted in the last year. *Canadian Mennonite* Editor/Publisher Dick Benner proclaims himself as the "denominational gatekeeper" in an October 31, 2011 editorial, which outlines why it is important for the publication to feature stories on sexuality (Benner, 2011a). Benner explains that it is not out of any urging or even subtle encouragement from MC Canada officials that the Canadian Mennonite is now making space for articles on sexuality. Rather, it is out of commitment to the BFC3 process and need for beginning a dialogue on sexuality which is non-exclusionary (*Ibid.*).

It is not surprising that the majority of the articles which have been published in the last year on the topic of sexuality, and specifically LGBTQ people, have emerged on or after Benner's proclamation. And it is perhaps also not surprising, although very disconcerting, that as of February 2012, none of these articles have been written by LGBTQ people nor have any of them made a specific effort to tell the stories of LGBTQ people. Furthermore, these articles have failed to create a new, non-exclusionary dialogue.

A few articles have provided sympathetic coverage of Harmony's work[4] or have presented the complexity of sexuality in a variety of ways.[5] Other articles have brought together a number of topics related to sexuality in a con-

4 See for example Bergen (2011).
5 See for example Graber Miller (2011).

fusing way, grouping all issues remotely related to the topic together.[6] An example of this are the discussion points offered in the October 31, 2011 issue of the magazine which asked whether "infidelity, too-early sexual engagement, promiscuity, sexual objectification, sexual exploitation and sexual violence are more of a threat to our churches than same-sex sexuality?" (Canadian Mennonite, 2011). It is problematic to me that same-sex desire and attraction would be placed against or somehow in comparison with something that is more about the timing of and choices in partners people make. Furthermore, this comparison is made without any analysis or engagement with the concepts of 'too-early sexual engagement' or 'promiscuity' being explained. It is also disappointing that same-sex desire and practices would be contrasted and compared to sexual violence, which again is quite another thing.

Also of note is a three part series of articles entitled *Letters to My Sister* (Linton and Gladwell, 2011a; 2011b; 2011c), which were published between October and November 2011. The series followed a written exchange between two elderly heterosexual, married Mennonite sisters, Elaine and Joyce on the topic of homosexuality. The sisters have very different opinions on the topic and I would suppose that the purpose of the series was to demonstrate the way that people can disagree and still love each other. This comes through particularly strong in the very last lines of the series where Elaine writes that "the wonderful thing is that we have been able to share deeply and frankly. We have both benefited from each other's insights and knowledge, and we have tested and proved the strength of Christian—and sisterly—love" (Linton and Gladwell, 2011c). Problematically, while the sisters can discuss the topic and be on good terms, many of the statements made by both of them reinforce dangerous assumptions and prejudices that position LGBTQ people as abnormal.

For example, the argumentations provided by each sister fall into predictable dualisms of gay/straight, man/woman and at times the biological determinism of gay identity. Both sisters use language to refer to LGBTQ people, which suggests a significant removal from the realities of LGBTQ people today by using words like 'homosexuality' and 'gays' and without recognition of the diversity of identities. The articles also suggest that youth are sometimes pressured into being gay after experiencing same-sex attraction as an adolescent. The series ends with an agreement between the sisters that holding same sex or gender attraction is somehow an accident of God. Of course

6 See for example Benner (2011b).

the sisters disagree on what a response to such accidents should be, but nevertheless same sex/gender desire is positioned as abnormal (Linton and Gladwell, 2011a, 2011b, 2011c).

Yet another development is the growth of Harmony. The organization now has a clearly defined mission statement and a number of new projects in progress. This includes the development of a 'Blue Book' of questions and answers on LGBTQ topics as a resource for MC Canada churches. They also have a formalized 'Speaker's Bureau' which connects people who are available to give presentations on LGBTQ topics with churches and other Mennonite institutions (Harmony: Mennonites for LGBT Inclusion, 2011c; 2012a). Furthermore, a newly developed Resource List will be launched on the group's website to connect people with other online, print, and media sources about being LGBTQ Mennonite (Harmony: Mennonites for LGBT Inclusion, 2011d).

Other work and developments are also underway. In 2011, Rebekah Enns, a lesbian student at Westgate Mennonite Collegiate in Winnipeg, was honoured with a human rights prize for starting a gay-straight alliance in her school. The Sybil Shack Human Rights Youth Award recognizes young people under 25 who have promoted respect for fundamental freedoms and human rights in Manitoba. The award is given annually on behalf of the Manitoba Association for Rights and Liberties, the Canadian Human Rights Commission, and the Manitoba Human Rights Commission. Enns was the first to receive the award for combating homophobia (Bergen, 2012). Enns's efforts are just one example of the many LGBTQ Mennonites working for change alongside allies. Combined with changes in individual congregations, church conferences, and institutions, the story of sexuality and being Mennonite is clearly always evolving. It is a dynamic topic which necessitates the need for a continual academic and analytic presence in this field of study.

This book offers one of the first academic studies of LGBTQ Mennonites. In the coming years, I hope that many more perspectives are shared in academic and non-academic contexts on this highly under-researched topic of lesbian, gay, bisexual, transgender, and queer Mennonite identities. The discussion on LGBTQ Mennonite identities must begin to happen, particularly in an academic context, for the sake of LGBTQ Mennonites and their families and for the sake of all Mennonites. The silence on LGBTQ Mennonites and sexuality, more generally, is so deafening within academic discourses that by its very non-existence it perpetuates a less than subtle violence upon diverse sexualities and ways of being.

This would not be the book it is without the contributions of each and every interviewee who agreed to take part in this project. I am grateful for the openness and honesty that each person offered. I am particularly thankful to the lesbian, gay, and queer people who shared their personal stories with me. Their enthusiasm for the project and dedication to living authentically inspired me during some rather difficult moments of research and writing.

I want to extend deep and heartfelt thanks to Dr. Josefina Echavarría, whose rigorous questioning and editing throughout the process of writing was central to the fashioning of the style and also the content of this book. Dr. Echavarría's enthusiastic support for this work and my personal well-being was unwavering without which I know this work would not have come to the light of day. I also am grateful to other faculty members of the Innsbruck Peace Studies program, Dr. Norbert Koppensteiner, Prof. Wolfgang Dietrich, and Dr. Andreas Oberprantachter. Dr. Koppensteiner and Prof. Dietrich's classes challenged me to think in ways that opened the spaces I needed to explore sexuality and identity in new perspectives. They also helped me to see the highly interrelated nature of the personal and the academic, encouraging me to explore that about which I was passionate, an opportunity for which I am forever grateful. I also extend my thanks to Dr. Oberprantachter whose feedback as a second reader on my thesis was thorough, thoughtful and has helped to deepen the content of this book. Furthermore, I would like to express gratitude to the University of Innsbruck for awarding my thesis the Recognition Award for Women's and Gender-Specific Research of the University of Innsbruck 2011 which provided the financial support to publish my work in book form.

There are countless other people who have been part of my personal and academic journey whose presence in my life has been an essential part of the process that has cumulated in this publication. I count among these people many friends, family, colleagues, and professors in my past and present. In particular, I extend my thanks to the friends around the world who make up my peace family from the University of Innsbruck or Universitat Jaume I Masters programs in Peace Studies. You have challenged me, loved me, and gave me the courage to begin this process in the first place.

Introduction

1: Author's Perspective

1.1 Shame, Silence & Confusion

For much of my life, I have felt ashamed of my sexuality and confused about what it meant to be woman. Sexuality as I use the term here, refers to a broad range of actions, feelings, and thinking about my body, who I am as a person, sexual practices, sexual desire, and gender. The reasons for the shame, silence, and confusion came out of both the setting within which I was raised and my own thought and behaviour patterns.

My evangelical Mennonite parents and, in fact, no one in my family ever spoke about sexual practices, body parts related to sex or reproduction, or sexual desire during my childhood or teenage years. Outside of a brief talk from my parents right before my grade 12 graduation dinner, in which my parents said that I should not let my boyfriend pressure me into having sexual intercourse, no other conversation on the subject was ever openly breeched. In elementary school, when all of my classmates were taught the family life unit in health class, which covered safe sex, the functioning of the sexual organs, and basic anatomy, I went to the library to do homework. My parents, fearing that the classes would teach me that sex outside of marriage was acceptable,[7] did not allow me to participate; and so during the several years the family life classes were taught weekly, I stayed apart from my classmates. The lack of communication about sexuality itself provided me with a very clear message: the things that the other kids were learning were bad, un-Christian, and topics that should not and could not be discussed.

In the evangelical Baptist church within which I grew up, sexuality was not spoken about outside of the very clear pronouncement that sexual inter-

---

7 I dislike the term 'premarital' sex which clearly implies that all sexual activities which are not taking place inside a heterosexual marriage relationship is pre-marriage or before marriage suggesting that everyone will one day succumb to heterosexual marriage. Further, the terms premarital and extramarital sex, both tie sexual practices to marriage as though the only pure sex, the only sexual practices which do not require a prefix for clarification, occurs in marriage. I therefore use the phrase 'premarital sex' and 'extramarital sex' when specifically referencing authors or discussing documents which make use of the terms.

course was only for monogamous heterosexual marriage. Not surprisingly, my experience with sexuality during my childhood and teenage years reflected the silence, fear of opposite sex relationships, and the relegation of sexuality to the confines of marriage that were articulated around me. Such was my shame and self-consciousness that my sexual attraction to other boys and girls was simply not present during almost the total duration of my childhood and teenage years, or if it was, I did not recognize it. I certainly did not understand the desire to have physical contact with a male through sexual intercourse or even kissing. All in all, I was not conscious of my own body and desires.

Confusion abounded also about what it meant to be a woman. In my conservative church and among my evangelical Mennonite family members, clear religious pronouncements dictated that women were not to be leaders in the church and were to be submissive to their husbands within the home. Cultural and familial examples clearly delineated the task of raising children and taking care of the home to women. Yet, I also saw clear examples of leadership among the women in my life and the subversion of and/or deviation from typical gender norms. Within my immediate family, the message too was mixed. After a Sunday sermon on women's submission to their husbands and silence in the church, my parents would challenge my brothers and sister and I to question those ideas. At the same time, gender stereotypical behaviour and actions were encouraged and fostered.

I noticed myself seeking in my late teenage years and early adulthood to 'act like a female', 'be a woman', and at times felt overwhelmed by expectations to fill a particular gender. I remember the conscious decision I made one day to get a purse, to bake, to crochet, not because I was particularly captivated by fashion or anything about the activities themselves, but rather because I saw these as ways to become a woman. I had often thought of myself as a progressive and religiously liberal person, having balked at the many pronouncements of gender from the church. Yet, frustratingly, I found myself at times feeling very much that I needed to be more female, be more of a woman and behave in ways that I thought would somehow help me secure that all important relationship with someone of the 'opposite sex'.

1.2 Shifting the Story in Adulthood

In light of the religious nature of my upbringing, the story above may sound quite typical and the fact that I have had difficultly speaking about sexuality and exploring what it means to me, is hardly surprising. I fully embraced the notions of my church and family on sexuality throughout many of my early adult years as well. Sexuality, as I understood it at the time, involved sexual intercourse and genital stimulation. My gender, sexual energy, attraction, and my body were not even on the radar screen of my mind until my first sexual relationship at the age of 22.

Suddenly, for the first time in my life, I experienced intense desire and I could feel the response of my body. I became very confused. Where was the line between sex and abstinence? Should I control the sexual energy I felt? The rule of no 'premarital sex' was no longer so straightforward. In Christian books, among Christian friends, and from the sermons on the pulpit, talks on sexuality provided little meaningful guidance for me as a living, breathing and sexual person.

Confusion about sexuality and gender abounded. I distinctly remember one seminar given at Canadian Mennonite University, which I attended for one year on developing sexuality outside of marriage. Sexual attraction, the single Christian facilitator told us, was something dangerous for single women because we could be led into sexual intercourse outside of marriage, particularly with married men. To celebrate our sexuality outside of marriage she suggested that we buy nice underwear for ourselves and take bubble baths with candles. So into my adult life I went armed with the steel certainty of chastity and the tools of lingerie and soap. Some of the churches I attended in the meantime offered sermons about how non-married people were the like brides of Christ and were married to the Church. Instead of sexuality, we could foster deeper relationships with God and provide more service to our church community.

I became increasingly frustrated with this message from the church, which manifested itself primarily in an outrage against the prominence of marriage in the church and within the Mennonite community at large. I felt very deeply that the diversity, depth, and intensity of love in friendships and familial relationships outside of marriage were not appreciated or celebrated. Marriage, which was termed often as the most significant relationship in life next to a person's relation to God, was the focus of most books, sermons, and discussions about human relationships. One of my closest female friends and I formed our own pseudo Non-Governmental Organization called Singleness and Marriedness In Dialogue (SAMID) out of these feelings. The goal of SAMID was to promote dialogue within the church about and between single and married people; to provide a more inclusive environment that better embraced and celebrated all types of relationships. SAMID never left our living room, but it did spark in-depth discussions among my friends and within myself about the value of being single and married in the church.

At the time I did not identify my frustration with marriage in the church as something coming out of the struggle I had with not being allowed to be expressive about my sexuality, my desire for being in intimate relationships with women, and the difficulty I had fitting into the mould of woman as it was presented to me. The strong linkage between sexuality and marriage, not surprisingly, added an additional dimension to what I experienced within Mennonite communities, and I would also argue within evangelical Christianity as I experienced, that marriage is a rite of passage into adulthood and into womanhood.

Throughout my childhood, I was teased when watching a film or movie if someone was kissing on the screen. As the youngest child in the family, I probably sustained the most teasing in this regard as my parents, brothers, or sister would say, 'cover Alicia's eyes'. At the age of 25, a married friend came over for the evening to hang out and watch movies with my parents and I. When the conversation turned to discussing something related to kissing, my mom piped up with a teasing laugh, 'Well, only married people understand that' and she winked at my friend. Surely at 25, I can understand a conversation about kissing. The message, however, was clear to me: I was not married and therefore my maturity level was still no higher than when I was at six and the realm of sexuality was completely off limits. And womanhood too, was somehow also not fully available to me because I did not fit the behavioural code, such as being married to a man. I simultaneously felt as though I did not fit into the white middle class Canadian mould of being a woman either. I did not have experience with penetrative heterosexual intercourse and according to many societal definitions that would still make me a 'virgin', [8] all too commonly portrayed in popular culture as innocent, immature, and not yet fully a woman.

I continue to struggle specifically with being a bisexual, unmarried woman within the communities of which I am a part. I wonder how much of this has

---

8 I do not like the word 'virgin' as it is most commonly used in contemporary Christian and Western discourse; Frequently, the term is used without sensitivity to its culturally conditioned meanings and is a label which is often used in an ambiguous, heteronormative, and sexist way. There are many scholarly works which provide a history of the concept of virginity, its origin, changing meaning through time and the contemporary use of the concept. One excellent discussion of early meanings of virginity can be found in the work of Barbara Walker (1983a). For a more general overview of the history of the concept, please see *Virgin: The Untouched History* (2007) by Hanne Blank. Jessica Valenti also provides a captivating discussion on the contemporary gender biased virginity and purity norms placed upon young women in the United States in her book, *The Purity Myth: How America's Obsession with Virginity is Hurting Young Women* (2009).

to do with hard and fast pronouncements on acceptable behaviour for belonging from my family and community and how much of this is my own perception and a reflection of my struggles surrounding my self-identification. I observe with great indignation, for example, when my grandmothers give different Christmas gifts to my cousins who are married than those who were not. I flare in anger when being 'straight' is assumed and pushed upon me with recommendations from friends and relatives on 'how to get a man' and 'be a good wife'. I make a choice to see and hear that rather than other expressions of affirmation and support that may in fact celebrate my singleness, my personhood, and affirm my adulthood.

What does my sexuality mean for me? Religiously, I would no longer consider myself as someone who holds to a literalist reading of the Bible and therefore, I reject many of the core precepts of Christian or religious Mennonite practice. Tracing back to some of the major causes for my disillusionment with religion, generally, new ideas related to sexuality and gender were a big factor. I now look at my own sexuality, including my body, my desires, and my identification as a woman, as something that is not necessarily fixed or static. Certainly for me, sexuality is not only confined to sexual intercourse, to the dichotomy of male-female, the absolutes of homo- and hetero- sexual. Sexuality is about the way I feel and think about who I am, my body, my gender. It is about how I feel and think about relating to other people, how I desire others. It is about how I think, feel and practice sexual acts. As I read more and more feminist literature, I am beginning to see that the story of my sexuality and the questions arising from that, is not one which is only mine, nor is it a strictly religious one. It is a wider, much more fundamental question of what it means to 'pass', to 'belong', and to 'be'.

1.3 Why Write?

The question that has been forming within my mind as I have gone through the process of thinking about my sexuality has been: why write? Do I do so to convince others of my ideas of my truth? Or rather, do I write to invoke changes within Mennonite scholarship or institutions? Although to a certain extent both of these play into my motivation for writing, in reading philosopher Ladelle McWhorter (2004), I was brought back to the core of my interest. McWhorter traces her own journey through feminist theory towards a realization that philosophy and intellectual endeavours cannot be separated from life lived. In her readings, intellectual discussions, political and social action, she discovered that "the body my culture had handed me was not the only one I might have and that with time and effort my corporeal existence could be otherwise, even radically otherwise" (McWhorter, 2004: 147). It was an otherwise which was not a rejection of false ideology to be replaced by a new truth, but rather an opening to new conceptual possibilities. "This transformation was not something that took place just inside my head," she notes (Ibid.). For in seeing new conceptual possibilities she was able to enact "new behavioural possibilities and then saw new conceptual possibilities in turn" (Ibid.). It is through the process of reading and writing on sexuality that I, like McWhorter, hope to gain new conceptual possibilities and in turn transform my own actions and perceptions.

2: Research Interest and Question

Coming out of these interests in sexuality, identity, singleness, marriage, and religion, my research problem is that there is a silencing and suppression of sexual processes of identification outside of the heterosexual norm of marriage within the Mennonite community. There is a limited space, and sometimes no space at all, to practice other ways of living or discuss that which is outside of this norm. For me, this is problematic because sexuality is an integral aspect of identification and when limited, not recognized or discussed, lesbian, bisexual, or single Mennonites or any other Mennonites who deviate from the heterosexual marriage norm are left, in some respects, on the outside of belonging, and without the opportunity to hold a multiplicity of identifications.

Further, it is problematic for me that Canadian academic scholarship on Mennonites has offered few studies of Mennonites whose gender and sex identifications or desires have varied from the heterosexual marriage normative. In recent years, increasing attention has been given to Mennonite women and also Mennonite single women. Yet, a systematic deconstruction of the category of women itself has not taken place and been applied to notions of Mennonite belonging. Except for a few lone, scattered accounts of a biographical nature, academic publications on Canadian lesbian, gay, bisexual, transgender, and queer Mennonites in particular, are non-existent.[9] This

9 The published studies which exist on sexual processes of identification, which move beyond the heterosexual norm, are of a personal, autobiographical nature. These studies are important in bringing attention to the difficult and alienating experiences of many Mennonites. See Braun (2008), Showalter Kreider (2004; 2003; 2002). One exception is the

study aims to bring attention to this important topic and present opportunities for re-imagining Mennonite identities. Also, I aim to bring a concrete analysis to the way in which sex, gender, desire, and sexual practices are framed within the Mennonite community.

2.2 The Heterosexual Marriage Norm

I have experienced and continue to witness in the Mennonite community that heterosexual marriage is most often the only sanctioned context for sexual desire and gender identification as a man or a woman is always coherent with one's sex. Sex is posited as a biological binary of male/female and a stable, core essential of being. Further, desire comes forth out of a person's sex and gender. Sexual attraction to a person of the same sex or gender is, although perhaps recognized by some as a 'natural' tendency, most frequently something that should not be acted upon lest that person wants to become a 'sinner'. Besides same-sex sexual practices, it is, in fact, the case that all sexual practices are subject to the heterosexual marriage norm, with sexual practices outside of marriage largely condemned or, in the case of solo masturbation, not spoken about at all and implicitly relegated to that which is not sanctioned.

Gender practices vary greatly across different Mennonite groups and circles as does the degree to which critical feminist analysis has been applied to gender and gender practices. In many groups, however, there remains a consistently strong message communicated about the types of behaviours and practices which a man or women should do, which is based on their gender. There are of course some notable exceptions to this norm, which will be addressed further in Chapter 1 and Chapter 2.

When I refer to the heterosexual marriage norm, I am referencing a range of norms that govern sex, gender, desire, and sexual practices. In this case, norm both refers to the 'everyday' sort of violence perpetrated by ideals that govern sexuality as well as the ethical justification surrounding heterosexual marriage, how it is established, and the consequences that flow from not following the ideals (Butler, 2008: xxi). Said in another way, the norms which speak heterosexual marriage as the only space for sexual practices, single celibacy as the desirable way of being sexual outside of marriage, and same-sex sexual practices as wrong, not only perpetrate an everyday structural vio-

work of Pamela Klassen (1998) who examines a lesbian Mennonite wedding in an academic frame.

lence upon people (including those who do and do not follow these norms) through limiting the field of possibilities for being. These norms are also instrumental in framing what it means to be ethical and to live an intelligible life. The heterosexual marriage norm then becomes the normative frame of "what will and will not constitute an intelligible life" and who qualifies as "human" (*Ibid.*: xxiii).

But these norms, while violent, are not exclusively repressive. Foucault confounds the "repressive hypothesis", which characterizes so much of the scholarship and debate surrounding sexuality in *Volume I of The History of Sexuality* (Foucault, 1978: 4-6). To be repressed assumes that there is a basic something that is being repressed. Such a view suggests that the 'problem' is that prohibitions on sexuality and its expressions must be overcome. In this case, sexuality is pre-existent of social relations and emanates outward from bodies. Power in such a conception is what keeps and controls sexuality from the outside and must be overcome. If taking Foucault seriously, however, a different conception of power is reached, one in which power produces resistance and resistance produces power, leading to the conclusion that power has actually leant itself to the explosion of polymorphous sexualities (*Ibid.*: 12). In other words, it is by our very participation in discourses through which we observe, discipline and organize our thoughts and actions that we become our sexuality. And so the distinctions between external social order (society) acting on the autonomous individual person, are not so clear cut (Neitz, 2004: 396).

Foucault does not deny the violence and silencing of sexuality norms, yet argues that the issue which needs attention is not "why are we repressed" but rather, "why is it that we say that we are repressed?" and how might we understand the relationship of power, knowledge, and sexuality in a new way? (Foucault, 1978: 8). The concern is not

> whether one says yes or no to sex, whether one formulates prohibitions or permissions, whether one asserts its importance or denies its effects, or whether one refines the words one uses to define it; but to account for the fact that it is spoken about, to discover who does the speaking, the positions and viewpoints from which they speak, the institutions which prompt people to speak about it and which store and distribute the things that are said. (*Ibid.*: 11)

According to Foucault, the Victorian prudery that suggests sexuality is oppressed is, in fact, an indication that sex has been channelled into specialized confessional discourses (Bernstein, 1997: 19). So drawing on Foucault, my concern is to look at the way in which sex, gender, desire, and sexual practices are spoken about, who speaks, how that relates to the heterosexual marriage norm and how people interact with these discourses to fashion identities.

2.3 Research Question

Flowing out of these interests, I endeavour to ask the following questions:

> ***What sexual processes of identification are made possible within the discourses of the Mennonite community and how do LGBTQ Mennonites interact with these discourses to articulate identities?***

In order to answer these questions, I structure my work to ask a number of related queries. Methodology, definitions of words and concepts used in the course of this work are addressed in Section 3 of this Introduction. In Chapter 1, I examine literature in Mennonite Studies on Mennonite identity and gender to understand the place of this study in the broader context of literature. I also look at gender, queer, and peace studies theory to better position this work. Following this, in Chapter 2, I ask what contemporary idealized discourses of sexuality are found in Mennonite church conferences and institutions. In Chapter 3 and 4, I examine how these idealized discourses of sexuality are invested in, re-signified, and contested by individuals and groups in order to articulate a multiplicity of identifications.

2.3.1 Why Mennonites?

One very obvious question coming out of this research interest is why do I want to focus on Mennonites? Although my familial background is within the Mennonite community, I would no longer consider myself someone who follows many Mennonite-Christian religious teachings as part of my spiritual practice. Nevertheless, I do consider myself to be Mennonite. It is for this reason that I am interested in understanding how it is that I can be Mennonite, how others can be Mennonite, and especially how LGBTQ people can be LGBTQ Mennonite given the fact that being that which is outside of the heterosexual marriage norm challenges some of the very fundamental precepts of what it means to be Mennonite in the first place. As it is possible to become Mennonite and many people un-become Mennonite, the question of how LGBTQ people can be Mennonite finds a central place on any research agenda concerning Mennonite belonging.

Why is it that I choose to identify myself with this grouping? There are many reasons. In part, I do so because almost all of my family and extended family also identifies as Mennonite and I seek to belong alongside. Many of my closest adult friends are also Mennonites –not a difficult accomplishment in a place like Winnipeg, Manitoba. So identifying as Mennonite comes forth out of a need I have to be included, to count as part of something greater than myself and to find a connection with others in my life. Also, it comes out of an unabashedly emotional connection I have to the real and imagined collective past. I find a great deal of pleasure being a part of that shared memory, even at times if I know that it is invented, imagined, and certainly not based on my own concrete experiences in the world. I like laughing loudly at Mennonite jokes and I can sit for hours listening to my parents relating all of the joys, trials and tribulations of their second, third, and fourth cousins –twice removed –during their growing up years in Manitoba's Interlake, the Southern Menno Belt, or the Mexican colony. I enjoy learning how I am related to every Dueck, Friesen, or Plett in the Manitoba phone book and the story of other second cousins who married each other because certainly my parents were not the only ones! Furthermore, I am also Mennonite because I hold strongly to many Mennonite convictions, particularly that of seeking peace and justice in the world. It is for those reasons that I can explain and many more I cannot, which tie me intimately and forever to being Mennonite, an identification which I will never give up.

2.3.2 Who are Mennonites?: A Performative Approach

Mennonites are not only a religious church group, nor are they an ethnic group, but rather a performatively constituted community. It is not without consternation from some religious Mennonites, yet I would argue that religious practice alone does not make a Mennonite; nor does eating borscht, varenyky, and zwieback.[10] Rather, being Mennonite is a process of identification, in which different idealized discourses on the meaning of being Mennonite are performatively constituted and re-signified and reproduced. There is nothing stable about being Mennonite.

The fact that I use the word 'being' suggests a constant creation and becoming. I might say that I am Mennonite and this is true in so far as it is my articulation of the performance of Mennonite. There is no essential, core, unchanging markers that make me a Mennonite. True, I have parents and grandparents who also identify as Mennonite and who trace their ancestry to other people who identified themselves as Mennonite. I enjoy eating Mennonite food, going to visit my grandparent's farm and singing Mennonite German hymns, not because I have a Mennonitism which is embedded

10 Often thought of 'traditional' Mennonite food ways, adopted by some Mennonites in different forms from their Ukrainian, Russian, and German neighbours as Mennonites moved around in Europe between the 16th and 20th centuries.

within the very essence of my soul (assuming such a core exists) but rather because I have learned these ways of being Mennonite.

When I label Mennonites as a performatively constituted community, I am referring to the summation of performatively constituted identifications of individuals. Mennonites are a community in so far as individuals identify themselves as part of that community and performatively constitute that which allows them to be Mennonite. I resist here the popular postmodern Mennonite Studies summation of Mennonites as an ethno-religious community or grouping. Although this framework also points to the constructed nature of identity and community, it gives primacy to ethnic and religious discourses in understanding this construction. Why not label Mennonites as an ethno-sexual or, even better, an ethno-heteronormative community? Or a religious-racial community? Are ethnicity and religion truly the cornerstones to understanding being Mennonite? Is it primarily through interacting with the discourses of ethnicity and religion that one can ensure their 'passing' as Mennonite? I will argue that they are not and that in every pore of being Mennonite are racial, class, ethnic, religious, and in particular gender, desire, and sex considerations.

Certainly, Mennonites have a historical narrative from which the clues are taken as to who are Mennonites. Following that history, Mennonites can trace their roots to 16th century radical Anabaptists emerging during the Reformation in Switzerland. Mennonites sought a more radical following of New Testament Christianity than was practiced in the Reformed Church (Miller, 2000: 275). From these Anabaptists, so named because they believed in adult baptism or the re-baptism of adults, there emerged a number of leaders who espoused values of non-violence; it is from one of the first to advocate non-violence, Menno Simons, that Mennonites got their name. The core beliefs of the first Mennonites included non-violence, simple living, refusal to take oaths, and adult baptism (Bender and Sawatsky, 1989). The Mennonites radically believed that when any group of believers gathered together to study the scripture, pray, and ask for the Holy Spirit to guide them, they could live a life reflecting the will of God (Miller, 2000: 276).

The earliest Mennonite groups existed in Switzerland, Germany, and the Netherlands but because of their controversial stance of non-violence and faith practice, they were often forced to move around in order to find governments sympathetic to their cause. Mennonites migrated from Europe to the United States and Canada throughout the 18th, 19th, and 20th centuries and later to various countries in South and Central America in the 20th century. Today, due to evangelical, peace building, and development efforts, Mennonites can be found throughout the world (Bender and Sawatsky,

1989). In fact, today there are more than one million Mennonites, Brethren in Christ, Amish, and Hutterites around the world (Miller, 2000: 275).

Due to their religious principles, Mennonites were forced or voluntarily undertook migration and formed inwardly focused, isolated communities. Frequent migrations removed Mennonites from a sense of national identity. Also, their "vision of the true church in peace and quiet and to separate themselves from a hostile and evil world" (Bender and Sawatsky, 1989), encouraged them to seek strategies of geographical and ideological withdrawal. Further, the practice of endogamy, or marriage within their own group, assisted in the formation of a distinct set of traditions, beliefs, and life practices (*Ibid.*).

2.4 Relevance of the Research Question

Perhaps as a reader, you are wondering whether it could be argued that the limiting of sexual process of identification occurs in many religions and that it is a matter of holy text interpretation, theology, or religious practice to determine what sexualities are sanctioned. If that is the case, what place does a non-theological research agenda have in understanding sexuality in the Mennonite community? Certainly, there are discussions to be had on the hermeneutics of the Bible. I believe, however, that it would be misleading to step aside from a discussion of sex, gender, and desire to leave the matter as an untouchable realm of inquiry for all but the theologian. As I will argue, I hope convincingly, the relevance of my research extends through, as well as beyond theology to questions of identification and the social and familial consequences, which emerge from the construction of the subject in modern discourse.

For me, the importance of my project lies in redefining the very frame within which discussions of sex, gender, desire, and sexual practices in the Mennonite community are framed. Here, I draw on Mary McClintock Fulkerson (1997) and her application of Judith Butler's critique of gender, sex, and desire to the question of homosexuality[11] in church contexts. McClintock

11 I am not inclined to use the term 'homosexual' or 'homosexuality' as it has associations with somewhat derogatory discourses, implying pathology and of an inherent/stable identity. It is also not a term generally used by gay, lesbian, or bisexual persons to self-identify. Furthermore, the word is ambiguous in its scope and tends to be associated with men. Therefore, I use the term 'homosexual' and 'homosexuality' when I am discussing works which make use of this particular word to describe gay and lesbian persons. The use of the word 'homosexual' is particularly common in Christian church discourses, hence the

Fulkerston convincingly argues that within religion, both 'sides' of the debate on homosexuality –those who argue for the full inclusion of gay and lesbian people into the church and those that would restrict participation and inclusion in some way –focus their argument around an understanding of identity which tends to assume a stable, "fundamental status-determinative reality" about the subjects (McClintock Fulkerston, 1997: 189). This frame, she argues, comes from the scientific discourses of modernity, and insists that people have a sexual identity and preference and that for good or bad it is a fixed and core, fundamental identity.[12] She challenges this position, drawing on Judith Butler's proposition that the sexed body is a discursive construction and that gender and desire, also performatively constituted categories of identification, cannot be automatically linked to the sexed body or a stable, essential identity. Such an approach is imperative, says McClintock Fulkerston, to "challenge heterosexuality as the 'real'" (*Ibid.*: 197).

Therefore, the fundamental issue at stake here both in religious and non-religious contexts is one and the same. The question is not what is right or wrong in terms of biblical hermeneutics or ethical prescriptions, but rather I am interested in re-thinking the frame within which Mennonite sexual identities are conceived; is identity fixed, inherent and status determinative or is it conceived of as a social construction? Are identities performatively constituted as the individual negotiates a relationship to discourses? And of course, what are the implications of framing identity in these different terms? What is ethical and intelligible when conceiving of identities as performative?

---

reason that McClintock Fulkerston addresses directly what assumptions about identity the term homosexuality implies.

12 Melissa Wilcox (2003) provides a detailed overview of literature on lesbian and gay Christians as well as Christian church practices and statements concerning lesbian and gay Christians. She also points to the way in which sexual identities are often framed as stable, inherent, and given from birth by lesbian and gay Christians. Wilcox argues that for lesbian and gay Christians, it is necessary to keep such a frame of understanding identities as inborn and fixed, for political purposes and in order to combat the way in which "most anti-LGBT [Lesbian, Gay, Bisexual, Transgender] Christian groups consider minority sexual or gender identities to be false, brought about through bad influences, misperceptions, poor upbringing, or even the devil" (Wilcox, 2003: 70).

3: METHOD

3.1 Defining Relevant Concepts and Propositions

To begin any discussion of sex one must speak of gender, and any discussion of gender must also speak of sex, desire, and sexual acts. Most commonly, gender and sex are divided into two different concepts –sex being conceived of as the innate, inherent, biological characteristics of people which allow us to conceive of two sexes, male and female and gender being the social construction of roles and behaviour onto that stable sex. Indeed, within medical science a person's sex has been distinguished at the genetic level (sex-specific gene expressions in x and y chromosomes), at the anatomical level (genitals and other sexual characteristics), and/or at the hormonal level (during fetal development, childhood, and puberty) and attempts are made to assign people a sex based on these facts (Fausto-Sterling, 2000b).

Gender then emerges from this sex and correlates with its biological basis. The divide, therefore, between sex and gender becomes a divide between what is real and constructed. As Judith Butler explains:

> In other words, acts and gestures, articulated and enacted desires create the illusion of an interior and organizing gender core, an illusion discursively maintained for the purposes of the regulation of sexuality within the obligatory frame of reproductive heterosexuality. (Butler, 1999a: 417)

Such an approach assumes that "a person is a gender and is one in virtue of his or her sex, psychic sense of self, and various expressions of that psychic self, the most salient being that of sexual desire" (Butler, 2008: 30). In this case, gender is presumed to flow from sex, desire from gender, and sexual practice from desire (*Ibid.*: 31).

Eminent scholar Judith Butler contests the division between gender and sex, arguing that both sex and gender are culturally inscribed, socially constructed, and with a particular history. "Taken to its logical limit, the sex/gender distinction suggests a radical discontinuity between sexed bodies and culturally constructed genders" (Butler, 2008: 9), yet this is simply not the case. Biologist and feminist scholar Anne Fausto-Sterling (2000a) provides a compelling look of the socially constructed nature of sex in her book *Sexing the Body: Gender Politics and the Construction of Sexuality*, demonstrating the culturally imbued nature of sex. She notes that

> The more we look for a simple physical basis for 'sex,' the more it becomes clear that 'sex' is not a pure physical category. What bodily signals and functions we define as male or female come already entangled with our ideas about gender. (Fausto-Sterling, 2000a: 4)

Indeed, Fausto-Sterling points to the diversity of intersex bodies to show the way in which the designations of 'man', 'woman', 'female', and 'male' are not always so straightforward.

With approximately one in every one hundred persons born with one or multiple 'sex identifying' characteristics it is common that

> one can find levels of masculinity and femininity in almost every possible permutation. A chromosomal, hormonal and genetic male (or female) may emerge with a female (or male) gender identity. Or a chromosomal female with male fetal hormones and masculinized genitalia—but with female pubertal hormones—may develop a female gender identity. (Fausto-Sterling, 2000b)

Fausto-Sterling goes on to lay out how hormones, the study of 'men' and 'women's' brains, and the classification of people as 'men' or 'women' itself is fraught with difficulties and imbued with gender at every step of the way. From work such as this, there is a call for the multiplicities of genders.

Judith Butler argues that gender itself needs not be conceived as a binary of either female or male. Even if sexes were unproblematically binary in their constitution, which they are not, it still would not follow that gender should necessarily only remain as two (Butler, 2008: 9). Gender is performative, Butler proposes, in that gestures, enactments, and acts that purport to articulate a particular identity are, in fact, inventions sustained through bodily signifiers and discourse. It follows that these gestures and enactments of gender, which are said to be the manifestation of sex, are actually involved in the very constitution of sex (Butler, 1999a: 417). Performativity is then a practice by which "discourse produces the effects that it names" (Butler, 1999b: 236). To paraphrase Friedrich Nietzsche, in the case of gender, and indeed in the case of all identities, there is 'no doer behind the deed' (Nietzsche, 2003: 26). "Gender is always a doing" and "there is no gender identity behind expressions of gender" (Butler, 2008: 34).

Sex, too is not only a physical description of what a person is but a standard by which all bodies are positioned in order to be culturally intelligible (Butler, 1999b). In other words, "sexual difference… is never simply a function of material differences which are not in some way both marked and formed by discursive practices" (*Ibid.*: 235). She is very clear that in the end it is not possible to reference 'a pure body' which is not at the same time acting in the formation of that same body (*Ibid.*: 240-241). The categories of man and woman, therefore, are not straightforward in their constitution. As scholar Ladelle McWhorter suggests, it might be possible to learn "to think woman not as a category of human being, not as an identity, but as the name for a locus of creative formation" (McWhorter, 2004: 156).

Desire, which I define as the sense of being drawn towards some type of practice, something or someone, is intimately tied to both sex and gender. All of these work together in a performative way in order to constitute the materiality of bodies and sexual differences "in the service of the consolidation of the heterosexual imperative" so that the designation of 'man' is inextricable with expectations of who and what you should desire (Butler, 1993: 2). This does not mean that 'sex' is artificial, certainly not. However, it is the case that the designation of female, male, heterosexual, man or woman is never fully realized yet all interconnected (*Ibid.*: 187-188).

Sexual practices, as I use the term in the course of this book, refers to a range of practices having to do with the sharing or articulation of desire. Whether that be on one's own through thoughts, actions, or words or whether that be with others. Sexual practices may involve the sharing of bodies or fantasies, for example. From my perspective, there is a range of practices which could fall under the label of sexual practices including anything from penetrative sexual intercourse to kissing, hand holding to masturbation, or having fantasies about any of these practices might fall under the category of sexual practices.

I frequently use the word discourse in the course of this book. According to well-known discourse studies scholar, Teun van Dijk, critical discourse studies is "the systematic and explicit analysis of the various structures and strategies of different levels of text and talk" (van Dijk, 2007: 5). Discourse itself is therefore the many layers of text and talk which communicate particular meanings. A discourse analysis is concerned with grammatical structures as well many other layers of understandings embedded in practices of language.

Van Dijk explains that

> There are many more aspects of discourse meaning that need systematic analysis and that cannot simply be reduced to the semantics of words and sentences. For instance, discourse may describe (prescribe, account for, etc.,) events, actions and actors and may do so in many ways: more or less explicitly or implicitly, more or less generally or specifically, more or less precisely or vaguely, with many or few details, as background or as foreground, and so on. (*Ibid.*: 5-6)

Discourse, in that case, is not just descriptive of reality but also a way through which meaning is itself made. Judith Butler writes that "what is constituted in discourse is not fixed in or by discourse, but becomes the condition and occasion for further action" (Butler, 1993: 187). It becomes therefore impossible to act outside of discourses, for the effects of all of this text and talk leads back to itself again so that it is actually quite impossible to understand discourses at all without the use of discourses.

Another way of thinking about the effect of discourses is in terms of performativity. I can think of myself as a woman because I have been told that is what I am and I have thought that and lived as a woman each day. I hold particular physical markers as I do ways of speaking, dressing, and acting which allow me to be seen as a woman by other people and myself. The meaning of being a woman, as practiced in my day to day life is not simply a description or display of some innate essence of womanhood deep within me but rather constituted through the constant repetition of acts and meanings of being woman that I have heard and also created and re-stylized myself. And so I am left with the question of whether the category of woman itself exists apart from my involvement in being women and indeed the involvement of the totality of women and men everywhere throughout history. This does not mean that I can arbitrarily choose not be a woman or a man or to be neither at all. Indeed, the normative power of these discourses is pervasive and they are performative in that they "enact what it names" and have done so throughout history (Butler, 1993: 187).

Within the course of this work, I utilize the term queer to characterize types of scholarship and theoretical approaches. For me, queer is used to speak of people and approaches of scholarship which embrace the pluralities of sexualities, genders, and desires as performances which constitute what it purports to be, ever changing, re-signified, contested, and invested upon in varying degrees and ways over space and time. Identities in a queer perspective are not fixed, stable, or inherent. As feminist theologian Elizabeth Stuart posits, "'Queer' then is not actually another identity alongside lesbian and gay… but a radical destabilizing of identities and resistance to the naturalizing of any identity" (Stuart, 2003: 10). It is a means through which "the specificity, materiality, and variety of sexual practices, along with their diverse meanings for individual lives, can be done better justice" than dividing up all persons and sexual acts into the categories of 'homo' or 'hetero' (Kosofsky Sedgwick, 2008: xvi).

Some people choose to identify as queer, as a sort of non-identity identity or as a way to identify themselves as that which does not fit into the labels of gay, lesbian, or bisexual. Particularly, for young people the term queer has salience as a way to resist the more institutionalized politics signified by gay and lesbian (Butler, 1993: 228). Queer can also be used more generally as a term to encompass a coalition of lesbian, gay, bisexual, and transgender identifying individuals for political purposes.

The terms lesbian, gay, bisexual, and questioning are used as encompassing those peoples who self-identify as such. Although these terms are often associated with people holding sexual attractions to people of certain sexes or genders who engage in particular types of sexual practices, unpacking any one of these terms often reveals a much more complex and nuanced reality. Lesbian denotes women who self-identify as such who are sexually, emotionally, and/or physically attracted to other women. Gay can refer to self-identifying men or women who are attracted to other people of the same sex or gender. Bisexual is again a term used to self-identify as a person who is attracted to both men and women. This is not to say that a lesbian woman will enter into sexual intimacy exclusively with women or will necessarily be attracted only to women; the same goes with the designation of gay. Likewise a bisexual identifying woman may have exclusive sexual intimacy with women and be primarily attracted to women, yet identify as bisexual. Questioning is a term to designate those who, just as the title suggests, are questioning their sexuality or gender and would not identify within the labels of LGBT nor as heterosexual. This questioning may be carried out in a diversity of ways with a variety of gender practices, desires, and sexual practices.

Transgender is used to refer to those who self-identify as such. This term is usually used by people who express, to varying degrees, aspects of a gender commonly associated with a sex which is different than their socially assigned sex at birth, or who see themselves holding multiple genders simultaneously. Transgender people may or may not undergo hormone or surgical therapies to alter some of their sex markers. Transgender people may hold a multiplicity of desires or be exclusively interested in one particular manifestation of gender or sex.

In the course of this work, I use the word homosexual when it is used by an individual holding same sex or gender attraction as a self-descriptor and I also make use of this word when discussing documents which use the term. As the word homosexual has some negative connotations of a pathological bend and is ambiguous as a descriptor, I do not use it as my primary descriptor of persons holding same sex or gender attraction. Heterosexual is a term used in reference to those people who self-identify as such which can refer to holding primary sexual attractions and/or engaging in sexual practices with persons of a different sex or gender.

Sexuality as I use the term in the course of this book refers to the summation of practices, ideas and discourses related to gender, sex, desire, and sexual practices. Also sexuality refers to the way we think about the positions we hold in society in relation to others and also in relation to our own selves. Michel Foucault argues that although sexuality is often seen as a constant, manifested in singular forms throughout history, it is in fact a modern phenomenon to look at oneself as the subject of sexuality and to be able to decipher and recognize for oneself the truth of one's desiring being (Foucault, 1985: 5).

Following Foucault, the rise of the term sexuality is a recent one intimately connected with the rise of other phenomenon including the emergence of new knowledge (reproductive and social variants in behaviour and desire) and sets of norms which changed the way in which individuals assigned meaning to their feelings, sensations, pleasures, conduct, and dreams (Foucault, 1985: 3-4). Foucault's argument is considered to be a postmodern one in that it challenges the transcendental 'Cartesian' subject, which holds a universal, unchanging set of traits, and thereby a sexuality of a similar nature; he argues that 'I' as it is understood in our world and in discourses on sexuality, is a contemporary, historically specific notion (Stanton, 1992: 4). It is in that frame that I launch my own discussion of sexuality in the Mennonite community.

3.2 Courses of Action

I gathered together three main different types of information during the course of research for this book. One type of data comes from secondary academic sources on my topic that provide the theoretical basis from which my primary data is analyzed. In the literature review section of this paper, I lay out further exactly what type of sources I used in this regard. The second type of information I gather together in the book are primary source documents from church conferences and Mennonite institutions, such as church and church conference documents, publications, website postings, and newsletters which address sexuality. I use this information to answer part of the research question of what processes of sexual identification are made possible in the Mennonite community.

Thirdly, I examine the results of nine interviews with lesbian, gay, and queer (LGQ) self-identifying persons on how they can be LGQ Mennonite. These interviews were collected using a digital recording device, transcribed and can be found in Volume Two of this work published on the website of the UNESCO Chair for Peace Studies (UNESCO Chair for Peace Studies, 2012). Major themes present in the narratives were identified and de-codified for integration into the book. The narratives of these LGQ Mennonites can be read as representative of an emerging, and largely marginalized discourse within the Mennonite community. Their experiences, thoughts, and feelings constitute important stories on the processes of identity formation and on the interaction of individual people with wider Mennonite narratives on belonging. In addition to these interviews, I also conducted interviews with representatives of five different Mennonite organizations as well as an interview with two activists for LGBTQ inclusion in the Mennonite community. These interviews were captured using a digital recording device which were synthesized into notes with the transcription of key statements or phrases. Notes were then grouped around themes and integrated into the book. To supplement these interviews, some email correspondences were made between the author and the interview participants, which is clearly indicated in the text references.

All research took place within Winnipeg, Canada between April and December 2010. Adequate secondary materials were available in many of the city's university libraries or for purchase. Church and conference documents were available online or by contacting individual organizations. Interviews were collected from persons residing in Winnipeg or where specified, were conducted via telephone.

3.3 Approach and Frame

In the course of this work, I use the term identification to refer to the way in which people articulate allegiances, affiliations, and a sense of belonging to certain groupings. Shared identity is commonly conceived as based around shared characteristics, homogeneity, and solidarity. However, identification, as I conceive of it here, will draw on Stuart Hall's conception of the term, as the process by which people temporarily attach themselves to subject positions which are constructed by discursive practices. For Hall, the pertinent question is how

> subjects identify (or do not identify) with the 'positions' to which they are summoned; as well as how they fashion, stylize, produce and 'perform' these positions, and why they never do so completely, for once and all time, and some never do, or are in a constant, agonistic process of struggling with, resisting, negotiating and accommodating the normative or regulative rules with which they confront and regulate themselves. (Hall, 1996: 14)

In other words, identification is the process of articulating the negotiation that takes place between the ideals of belonging found in discourses and the reality of life daily lived in which people invest in, resist, twist, and/or perform these ideals.

3.4 Primary Source Considerations

I gather together a number of church and church conference documents as well as those of Mennonite institutions to understand some of the discourses surrounding sexuality and what it means to be Mennonite. There are a large number of different sources that I could have drawn on given the wide number of different Mennonite groupings and Mennonite and Mennonite inspired institutions. Such an investigation, however, is beyond the scope of this inquiry. I therefore surveyed this material choosing to look at three particular Mennonite conferences including Mennonite Church Canada (MC Canada), Canadian Conference of Mennonite Brethren Churches (CCMBC), and the Evangelical Mennonite Conference (EMC) as well as their provincial bodies, if any. In addition, I looked at five Mennonite institutions including Mennonite Central Committee (MCC) and Canadian Mennonite University (CMU), as well as Mennonite Economic Development Associates (MEDA), Mennonite Heritage Village, and Concordia Hospital.

These three particular conferences were chosen because both MC Canada and the CCMBC are the largest Mennonite church conferences in Canada and hold a very prominent role in the Mennonite community. Further, all three hold strong personal connections for me as I attended a Mennonite Brethren Church of Manitoba (MBCM) supported high school, spent my childhood in a choir directed by and filled with MBCM members, attended a joint MC Canada/MBCM rooted university college, and have strong familial connections to the EMC.

In addition to these three church conferences, I also draw on documents and interviews with administrators from five different Mennonite institutions. These institutions were selected for the diversity of the relationships that they hold to Mennonite church conferences and their prominent role in the Mennonite community at large. Some of these organizations are more direct bodies of the church whereas others, although founded by Mennonites, no longer have formal connections to church bodies. Yet another organization is primarily concerned with historical representations of Mennonites. Only two of these organizations, Mennonite Central Committee and Canadian Mennonite University, receive prominence in the course of this book. These institutions were the Mennonite institutions most regularly referred to in the individual interviews I conducted with LGQ Mennonites and an in-depth investigation of all of these organizations was simply beyond the scope of this work.

3.5 Interviews

I conducted interviews with nine persons who self-identify as lesbian, queer, or gay Mennonites in addition to the interviews I conducted with Mennonite organization representatives and two Mennonite activist allies.

PARTICIPANT SELECTION

I contacted those LGBTQ Mennonites that I knew personally and then utilized snowball sampling in order to collect the names of other possible participants.[13] I was also able to spread news about my study through friends and families who were connected to lesbian, gay, bisexual, transgender, queer, or questioning Mennonites as well as through forwarding information about my study to various community and church groups. I wanted as much as possible to have a diversity of perspectives, including the voices of Mennonites active in different denominations of the Mennonite church, as well as Mennonites who were involved in Mennonite institutions and Mennonite ethnic, cultural, or familial groupings. I also sought as much as possible to interview Mennonites who had a range of (un-)involvement or (dis)affiliation with the Mennonite community. In the end, no transgender, bisexual, or questioning Mennonites expressed interest in being part of the study and so the voices of these groups of people are unfortunately not present in my work. Likewise, the majority of people that I interviewed were from a MC Canada background and remained in the Mennonite church and so the voice of atheist, agnostic, and Mennonites of other faiths or religions was limited. Furthermore, only one interview participant self-identified as holding an additional racial or ethnic identity, that of Aboriginal. I received the names and contact details of the allied activists who participated in my study from one of the interview participants.

In order to secure interviews with different Mennonite institutions, I contacted each of the organizations I was interested in gaining information about via email or phone and either corresponded directly with a senior administrator regarding my study or with an administrative assistant who could direct me to the appropriate person with whom I could speak. In the end, I met with senior administration or staff in each of the five organizations all but one whom were Caucasian males and none of whom self-identified as belonging to the LGBTQ community.

13 In snowball sampling, a number of individuals are identified for interviews who fit the relevant group of study and then the researcher asks these subjects for the names of other persons who possess the same attributes as they do (Berg, 2004: 36).

TIMELINE & INTERVIEW COLLECTION APPROACH

I secured the list of possible participants during the month of September and October 2010 and proceeded to conduct interviews during the month of October. I corresponded with all participants over email initially to outline my study, its purpose and objectives, and offered to answer any questions before setting up an interview. At the initial interview with participants, I outlined again the purpose of the study and went through a process of securing written informed consent. This was immediately followed by a semi-structured interview of approximately one hour. Depending on the participant, I asked follow up questions through email correspondence.

Likewise, in my contact with institutions, I outlined my areas of interest and the purpose of my study through email and offered to answer any questions. At our initial meeting, I proceeded to outline again the nature of my study, answer any questions remaining, and secure written informed consent. This was followed immediately by a semi-structured interview averaging one hour in length. Again, additional follow up questions were made via personal email correspondence.

QUESTION SET

The main question that I asked the individual LGQ participants was whether the participant could share with me their story, their life experiences around the theme of being Mennonite, whatever that meant to them. Based on the responses gained, I then asked specific follow up questions or prodded for further expansion. If it was not apparent in their story, I also asked participants to tell me how they heard the Mennonite community speaking about LGBTQ people, if there was a particular moment where they felt challenged or affirmed in being Mennonite, how they be Mennonite in their everyday life, and how they see the way forward for the Mennonite community regarding the inclusion of LGBTQ people.

In each of the interviews conducted with institutions, I was primarily concerned with three main topics including: a) the relationship of the organization with the Mennonite community at large, both in formal and informal structures and practices; b) ideas and values surrounding sexuality in the workplace and in the organization as a whole and how this affects hiring, firing, staff expectations, and general day to day operations; c) any programs or services offered as they relate to sexuality. I asked for further details and information as appropriate during the course of the interview.

A semi-standardized interview was appropriate for the data I wished to acquire. As a semi-standardized interview, I had a number of predetermined questions and topics in mind but there remained significant freedom to digress from the questions at hand (Berg, 2004: 81). In this way I was able to adjust the level of language formality, re-word questions where appropriate, and reorder questions depending on the flow of the interview.

ETHICAL & PHILOSOPHICAL CONSIDERATIONS

Ethically, it was important to get informed, written consent from interview participants. Each potential participant received an informed consent form that contained a written statement on the purpose of the research, potential risks and benefits of their participation, information on what the research would be used for, and noted their option to withdraw from participation or refuse to answer any specific questions at any time. I presented each participant with the choice to request anonymity as well as access to the digital recording of the interview and a final copy of the work.

3.6 Summary

This study comes forth out of a deeply personal journey to understand my sexuality as it intersects with my identity is a Mennonite. From this springs my wider research question of what sexual processes of identification are possible in the discourses of the Mennonite community and furthermore, how do LGBTQ Mennonites interact with these discourses to be Mennonite? In the course of this introduction, I laid out my method to answer these questions and defined key concepts as well as approaches which ground this work.

Beyond these practicalities, is of course, the question of where this study fits into the broader realm of academic literature. This question is explored thoroughly in Chapter 1, which delves into Mennonite Studies, Peace Studies, Queer Studies, Theology, Religious Studies, and History to provide a broad look at many of the discussions currently surrounding identification and Mennonites.

1. State of the Art of the Discussion

Understanding Mennonite studies literature as well as literature on feminism, gender, and peace is important to understand what this work might contribute in various fields of academic scholarship. In the next section, I outline some of the literature in Mennonite Studies that deals with questions of identity, sex, gender, and desire. Further, I look at literature within Peace Studies, as well as feminist and queer theory in order to better understand how sexualities are approached within Mennonite Studies and possibilities for re-reading and re-approaching the study of Mennonites.

1.1 Re-reading the Mennonite Ethno-Religious Designation

As early as 1956, Winfield Fretz wrote on the changing nature of Mennonites stating that "where Mennonites have gone into the cities, the solidarity of the communities has been shattered… [and they] lost their identity as Mennonites" (Fretz quoted in Loewen, 2006: 204). T.D. Regehr's *Mennonites in Canada 1939-1970* (1996), presented an alternative conception of identity, not lost but strengthened, in the process of urbanization where whole communities of Mennonites made major changes and adjustments while still maintaining their own traditions, customs, and identity (2-3). Indeed, the question of Mennonite identity and how it is changing and how it has changed has preoccupied scholars for decades, particularly concerning how it has changed in the latter half of the twentieth century with the advent of widespread urbanization. What is the nature of this identity? Are Mennonites a religious group? An ethnic group? A cultural group? An imagined community? A self-constructed identification? And what in the world does Mennonite identity have to do with sex, gender, and desire?

Historian Marlene Epp notes that the question of what a Mennonite is has received significantly more priority and discussion as the question relates to ethnic, political and theological difference than those questions of gender (and I would add desire and sexual practices) (Epp, 2008: x). Indeed, scholarship abounds on making sense of Mennonite identity in relation to differences in historical national origin (such as Swiss Mennonites or Russian Mennonites), theology (such as Mennonite Brethren, Mennonite Church Canada, and Kleine Gemeinde Mennonites), political involvement or separation from the world, or the splits between urban/rural Mennonites. This type of attention to the theological, ethnic, and political differences within scholarship and in the community itself, however, sets a frame which tends to ignore the gendered and sexed nature of these groupings and also of being Mennonite.

That is why I have chosen to leave aside the popular postmodern conception of Mennonites as an ethno-religious community holding to a symbolic and invented ethnicity and sense of belonging. Rather, I see Mennonites as a performatively constituted community, which is sexed, racialized, ethnicized, religiosized, and gendered. I will expand on this during the course of this chapter. Firstly, however, it is necessary to outline the literature on Mennonites and gender which informs my understanding.

Scholar Katie Funk Wiebe describes important texts in Mennonite history as seeing women "mostly through a low-lying fog" (Funk Wiebe, 1999: 10). Indeed, bringing a gendered analysis to a reading of Mennonite history and identity is a relatively new venture. To date, the most significant cumulative effort to do so in the Canadian context is Marlene Epp's 2008 book, *Mennonite Women in Canada: A History*. Here, Epp crafts together the complex and diverse story of Mennonite women's lives, significantly noting that the story of Mennonite women is not a simple one of oppression under a patriarchal religious culture but that "sources reveal that women were constantly acting in ways that unsettled a clear delineation of their roles" (Epp, 2008: 5). A quick and superficial reading of Mennonite history and religious practice might suggest that women were oppressed within the structures of patriarchal church leadership and private roles within the household. Yet, as Epp notes, Mennonite women cannot so simply be characterized. She argues that:

> in virtually all realms of women's public and private lives, I have found a juxtaposition between ideals of women's nature and behaviour with the exigency that allowed those ideals to be permanently or temporarily bypassed or subverted. (*Ibid.*)

Similarly, Michael Driedger points to the fact that the official standards of Mennonite identity even among 17th century German Mennonites were "contingent, dynamic, emergent, and situational" (Dreidger quoted in Epp, 2008: 5).

Epp and several other Mennonite scholars highlight much of what both Michel Foucault wrote on power and Judith Butler's assertion of identities as performatively constituted. It is from this understanding that I launch my own discussion of Mennonites to argue that Mennonite identity is constituted through contingent processes of negotiation between idealized discourses and the subject's stylized repetition, contestation, and re-signification of these ideal representations. I will show the need to expand this frame within Mennonite Studies to delve deeper into investigations not only of gender, but also on the creation of norms on sex, desire, and sexual practices in Mennonite history and contemporary analysis.

1.2 Examining Gender in Mennonite Studies

For the purposes of my study on LGBTQ Mennonites, the relevance of gender and specifically women in Mennonite scholarship is quite acute. It is, I believe, the key to understanding the place of this study in the broader context of Mennonite Studies because these writings on women are the first steps towards a comprehensive analysis of gender, sex, sexual practices, and desire in the discipline. And so, I will outline here some of the challenges of writing women into Mennonite history, the general trends found in the historical and sociological studies of gender and Mennonites, and briefly examine how academic writings reveal the changing nature of gender norms in Mennonite communities.

As Marlene Epp argues, it is only recently that the historical narrative of Mennonites and the often taken for granted ideas about who Mennonites are, are being read in gendered ways. Epp provides the example of the common adage found in Mennonite scholarship that the Mennonites were the 'quiet in the land'. The passivity, humiliation, and self-denial that characterized the Mennonite worldview according to dominant historical narratives can be unpacked to reveal additional, intensified, and overlapping gender pronouncements which have different implications for the situation of Mennonite women than Mennonite men (Epp, 2008: 11-12).

Indeed, there are a number of scholarly works which point to the compounding and different gendered religious and cultural teachings which shape the lives of women and men. For example, Ruth Derksen Siemens, in her study of domestic Mennonite single women in Vancouver between 1930 and 1960, found a prevailing concern for purity in the proverbs which women stitched on quilts, particularly sexual purity (Derksen Siemens, 1999: 125). A proverb communicated things on several levels so that the declaration to "think on pure things" was understood by these women to mean "Be pure!" and "if something happens –keep silent!" (*Ibid.*: 126). There were certainly some women who had 'troubles', such as unwanted advances from men and Derksen Siemens even implies that rape or sexual abuse may have been a reality for many of these women, yet such abuses were largely not spoken about. Compounded with teachings to strive to live at peace with everyone and submission to authority, these women were socialized into an unquestioning acceptance of parent's, matron's, church's or elder's authority (*Ibid.*).

Carol Penner's (1992) study of Mennonite theology explores that which is at the root of these social practices. She finds that teaching on subject of suffering among Mennonites "has conveyed a message which dis-empowers women suffering from patriarchal violence, destroying their hope and spreading confusion rather than understanding" (Penner, 1992: 99). Penner argues that in these suffering pronouncements no distinction is made between suffering in sickness or in sexual assault. Rather, the "common message in Mennonite thought is often that suffering, all suffering, should simply be endured, just as Jesus endured the cross" (*Ibid.*). Increasingly, in a church context, Penner argues that feminist theology has begun to educate the Mennonite community about the specific suffering of women and provide worship resources that reflect this as well as a re-reading of scripture in which the resurrection is balanced with the crucifixion (*Ibid.*: 107). The work of Epp, Derksen Siemens, and Penner suggests that the teaching of suffering and submission is an important factor in the story of gender and Mennonites and, in addition, may have a continuing role in the very writing of gender history.

Recognizing the gendered nature of key historical paradigms, such as 'the quiet in the land', is one part of uncovering the story of gender. And also, in challenging commonly held understandings of Mennonites, it is possible to ask what the current influence of such thinking is on the very act of studying Mennonites. Kimberely Schmidt and Steven D. Reschly (2000) suggest that the late engagement of Mennonite scholars with gender may be due to the very socialization of women in particular into silence and submission. Since most historians who write on Mennonites are themselves Mennonites, "[i]t is still unclear how the many manifestations of being 'the Quiet in the Land' in Mennonite and Amish culture have affected women historians," write Kimberely Schmidt and Steven D. Reschly, noting that several Mennonite women poets have pointed to their difficulty writing until their father died (Schmidt and Reschly, 2000: 30).

More than ten years prior to this, Marlene Epp (1987) echoed a similar sentiment, suggesting that Mennonite women have shied away from associations with the women's liberation movement or feminism generally because "their conditioned modesty, humility, self-denial and obedience often prevents a wholehearted and assertive embrace of issues that concern injustices which are very personal" (Epp, 1987: 93). Rachel Waltner Goosen (1999) similarly notes that feminist or gender theory is often positioned as oppositional to Mennonite servanthood theology and seen as individualistic in its call for gender equality. The idea that the personal is political is hard to manage, she argues, and "difficult to absorb into a religious ideology that has tended to prize communalism over individualistic expression and counter-cultural witness over and against political power" (Goosen, 1999: 545). I would certainly contend with the notion that feminism or gender theory is necessarily individualistic or culturally mainstream. Nevertheless, it is the perception of feminism in such a light and the deeply entrenched gender pronouncements which no doubt help foster resistance to feminism, gender theory, and queer theory both in scholarly circles and more generally in the Mennonite community. As Pamela Klassen asks, given that Mennonites study Mennonites, "how does it shape how gender, sexuality and race are seen or not seen by scholars, and how theological and ideological issues are treated in comparison to issues of everyday practices –of dressing, of wedding, or lovemaking?" (Klassen, 1998: 240-241).

While these gender norms may keep Mennonites from seeing the pervasiveness of these rules in all facets of life, the difficulty in writing about women in history is also rooted in a lack of training in gender theory for many of the key academics in the field (Schmidt and Reschly, 2000: 30). Furthermore, the insights and accomplishments of women were not often formally recorded as women's work was largely in the private realm and those records that were kept of their lives (diaries, letters, journals) have tended to be housed within private family collections (Epp, 1987: 91-93). Women who are found in the historical record are often framed in terms of their husband and their successes without recognition of women's qualities and attributes (*Ibid.*)

1.2.1 Trends in the Historical Study of Gender & Mennonites

According to Schmidt and Reschley (2000), historical studies on Mennonite women and gender can be largely classified within the frames of compensatory history, contribution history, social history, and gender theory. The very first studies on Mennonite women were largely biographical in nature and fell into the frame of compensatory history in that they were focused on proving the existence of women in the historical record (Schmidt and Reschley, 2000: 31).[14] Following this, there emerged histories which focused on

14 See for example: Cummings (1978) and her collection of biographies of women entitled, *Full Circle: Stories of Mennonite Women*, (Unrau, 2008), and a similar collection originally published in 1986 entitled, *Encircled: Stories of Mennonite Women* (Unrau, 2008); Edited by Swartley and Keener, *She Has Done a Good Thing: Mennonite Women Leaders Tell*

the contribution of women to topics, issues, and themes already counted as important in general historical study (*Ibid.*: 32-33). These accounts tended to focus on institutions and public leadership and therefore did not cover the contributions of women in 'private' spheres of living in which they were greatly and primarily involved (Penner, 1991: 132).

The emergence of social history methods led historians towards a re-thinking of the very base of history and to challenge that which was considered important historical knowledge. Social history's focus on private lives, social relations, and work arrangements meant the use of new sources such as diaries and oral interviews, and also looking at material culture such as quilts or women's dress (Schmidt and Reschley, 2000: 35). Gradually being incorporated into Mennonite Studies was also gender theory which distinguished that sex and gender were different and that gender norms changed over time (*Ibid.*: 36-37). Increasingly, studies of changing gender norms and Mennonite men, also found their way into the historical discussion. Many different scholars make use of gender theory alongside social history methods including, for example, Snyder and Huebert Hecht (1996), Goosen (1992), Derksen Siemens (1999), Loewen (2006; 1993) and Epp (2008). Certainly these categorizations are not exhaustive or exclusive, nor are they used linearly. Still, it is a frame which is useful to understand the general progressions made in Mennonite studies over the years.

Unfortunately, there remains a glaring lack of contemporary academic studies of LGBTQ Mennonites or same-sex desire. There exist autobiographical accounts such as those collected in three different volumes edited by Roberta Schowalter Kreider (2004; 2003; 2002). The first of these books, *From Wounded Hearts* (2003) originally published in 1998 and then re-released in 2003, contains the stories of 31 Mennonites, 1 Catholic, and 1 Jewish LGBTQ persons and 7 stories from parents, families, and friends of LGBTQ people. The second and third books, *Together in Love* (2002), and *The Cost of Truth* (2004), continue along the same path with the former including 26 stories of LGBTQ couples as well as a number of single LGBTQ or allied voices. The latter contains 31 stories of Mennonite and Brethren in Christ LGBTQ persons who have served in church leadership positions or have felt called towards church leadership but gave it up because of strictures against LGBTQ participation in the church.

Their Stories (1999) offers an account of Mennonite women and like Unrau's book offers some critical analysis of the role of patriarchy in the church.

These works make an important contribution in Mennonite studies literature, in that they share the individual and very diverse stories of LGBTQ Mennonites. They challenge the notion that LGBTQ Mennonites do not exist. These stories show how LGBTQ Mennonites can be found in every type of congregation, from evangelical literalist to more social justice and theologically open groupings, to no religious grouping at all. It also shows that many LGBTQ Mennonites are not only deeply thoughtful, spiritual individuals, but also actively involved in and positively contributing to society and the church. I agree that telling stories is very important and there are many more left to tell. Yet, Schowalter Kreider's work includes only a handful of Canadian Mennonite voices and due to its biographical nature, does not frame these stories in a theoretical frame or make suggestions for moving forward the discussion on LGBTQ persons' inclusion into the Mennonite community.

In a similar vein, is Jan Braun's (2008) story published in the *Journal of Mennonite Studies* which provides a compelling personal account which is also interwoven with some discussion of changing pronouncements in Mennonite Church Canada on homosexuality and historical tidbits on the Brethren Mennonite Council for Lesbian, Gay, Bisexual, and Transgender Interests (Braun, 2008). Braun's account is a welcome Canadian, and indeed Winnipeg based contribution to academic Mennonite Studies and is interesting because it shows the deeply interwoven nature of church discourses on sexuality and individual experience.

Pamela Klassen's (1998) article on Mennonite weddings, which profiles a lesbian wedding in the United States, does integrate a personal story into a strong theoretical base and contextualizes this story in relation to the history of social practices. Klassen uses both the story of this lesbian wedding along with stories from two other weddings to demonstrate how weddings can be sites of conflict where individuals interact with idealized pronouncements on behaviour which often do not fit. She shows how this tension is mitigated or intensified through wedding practices but never resolved (Klassen, 1998).

Even studies of heterosexual sexual practices outside of the heterosexual marriage norm have been few and far between. Hans Werner's (2008) study on premarital sex among early Old Colony Manitoba Mennonites certainly provides an intriguing first glance into the multiplicity of sexual practices no doubt found throughout Mennonite history, but yet largely unstudied.[15]

15 Deviating from the norm of sexual relations within marriage, Werner argues that these couples were engaging in a mild form of deviancy, when such acts were followed by

Likewise Leo Driedger's (2000) sociological account of the sexual practices of Canadian Mennonite teens suggests that although norms surrounding sexual practices have loosened, Mennonite 'churched' teens continue to highly value and, by in large, practice norms which confine sexual activities to heterosexual marriage.[16] And so although everyday practices, including those relating to sexual practices, are gaining increasing attention, there remains a particular difficulty in seeing that which is unseen theologically or ideologically.

1.2.2 Where is the History of LGBTQ Mennonites?

As I think about the history of Mennonites, I cannot help but wonder where the stories on the multiplicities of sexualities, genders, and desires are in this great narrative. Where are the stories of institutional interactions with sexuality? The problem with the absence of historical memory in this regard is that, that which is outside the heterosexual marriage norm is often portrayed as something external rather than integral to Mennonite identity in a contemporary and historical setting. Gay Mennonites, queer Mennonites, and anyone else outside of the heterosexual norm are relegated to a solely contemporary context as an addition emerging out of Mennonite interaction with the 'wider, secular world' in the latter half of the 20th century. This is not to say there were (or were not) bisexual or lesbian Mennonites in a historical context. Any documents which might reveal the multiplicities of sexualities held by Mennonites in different periods of times likely do not use the words 'gay' or 'lesbian' and if they allude to anything outside of the heteronormative

---

marriage, the formation of a Mennonite household and contributions to village and church life (Werner, 2008: 144). Werner argues that compared to most other societies, Old Colony Mennonites were quite good at regulating sexuality, with significantly lower rates of premarital conception than other groups (*Ibid.*: 146). Interestingly, Werner notes changes in incidences of premarital sex with migration and with the seasons (*Ibid.*: 155).

16 From a sample of 3,795 'churched' youth from various evangelical Mennonite conferences, Driedger found that most Mennonite youth think God intended marriage to last a lifetime and do not expect marriages to end in divorce, three quarters want to be virgins when they marry and "those who no longer are virgins would like to be" (Driedger, 2000: 152). Driedger also looks to specific beliefs and practices of teens finding that most youth believe holding hands and kissing are acceptable in non-marriage relationships whereas one-third do not approve of French kissing while one-half engaged in it, one-tenth think it is acceptable to fondle breasts with one-third engaged in the practice. While 55 percent of Canadian youth engage in premarital sex, the number is significantly lower among evangelical Mennonite youth with between 8-16 percent engaging in sexual relationships outside of marriage although almost none approve of it in word (*Ibid.*: 157).

frame, it is possible that our understandings of those sexualities may fall inadequately short.[17]

I believe that there is a fundamental need to once again look at Mennonite relationships in a historical context and uncover the multiplicity of desires, of bodies, of gender performances imbedded within women to women and men to men relationships. Adrienne Rich's groundbreaking work, *Compulsory Heterosexuality and Lesbian Experience* (1996), argues that a compulsory heterosexuality has been forcibly and subliminally imposed upon women, which denies the importance of woman to woman relationships. These woman to woman relationships, Rich argues, are fundamentally different from those of man to man relationships due to the unique place and status women hold in society. Rich proposes that female friendship and comradeship should not be separated from the erotic, but rather included into a broadening of what counts as lesbian experience to form a lesbian continuum (Rich, 1996: 136).

Such a conception demands a re-imagining of the erotic in female terms which are not confined to one part of the body but which includes all aspects of existence. If taking such an approach,

> [w]e begin to observe behaviour, both in history and in individual biography, that has hitherto been invisible or misnamed, behaviour which often constitutes, given the limits of the counterforce exerted in a given time and place, radical rebellion. And we can connect these rebellions and the necessity for them with the physical passion of woman for woman which is central to lesbian existence: the erotic sensuality which has been, precisely, the most violently erased fact of female experience. (Rich, 1996: 137-138)

Jyoti Puri (1999), and her examination of women in post-colonial India, highlights the importance of claiming a history of alternative sexualities. It is all too common, she argues, for contemporary discourses in Indian-Hindu and Islamic communities to posit that "since homosexuality did not play a visible role in the Hindu scriptures, the fact that gay and lesbian women and men are staking a claim within the contemporary, post-colonial nation-state" is leading to "the degeneration of tradition" (Puri, 1999: 183). Utilizing a number of scholarly works on the queer history of India, Puri demonstrates

17 Great contention currently exists over how same-sex sexual practices and relationships have been viewed throughout different historical contexts. According to the well-known historian of sexuality, David Halperin, the contemporary labels of LGBTQ were not conceived in the same way in different time periods (Halperin, 2002: 3). Feminists have vociferously critiqued Halperin's work. Please see section 1.3.4 Re-thinking Theology and Religion for a more developed discussion of this question.

the illusionary nature of 'tradition' and a history which is constructed around the binaries of modern versus the ancient, or a liberal past versus the repressive present, for example. Queer historical narratives, she argues, allow for the claim "that queerness is integral, and not external, to Indian and especially Hindu cultural traditions" (*Ibid.*). Similarly, we must not think of LGBTQ Mennonites as a contemporary addition to the story of Mennonites, but an integral and indivisible part of the totality of Mennonite history.

What, for example, would happen then to the way in which women to women relationships were conceived if Mennonite scholars chose to apply Adrienne Rich's (1996) lesbian continuum to a reading of women's relationships with each other? Or what if Judith Butler's (1993; 2008) idea of gender performativity was seriously applied to a reading of Mennonite life practice? I do not doubt that it would become clear that the gender and sexual practices of Mennonites have not been nearly so clear cut as we have been led to believe. Certainly, same-sex eroticism would not only be seen as that which is external to Mennonite lived experience or simply a contemporary anomaly in the long history of the community, but an intricate part of everyday lived practices.

1.2.3 Relation to Broader Trends

Positively, scholars have demonstrated how gender norms among Mennonites are interwoven very intimately with broader regional, national, and international trends. According to Marlene Epp, the story of Mennonite women and gender norms goes in waves. "These waves can generally be compared to historical changes in society at large and are not primarily due to internal factors unique to the Mennonites" (Epp, 1987: 94). Epp notes that it may in fact be the case that "the underside of one cultural group has more in common with the underside of another group than with dominant elements in their own group" (*Ibid.*). She uses this to suggest that the situation of Mennonite women may have more in common with the situation of Jewish Canadian Women or other women than with Mennonite men. To what extent is this even more the case for LGBTQ Mennonites? How are the norms on desire and sexual practices in the Mennonite community tied to broader trends in Canadian and Western society? These are key and important questions which require further scholarship alongside any attempt to study the history of Mennonites and sexuality. Caution, however, should be exercised in that such investigations are not used to further 'other' LGBTQ Mennonites. All too commonly, as I will show in Chapter 2, LGBTQ Mennonites are talked about as though they are the result of an increasing secularization of Mennonites which has the danger of positioning LGBTQ Mennonites as a group which is somehow external to the core of the Mennonite community.

1.2.4 Challenging the Sex/Gender Binary

Certainly, there have emerged works of social history and sociology within Mennonite Studies which incorporate gender theory. And some of this work on the regulation of women's bodies could be read as a preliminary challenge to the male/female sex binary. A prominent scholar at the early forefront of the study of gender and Mennonites, Katie Funk-Wiebe, discusses the regulation of the body in her article, "Me Tarzan, Son of Menno –You Jane, Mennonite Mama" (Funk-Wiebe, 1999). Noting the impact of birth control on gender norms, Funk-Wiebe states "[t]he identity of women as child-bearers was rooted in their anatomy. They migrated long distances big with child. It was their duty. It was their lot in life" (Funk-Wiebe, 1999: 18). With birth control, she argues, the very structures of community life and family changed. Which came first, the increasing urbanization, worldly engagement and education of Mennonites or birth control, is not altogether clear.

The point Funk-Wiebe makes, however, which has also been made by several other Mennonite scholars (Schmidt and Reschley, 2000; Pederson, 2002)., is that Mennonite women have sustained a greater number of norms and regulations on their bodies than Mennonite men. "Long after men had moved in other directions, women were expected to be the social conservators of Mennonite culture, presumably based on Scripture, particularly clothing and hairstyles" (Funk-Wiebe, 1999: 16). Funk-Wiebe notes that

> [b]y their headcoverings, long hair, simple dress styles, worn long after men accepted current hairstyles and dress, Mennonite Janes were expected to reinforce women's traditional role of submission, modesty, and piety. It was important to keep gender hierarchy clear. (*Ibid.*)

Jane Marie Pederson (2002) notes a similar phenomenon. With Mennonite's increasing contact with wider society and changes to the economic livelihood of Mennonites in the latter half of the 20th century, Christian evangelical pronouncements developed an increasing presence in the formation of gender norms.

As cultural localism and separation structurally break down, an evangelical response follows: an aggressive effort to carry 'the essence' or core values and ideals of their ethnic and religious culture into the mainstream. For the 'modern' Anabaptists, 'the essence' of life is grounded in their gender system. The evangelical effort eases the inevitable sense of loss of control, of ambivalence, and of the conflict of values. (Pederson, 2002: 354)

Certainly there are many groups of Mennonites with different belief systems and practices. Some scholars argue that it is neither Mennonites who have assimilated into mainstream North American society nor Old Order Mennonites who sustain the strictest regulations on women's bodies; rather, that it is women within 'transitional' Mennonite groupings, where the community is negotiating between the two extremes, in which women face the harshest parameters on their bodies to sustain social stability (Schmidt and Reschley, 2000).

Although not explicitly explored, these academic works on the body could be said to set the base from which a more developed critique on the gendered nature of biological sex could be made. These authors look at the gendered nature of the biological distinctions attached to women, in the sense that they point to the particular norms and expectations attached to some women because of their ability to bear children. Further, calling attention to the regulation of other physical markers commonly ascribed to women, including long hair and body shapes through the use of head coverings and particular styles of clothing, suggest that there is something very gendered about the sex distinctions given to different bodies.

1.2.5 Sex Determinism and the Erasure of Gender

Although it is true that some scholars are challenging frames which posit sex as a neutral base upon which gender acts, it is also true that sex is viewed by some scholars as determinative and gender itself ceases to exist. On the side of biological determinism is Dr. James Urry, one of the few scholars of Mennonites who is, in fact, not from a Mennonite background. Urry, a graduate of Oxford University, professor at the University of Wellington in New Zealand, and a well respected scholar of Russian Mennonite history, argues that the scholarly concern with gender is a product of modernity and reflective of a glorification of the individual. Gender did not exist, he argues, in the lives of historical agrarian Mennonites. What the historian labels as gender is, in fact, a person doing that which is inherent in their biology. Particular divisions in labour therefore flow 'naturally' from particular inherent biological realities, particularly women's ability to bear children,[18] and Urry ex-

18 Urry asserts that "[g]ender roles are closely tied to the basic biological reality that only women bear children (after of course the minimal and momentary involvement of men). They are also responsible for the early sustenance of dependent infants" (Urry, 1999: 98). He continues, stating that "[w]omen are as capable as men at most physical tasks involved with agricultural production and could be more involved if pregnancy and the demands of

plicitly ignores the possibility of gender and sex distinctions being performatively constituted. This is very clear when he argues, "people are born into existing social systems and worlds of cultural meaning. They do not invent these social systems of cultural meanings" (Urry, 1999: 101).

In short, Urry works to deny or negate the very existence of gender in agrarian Mennonite society, asserting that these historical Mennonites had a different concept of personhood which was based primarily around age distinctions, community or "connectedness", and biologically determined sex. I disagree with Urry quite strongly, not only because I firmly believe in the necessity of looking at the constructed nature of sex and gender, but also because he simply does not substantiate his argument with convincing evidence. Urry looks at the single person as representative of a different and more individualistic way of viewing the self in agrarian Mennonite society. The single person, he argues, was by in large considered childlike when they did not marry,[19] and was disconnected from regular family structures and therefore more able to deviate from their biological purposes and be more individualistic. Single people "could self-define themselves…[and] [i]n many ways they were the only true individuals in the agrarian Mennonite world. Of course ties of kinship still existed but not in a truly connected sense" for "they would not become ancestors which children and grandchildren, would honour and later genealogists would assign them only a minor footnote in their listings" (Urry, 1999: 105).

A number of studies on single Mennonites show that these Mennonites were, in some cases, able to exercise greater freedom in choosing different possibilities for service, work, or living arrangements and therefore challenge gender norms, but these in no way suggest that the kinship ties these people held were any less 'connected' nor meaningful (Klassen, 2008). The fact that

---

infant children did not take first call upon their time" (*Ibid.*). My question is of course, why it is that women are commissioned with devoting their time in this way? How did it come to be that Mennonite women in agrarian society had to sustain such a great number of pregnancies? How was agrarian living an inherently gendered system which required women and men to take on different roles? Were these different roles based around biology alone or was there social factors which made any biological realities the primary focus of organization? What structures could have made it possible for men to take a more active role in the demands of caring for infant children? Why is men's involvement in the creation of children conceptualized as minimal?

19 Urry briefly outlines the story of two bachelor brothers who dressed poorly and kept a dirty house, as an example of this designation of 'childlike' not being without basis. What is missing from Urry's analysis, however, is any mention of whether this type of bachelor behaviour is performative –that is, is it constituted by the very discourses which speak singlepeople as childlike?

deviations from the marriage norm are at the root of the individualistic gendered person according to Urry, reveal how very hidden and deeply imbedded gender was among agrarian Mennonites and its continual hold on Mennonite narratives which posit women's place in the home as that which is 'natural' and biological inevitable.

Of a similar bend is well-known Mennonite sociologist J. Howard Kauffman's (1994) study on Mennonite families. Kauffman, holding a PhD from the University of Chicago and long time professor at the Mennonite Goshen College in Goshen, Indiana, surveys Mennonites to determine how power[20] is distributed in marriages and its effect on the overall self perceived well-being of men and women in 'women directed', 'men directed', or 'equally directed' marriages. Survey results indicate the dominance of patriarchal (men directed) marriages among those surveyed and an overall greater satisfaction of people in such marriages compared with 'women led' marriages (Kauffman, 1994: 522).

Unfortunately, Kauffman provides little meaningful analysis of why satisfaction may differ across different types of relationships but this is perhaps not surprising given that in Kauffman's introduction he calls for a version of equality which does not aim for women to hold as many high power public roles as men as this is neither possible nor desirable; "[b]iology, cultural traditions, and the need for economic efficiency conspire to prevent its full realization" (Kauffman, 1994: 506). He argues that the greater strength of males results in unequal violence towards women and furthermore suggests that

> [t]he fact that childbearing and lactation are exclusively female functions means that certain domestic roles cannot be shared equally. Furthermore, the greater average strength and endurance of the male physique predisposes males to be assigned to heavier tasks associated with the production of food and shelter... This condition may partially explain social inequalities, since yielding to greater physical strength gets translated into greater female yielding... Sexual aggressiveness of males and their physical and cultural drives toward intercourse and impregnation, apparently due in part to hormonal factors, may also translate into greater yieldness on the part of females. (Kauffman, 1994: 504)

Kauffman's suggestion that women's 'yieldness' is natural and innate goes together neatly with his assertion that seeking power is not Christ-like and his call for both men and women in marriages to act as servants to the other

---

20 Power is defined by Kauffman as a linear exercise of control by one over the other, a definition which I will strongly contend with later in this chapter (Kauffman, 1994: 501).

and value equally different, biologically determined roles (Kauffman, 1994: 507). Theoretically, Kauffman's suggestion might sound like a call for equality and sharing. However, given the compounding way in which women are socialized into servanthood and submission, and the fact that certain types of labour are incredibly devalued in our society, this assertion helps to continue the structural and cultural violence inherent in men-women relationships based around biologically predestined roles.

In both of Urry and Kauffman's works, gender ceases to exist because sex is seen as determinative in how people relate, and their roles in families and society. Both fail to recognize the way in which 'tradition', 'efficiency', and 'biology' are used to legitimize a violence by which women and indeed men are controlled and their bodies, practices, and desires are subject to regulation.

1.2.6 Idealized Discourses of Sexuality and Life Practice

I will take neither Urry nor Kauffman's studies as the base from which to understand the way in which sexuality has taken its place in Mennonite history and contemporary life. Although these works are helpful to understand the diversity present in the application of gender analysis to Mennonite history, I will make use of those studies of agrarian and contemporary Mennonites which take the perspective that norms on the family, sex, gender, desire, and sexual practices are contingent, performative, and therefore constantly changing in relation to wider society and the particular individuals who interact with these norms. Several researchers have documented this phenomenon, suggesting that the community norms surrounding gender in particular, do not have absolute priority in dictating behaviors or practices.

Pamela Klassen (1994), outlines the stories of two Mennonite women who immigrated from Russia, asserting that it was not only formal religious norms and pronouncements which shaped the lives of these women. Rather, these women defined themselves in relation to the wider norms of the formal religious communities they joined and also through their own personal relationships with God. Further, Klassen argues that this was not a once given process, but a constantly evolving one (Klassen, 1994: 16).

Some years later, Pamela Klassen built on her earlier work and published an article in the *Mennonite Quarterly Review* on the conflict inherent in weddings as sites of practice in which "ambivalent and contested meanings" were sustained (Klassen, 1999: 225). Using oral history interviews with three different women, Klassen examined a 1962 wedding in a Bergthaler Mennonite church in which 'English' customs were introduced, a 1963 wedding which involved a prior confession to the women's home congregation to confess the sin of premarital sex with her fiancé, and a 1990s wedding of two women (*Ibid.*: 226). Klassen found that these women found ways to negotiate a response to the conflict inherent in weddings.[21] Lillian, who engaged in premarital sex, mitigated the conflict with the church by driving out of the city in which she was living to confess her sin in front of her home church in rural Manitoba, yet "she did not emotionally or intellectually assent to what the church was demanding of her" (*Ibid.*: 235). Further, for the same-sex couple,

> they strove to acknowledge their love before God in a Mennonite way: they were not willing to let go of being Mennonite, of being in relationship with God or of being in relationship with each other. Their tenacity in holding on to their Mennonite identities and their lesbian identities in this public declaration of love have caused both tumult and concord. (*Ibid.*: 235, 237)

The stories show that it is possible to live within conflict, interacting with particular norms in a way which does not demand either/or identities or practices.

Kimberely Schmidt's (2001) examination of the stories of two conservative Mennonite women further reveals the way in which Mennonite women have negotiated their own subject positions continuously in relation to idealized discourses of gender and sex. These women went against church norms and chose to work outside of the farm and home in the 1980s to support their financially strapped farm based incomes. "Although both women verbally supported church teachings on women's submission to male authority and the primacy of farm life in Mennonite beliefs," Schmidt argues, "their work lives reflect personal negotiation with such beliefs." (Schmidt, 2001: 95).

It is not only church institutions which communicated norms, in fact, research suggests that for many Mennonites the primary unit of allegiance in Mennonite communities was the family and networks of kinship ties; and these family units also communicated very clear norms of behavior and life practice (Loewen, 1993: 32).

> The family ordered one's very life: it determined the people with whom one would interact most often and most intensely during the course of life; it influenced the most important decisions in life; it shaped village settlement patterns; it comprised the sphere of influence and power for Mennonite women. (*Ibid.*)

---

21 Klassen identifies four main themes of conflict running through the women's narratives – contesting notions of worldliness, controlling sacred space, regulating sexuality and negotiating family relationships (Klassen, 1999: 226).

Of course, kinship norms were also contested and not always carried out as prescribed. Marlene Epp notes that the disruption to practices of family and kinship in the lives of women refugees, were sought to be normalized upon arrival in Canada. Because the practices of family had changed and become varied as men were killed, imprisoned, or joined in the fighting forces, Epp notes that "[t]he practical, if not ideological, definition of 'family' had become fluid throughout the Soviet period of Mennonite history" so that living units varied and were composed of people holding a variety of kinship relationships (Epp, 2000: 10). As a result,

> the roles that individuals played within their families and how duties and responsibilities were allocated was often in variance with Canadian and Mennonite norms. The way in which refugee families and their host communities attempted to create normative families out of fragmented ones was part of the process of integration. (*Ibid.*: 11).

Epp and Loewen's work is interesting in that it suggests that idealized notions of belonging are not only found in institutional frames, but in familial relationships and that the fulfillment of these norms is varied.

1.3 Ethnicity, Identification, and Being Mennonite

In the 1970s, it became increasingly common to refer to Mennonites as an ethno-religious community. Mennonite historian Royden Loewen argues that Mennonite ethnicity consists of "historically conditioned cultural constructions" (Loewen, 2008: 332). Loewen, a well-known Mennonite historian, received his PhD from the University of Manitoba and currently holds ones of several endowed Ethnicity Chairs spread across Canada. Loewen writes:

> Ethnicity for Canadian Mennonites is a cultural construction, established by time, tempered by space, and conditioned by social interaction. It intersects dialectically with religious teachings that are themselves in flux. The dynamic intersection of the two constitutes a 'poetic act' for the Mennonites. (*Ibid.*)

Loewen also draws on Gans's concept of 'symbolic ethnicity',[22] arguing that Mennonites took on more adaptable and discardable symbols of ethnicity

---

22 US-American Sociologist Herbert Gans coined the phrase, 'symbolic ethnicity', to describe third or fourth generation children of immigrants to the United States whose ethnic identity was not intense or frequent but who made use of symbols to hold to some feeling of belonging (Gans, 1999: 167). More and more, he argues, there are less behavioural expectations accompanying ethnic identification and therefore people have an increased freedom in role definition (*Ibid.*: 175). Gans argues that this allows ethnicity to be expressed

over time, which had less of a role in regulating family life (Loewen, 2008; Gans, 1999).

As scholar Joane Nagel notes, "ethnic boundaries are also sexual boundaries" (Nagel, 2003: 1) and so any discussion of ethnicity is necessarily also a discussion of sexuality. Ethnicity[23] and sexuality join together in forming what Nagel calls 'ethnosexual frontiers' which keep some people in and others out and help "to define who is pure and who is impure, to shape our view of ourselves and others, to fashion feelings of sexual desires and notions of sexual desirability" (*Ibid.*). Nagel argues that the 'sexual ideologies' of many groups set members of other groups as sexually different and usually inferior from the ethnic group in question (*Ibid.*: 9).

Nagel's work connects back to Judith Butler's assertion that identities are premised on differentiating oneself from the 'other' (Butler, 2008). In this process of identity formation, by asserting that which the group is not, some identities are rendered beyond existence. These identities do not 'exist' in the sense that within this particular context, they appear either as logical impossibilities or developmental failures. Such identities include those in which gender does not follow from sex and where desire does not follow from either gender or sex, including persons holding same-sex attraction identities (*Ibid.*: 24). It is for this reason that the ethno-religious label for Mennonites must be challenged and deconstructed so that the ethno-sexual frontiers embedded in being Mennonite become visible.

Further, dissecting ethnicity reveals that it is implicated not only with norms on sexuality but also with classism, the promotion of the market capitalist system and racism. In his 2008 book chapter in *Christianity and Ethnicity in Canada*, Loewen alludes to the connection of ethnicity to nationalism and contemporary free market economies noting that Mennonite symbolic ethnicity "easily complemented Canadian middle-class values and identities, and Canada's evolving embrace of official multiculturalism" (Loewen, 2008: 339).[24] Along these lines, an intensive deconstruction of the use of the term ethnicity itself needs to be continually pursued in Mennonite Studies.

---

in an individual way which does not conflict with other ways of life. Gans states, "ethnicity takes on an expressive rather than instrumental function in people's lives, becoming more of a leisure-time activity and losing its relevance, say, to earning a living or regulating family life" (*Ibid.*: 177).

23 Nagel uses the term ethnicity broadly to refer to differences between people solidified in groups around language, national origin, culture, geography, and race (Nagel, 2003: 6).

24 See Thomas Hylland Eriksen (1993) who raises the question of whether ethnicity is chiefly a modern phenomenon and notes that many of the processes by which ethnic identification emerges are modern. As a concept, Eriksen notes that ethnicity has replaced other

What exactly is ethnicity? According to well-known scholars Kathleen Conzen and David Gerber, ethnicity is a cultural construction which "incorporates, adapts, and amplifies pre-existing communal solidarities, cultural attributes, and historical memories" (Conzen and Gerber, 1992: 3). Although I agree that ethnicity is a culturally constructed notion, I would also assert that such 'pre-existing communal solidarities' as Conzen and Gerber identify, are themselves constructions and abstractions in the mind, as are shared cultural attributes and historical memories. Thomas Hylland Eriksen argues that ethnicity is generally a word used to describe groups which are biologically self-perpetuating or endogamous and most importantly groups in which the individuals have a shared ancestry and a shared religion (Eriksen, 1993: 34-35). Some conceptions of ethnicity discard religion altogether and focus solely on the connection shared through shared ancestry while other positions abandon both and define ethnic groups in terms of shared cultural practices (*Ibid.*). Using any of those three conceptions alone to define Mennonites–shared ancestry, religion, or culture–would be insufficient.

Within Mennonite Studies there are certainly scholars who dispute the ethnicity label ascribed to Mennonites. Scholar James Urry abandons the terminology of ethnicity altogether arguing that it does not capture the being and belonging of Mennonites "which is informed by a culture of faith rather than faith in culture" (Urry, 2006: 6). Instead, Urry chooses the term 'peoplehood' to describe the sense of identity based on faith and sense of belonging and being. This belonging, he argues, was (and is) based around confessions of faith, the core of which for all Mennonites were (and are) adult baptism, nonresistance, and separation from "the world" (*Ibid.*). Indeed, Urry shows convincingly how the term ethnicity is a new way of conceiving being Mennonite which is not only faith based, and which can be completely sepa-

---

anthropological terms, such as 'cultures' or 'societies' which tend to assume that more static and homogenous units of belonging (8-9). See also Peter Li (1999), who quotes Yancey, Ericksen, and Juliani (1976) noting "the assumption of a common heritage as the essential aspect of ethnicity is erroneous. Ethnicity may have relatively little to do with Europe, Asia, or Africa, but much to do with the exigencies of survival and the structure of opportunity in this country" (Yancey, Ericksen, and Juliani quoted in Li, 1999: 13). In other words, ethnicity may be more of an indication of adaptation to ensure access to the discourses of wider Canadian society than anything coming out of an inherent identification with a particular background. Further, Henry and Tator (1999) argue that with the organization of capital globally, corporate structures, and the rise of transnational labor "people all over the world have turned to ethnic and cultural identity as a means of mobilizing themselves for the defence of their social and political/economic interests" (Henry and Tator, 1999: 95) suggesting the intimate relationship between ethnic identification and the capitalist market economy.

rated from faith based practice. He points to the close relationship between the rise of ethnicity discourse and the Canadian national project of multiculturalism, increasingly divergent evangelical and neo-Anabaptist faith practices, urbanization and the disintegration of the farm based household economy (*Ibid.*: 223).[25]

Yet, almost contradictorily, Urry shows that one such core belief of "separation from the world" was less than absolute or simple and in fact, Mennonite experience was very much connected to the social and national contexts within which they lived. Urry posits that throughout history "those in power and their officials have insisted that they [Mennonites] subject themselves to identities other than those of their own choosing" (Urry, 2006: 13).

In a similar fashion, Marlene Epp notes that gender roles are of human creation, and made to service particular interests at different points of time (Epp, 2008: 5). It is imperative, Epp argues, that Mennonite women be studied in their local and national communities so as to understand them as participating in other forces than just their religious or ethno-religious allegiances. Epp goes on to quote M.J. Heisey who argues that "nonconformist Anabaptists have largely borrowed their gender expectations from the larger society" (Heisey quoted in Epp, 2008: 8) and suggests the same for contemporary Mennonites.

The question then, especially in light of Urry's own uncovering of the very political, but most commonly discursively apolitically framed Mennonites,[26] as well as writings on gender which show the very contingent nature of norms among Mennonites, is whether there are or were truly any 'core' aspects of being Mennonite; adult baptism, nonresistance, and perhaps also the heterosexual marriage norm, are all, to some degree, discursive idealizations

25 The idea of ethnicity and the development of a wider concept of Mennonite peoplehood within the world, rather than apart from it, was borne not only out of the urbanization of Mennonites. As James Urry points out, the wider sense of Mennonite peoplehood also had to do with the increasing movement among many Mennonites into evangelical, mainstream politicized Christianity or towards a neo-Anabaptist vision, as well as the promotion of the category of "ethnicity" by communities, individuals, and the government throughout the 1960s and early 1970s in Canada (Urry, 2006: 222). Ethnicity was a marker of personal and communal identity in addition, and sometimes also without, religion. The ethnic label allowed Mennonites to access government grants supporting multi-culturalism and for the development of Mennonite cultural programs. By the 1970s, Mennonites became known in official reports and academic descriptions as an "ethno-religious community", an ethnicity within Canadian nationalism (*Ibid.*: 223)

26 See James Urry (2006) for a captivating discussion of Mennonite political involvement through the 16-20th centuries.

of being Mennonite and that the story of what it means and what it meant in the past to be Mennonite is far more complicated, nuanced, and reflective of wider socio-political trends than often espoused.

1.3.1 What is Identification and Subjectification?

This is not to say that being Mennonite has no meaning at all. From my perspective, it is the believing in, feelings about, investment in, and association with the very subject position of 'Mennonite' which accounts for the formation of this 'ethnic' grouping. As Thomas Hylland Eriksen argues "[e]thnicity emerges and is made relevant through social situations and encounters" and ethnic identities are always defined "in relation to that which they are not" (Eriksen, 1993: 1, 10). To what degree is identification as a Mennonite then a social act of fashioning the 'I' in relation to the 'we' and the 'other'? And to what degree is being Mennonite entangled with not doing those things which are said to not be Mennonite?

To understand being Mennonite, it is important to understand the processes by which we are ascribed into and which we inscribe ourselves into particular groupings. With postmodernism, the term identity and identity groupings (such as ethnicity) have seen a radical deconstruction to the point where many scholars have argued that there is no identity which is not completely constructed and the term itself has reached the point of erasure (Hall, 1996: 2). Most commonly, when identity is not subjected to such deconstruction, it is believed to be premised on a shared characteristic or common origin with an ideal of allegiance and solidarity set on this foundation. Communities are commonly premised around this illusionary solidarity (*Ibid.*: 6).

Stuart Hall conceives of identity not as a fixed, stable state based on unwavering shared characteristics, but rather a process which he terms 'identification'. Identification occurs at the meeting point between the discourses which place us as subjects of particular discourses of belonging and the processes which allow for us to conceive of ourselves and others as subjects in the first place (Hall 1996: 6). Said in another way, identification is the "naming in discourse or language-of what it means or feels like to be a particular human among other humans" (Stern, 2005: 31). In this case, it is the process of naming what it means and feels like to be a Mennonite.

It is helpful here to say a word about what I mean when I write about 'the subject'. Subjectification, the making of 'the subject', is the process by which humans choose to apply "the technologies of relationality not just to the outside world and to its fellow human, but to itself in order to fashion the own subjectivity- in order to *become* (different)" (Koppensteiner, 2009: 79).

In other words, subjectification is the process through which the 'I' and the 'we' emerges as an entity in relation to other humans.

This way of thinking "challenges the assumption central to modernist thought, that in each of us there is an underlying person who is the same across different contexts" (Neitz, 2004: 396). As scholar Maria Stern argues, subjectivities are too large to be captured with any single representation or words and therefore it follows that one person has multiple subject positions and selves (Stern, 2005: 31). And these are not only self-constructed and defined selves. As Maria Stern argues,

> no matter what notions of multiple selves we may evoke to capture or stand for who we, as a person or a movement or 'a people' may be, attempts to secure these selves depend on a picture of being painted of 'us'. Such a picture demands boundaries and a content that resides within its contour, even if these boundaries shift and recompose themselves. (Stern, 2005: 31)

Here Stern is not only referring to the process by which the 'I' is formed but also the process by which 'we' or community is formed.

1.3.2 Community and the Possibilities of Performativity

Community is most commonly framed as something which is built around commonality such as a shared identity, purpose or belief. It is often assumed to be about a shared sense of obligation, emotional and affective ties (Sullivan, 2003: 135-136).[27] Very often within religious communities, this assumedly unambiguous nature of identities is commonplace (McClintock Fulkerson, 1997; Wilcox, 2003). Nikki Sullivan argues, however, that there is never a 'we' which is straightforward and not problematic (Sullivan, 2003: 140). A community based around the notion of an understandable 'we' and commonality "cannot really tolerate difference" in the end (*Ibid.*: 142). According to Sullivan,

> the fact that is central to the ideal of community and more with the idea that any attempt to achieve community will necessarily involve the giving up of one's freedom…in such a conception there is a fundamental tension between personal freedom and belonging or community- community is tantamount to conformity and to the loss of individuality. (*Ibid.*: 145)

---

27 According to Sullivan, there are most commonly two models of understanding community – the ascriptive model –which assumes that there is an innate, underlying something that all members of a community share and the non-ascriptive model –which although assuming that one chooses to be part of a community nevertheless positions identity as unambiguous (Sullivan, 2003: 139).

Rather, than seeing the 'we' through such a lens, community can be built around discourses which construct the 'we', and also the 'I' through processes of identification, where the 'I' and 'we' are in constant flux, creation, and recreation.

In the idealized discourses of the Mennonite community, there is a clear rejection of bodies and subjectivities from the community when they fall out of the frame of heterosexuality or gender/sex uniformity. Too often, it is impossible for the transgender individual to be Mennonite and even, in fact, exist in the consciousness of the community. Yet, when we look carefully at the stories of people within the Mennonite community, can we see that there are many ways of being Mennonite? Literature on Mennonite women suggests that women have consistently lived in ways which contended with or deviated from the familial, institutional and theological discourses which prescribe certain behaviours and reject others. Later, I will specifically highlight interviews with LGQ identifying Mennonites to see whether this also holds true in the case of LGQ identities and what this does to understandings of community.

According to Judith Butler (2008), when we recognize the performatively constituted nature of identities, in that identities are formed by the same expressions which are said to be its results, there is a possibility for great transformation. Butler suggests that it is in the very performance of any identity, in the continuous repetitions of being anything, where there exist spaces for re-signification and change (Butler, 2008).

Hall also highlights the contingency of the discourses of identity, which he argues, exist interdependently and are intimately connected to time, space, and the attachment of persons to these discourses. The attachment of a person to a particular subject position requires an investment of some sort in the position and can be thought of as an articulation on the part of the individual (Hall, 1996: 6). Identifications, then are always representations of discourses and ideals of belonging and such are always "constructed across a 'lack', across a division, from the place of the Other, and thus can never be adequate-identical-to the subject processes which are invested in them" (*Ibid.*). In other words, identifications are never complete, never fulfilling of the ideal discourses which they represent and thus while identifications always exist in relation to what they are not, it is simultaneously what it is not (Stern, 2005: 33).

For Mennonites, this means that while I might identify as Mennonite and being Mennonite has clear institutional and theological parameters such as being white, heterosexual, religious, and peace loving, these ideal discourses of belonging are never fully realized in my living. In fact, my being Mennonite exists very closely in relationship to that which is most commonly framed as not Mennonite –for example being black, gay, atheistic, violent.

So, if I look at the process of identification as just that, a process, performatively constituted, what does this do to my conception of community? Sullivan proposes that community can be imagined, not as a group of sameness and place of safety in uniformity, but rather a group with an allegiance to the destabilization of the logic of identity. This can be done through the recognition of multiplicity, difference and through the transgression of boundaries and categories (Sullivan, 2003: 148). In a Mennonite community such as this community becomes a place where difference is recognized and celebrated and all identifications, including that of Mennonite, are recognized as ever evolving and never possible to fully represent. In chapter 2 and 4 I will investigate how community is conceptualized among Mennonites and the possibilities to change this understanding.

1.3.3 Making Sense of Mennonite Ethnicity and Identification

A 2010 debate raging within the Viewpoints (letters to the editor) section of the *Canadian Mennonite*[28] demonstrates the divergent and sometimes heated debates within the Mennonite community on what it means to be Mennonite or have a Mennonite identity. The source of contention in this case was the Mennonite DNA project, a collaborative effort by Chemistry professor, Glenn Penner and physician, Tim Janzen, to establish a DNA record of the population of Low-German ancestral background Mennonites. The aim was to determine how many common ancestors there were for present day Mennonites and the number of common ancestors for each present day Mennonite family name (The Mennonite DNA Project, 2010; Epp, 2010). Letters to the editor published in the March 8th, 2010 *Canadian Mennonite* highlight the offence taken by some Mennonites from a non Low-German ancestry that such a project was launched and the implication that having a Mennonite identity was somehow tied to a genealogical history (Metcalfe, 2010; Morton, 2010). Dave Metcalfe wrote, "I believe that my Mennonite, or Christian, identity can only be found to exist within a faith-and not a biological-context" (Metcalfe, 2010).

Although the DNA project was never designed to find the true Mennonite DNA strand and decide who was in and out of the Mennonite fold, it is telling that for some Mennonites, historical roots are not part of the way in

---

28 The *Canadian Mennonite* is a biweekly publication of Mennonite Church Canada.

which they think about being Mennonite and that identification as a Mennonite and Christian are synonymous. Similarly, there would be other Mennonites who would not subscribe to any religion at all yet still identify as Mennonite.

According to Royden Loewen (2008), there are seven different ways to be Mennonite ranging from those who embrace being Mennonite ethnically, yet de-emphasize/critique/reject religion. Yet others ways to be Mennonite include embracing Canadian evangelism, having a strong distain for traditional Mennonite religiousness, and all the while celebrating elements of ethnicity. Taking Loewen's argument even further by applying Hall's concept of identification and Butler's notion of performativity, I see as many ways of being Mennonite as there are self-identifying Mennonites. Being Mennonite then, is to act out or articulate the constant negotiation taking place between idealized discourses that place 'I' and 'we' in a particular subject position and the subject and involved in the very constitution of the idealized discourses and their own position as a subject. In other words, being Mennonite is the way in which one repeats, re-signifies, and individually stylizes the performatively constituted identity of Mennonite and the idealized discourses which construct it as such. Mennonite identification is inextricable from religion, class, race, geography, sexual orientation, gender, and nationality/national origin; a fact which is quickly evident in what being Mennonite often entails. If we take such an approach to the meaning of Mennonite, the question of how religious or how ethnic a person is loses its relevance as a question of inquiry.

1.3.4 Re-thinking Theology and Religion

The question then of how performativity relates to sex, gender, desire and religious practice is an interesting one. Indeed, there are many scholars of religion who are looking at that question[29] and feminist theologians who are challenging the structure within which sexuality is framed in Christianity. However, for the most part, writes feminist theologian Margaret Kamitsuka, feminist theologians "tiptoe delicately around or avoid completely issues of

29 There are a great number of scholars who offer an different interpretation of the six main passages in the Bible which are often used to condemn same-sex practices and desire. See Miner and Connoley (2002) for a brief, easy to read introduction to the subject. Gareth Moore (2003) provides an analysis of biblical passages to argue, along the same vein as Foucault (1988) and Halperin (2002), that homosexuality as a concept did not exist in early Christianity and in the ancient world.

sexuality and are unwilling or unable to take on questions such as Judith Butler's" (Kamitsuka, 2007: 18).

Feminist theology, like feminism, is hardly a uniform or coherent category of study or approach as it has gone through many challenges and changes, imbedded within the larger frame of the feminist movement. First wave feminists in the 1970s and early 1980s focused on the experience of women's oppression under patriarchy as a starting point for their analysis of religion (Kamitsuka, 2007: 5). In the 1980s, the notion of an underlying common experience of all women was challenged, especially by black and post-colonial feminist scholars. Still, although most feminist theologians no longer "appeal overtly to a common women's experience, [...] they still tend to pursue an agenda of codifying women's diversity into symbols that assume some unified experiences and values" (*Ibid.*: 6). Rather than starting from an assumption of uniformity in the experience of women, Margaret Kamitsuka provides an alternative interpretation which deconstructs the male-female sex binary. She argues that selfhood is constructed performatively in relation to disciplinary conventions, and goes on to re-think sin as well as creation in light of this performativity[30] (*Ibid.*: 64).

There are also scholars looking at religious practice and LGBTQ identities through a sociological or ethnographic perspective. Edward Gray and Scott Thumma (1997) studied participants of a weekly gospel hour which brought together gay drag and gospel songs in an interactive performance. In this fo-

30 Interestingly, Kamitsuka applies performativity in order to understand the nature of sin as either the maximization of cooperation with regimes of disciplinary power, making what might be relatively good into the supreme good, or the underdeveloped cooperation with disciplinary power by avoiding conditions necessary for resistance practices to emerge (Kamitsuka, 2007: 73-75). She argues that the way to respond to both undue and underdeveloped cooperation with disciplinary power is to widen "discursive performativity" (*Ibid.*: 77). Following Kamitsuka, many feminists continue to believe that maleness and femaleness are God given, biologically based, and self-evident for the continuation of the human species. It becomes gender (as the cultural inscription upon bodies) which is problematic, rather than the dualism of sex itself. Further, it is often thought that only through unitary relations between males and females that humans can achieve their fullest capacity for reflecting the goodness of God epitomized in the emphasis on biblical passages in which 'the flesh become one' and all are commanded to 'be fruitful and multiply'. In such assertions, a prevailing sex binary is still at work. This creates a great deal of pain for those who find themselves outside of the heterosexual norm and leads to a fundamental rejection of bodies and subjectivities that do not fit with this compulsory heterosexuality, and often leads to exclusion from communities (*Ibid.*: 66-67). Kamitsuka re-frames the notion of being made in God's image to argue that "to be made in God's image suggests that our performativity can have the possibility of being 'an icon of who God is'" (*Ibid.*: 79). In other words, the image of God is "the graced possibility for godliness in every discursive identity performance, including gender, sex, and sexual desire" (*Ibid.*: 23-24).

rum, the performers and participants were able to "reclassify ordinary, taken-for-granted social relationships and cultural categories framing Christianity and gay sexuality" (Gray and Thumma, 1997: 81). In other words, it was a means through which they could contest, twist, and invest in the ideal discourses of both 'being gay' and 'being Christian' and in doing so they created a liminal time and space set apart from the everyday in which being gay and Christian was not odd, but normal (*Ibid.*). Although Thumma bases his argument around the notion that people have a core identity construct which resides in interplay with experiences, I think that it is possible to re-interpret this liminal space negotiation in the frame that Hall presents.

René Drumm (2005) examined gay and lesbian Seventh-day Adventists to look at the way in which gay and lesbian people negotiated their identities. Drumm found that some people left the church, others practiced celibacy while remaining in the church, whereas others stayed in the church finding welcoming congregations which affirmed their sexual orientation (Drumm, 2005: 61). Drumm notes that that majority of those he interviewed chose to remain Adventists and have a same-sex life partner with an emphasis on "monogamy and commitment in the heterosexual tradition as part of this choice" (*Ibid.*: 62). All of these self-identifying gay and lesbian Seventh-Day Adventists, no matter what their choices were for being, however, came to a sharper understanding of their beliefs, the types of behaviour that they would tolerate, and a sharper picture of what defined their Adventist identity (*Ibid.*: 65). Clearly, the concept of performativity is being applied in both feminist theology and religious studies, offering new ways to conceive of faith practice and texts.

Sexuality Norms and Christianity

How is it that there has come to be particular sexual norms in North American society, both in Protestant Christianity and the Mennonite church? Furthermore, why are these norms so focussed around sexual practices? Presumably, answers require going to the very root of early Christian thought as sexuality norms are intimately connected with the early Christian church. Some clues as to the interrelated nature of Christianity, Western society, and sexuality can be revealed by looking at some of the historical work surrounding the development of sexual regulations in the Greek and early Christian world. Of great importance in this regard, is the work of Michel Foucault in *Volume III, The History of Sexuality: The Care of the Self* (1988).

Foucault argues that Christian ethics which prescribe strict rules and norms on sexual acts (pleasure is reserved for heterosexual marriage alone, the primacy of reproduction, the control of pleasure and the glorification of celibacy) were borrowed from the philosophers of the first two centuries A.D. and reflected a new way of thinking about the self that climaxed in importance during this time. Foucault argues that there was an increasing concern about the self in relation to pleasures. It was a way of thinking of the self by which oneself became constituted as the subject of one's acts (Foucault, 1988: 41). Foucault writes

> what stands out in the texts of the first centuries –more than new interdictions concerning sexual acts –is the insistence on the attention that should be brought to bear on oneself; it is the modality, scope, constancy, and exactitude of the required vigilance; it is the anxiety concerning all the disturbances of the body and the mind, which must be prevented by means of an austere regime; it is the importance of self-respect, not just insofar as one's status is concerned, but as concerns one's rational nature –a self-respect that is exercised by depriving oneself of pleasure or by confining one's indulgence to marriage or procreation. (*Ibid.*)

Other scholars, building on the work of Foucault, demonstrate how both Plato and Aristotle were very suspicious of sexual passion because they believed that it distracted from the pursuit of knowledge and so praised nonsexual, intellectualized love (Wiesner-Hanks, 2000: 25). This was reflective of a more general dualistic view of the world in which the unseen realm of ideas came to be thought of as superior to the visual world. And so the individual was thought to contain two separate entities, the mind/soul and body (*Ibid.*). There is significant debate, however, surrounding Foucault's premise of a casual link between ancient Greece and Christian sexual mores. Whether or not one agrees with Foucault's premise, however, his work nevertheless helps point to the prominence of norms on sexual practices in western discourse.

According to Kathy Gaca (2003), a clear link cannot be made between early Greek discourses and the sexual mores of the early Christian church. Gaca shows that the ideas about sexual morality of many of the early Christian leaders including Paul, Philo, Tatian, and Clement, were markedly different from the ideas of Plato, the Pythagoreans, and the early Stoics (Gaca, 2003). However, while each of these thinkers had different positions, one key commonality was the aberration of sexual practices which were thought to honour gods other than the monotheistic Lord.[31] Among Gentiles and Greeks,

31 Scholar Richard Price notes a similar phenomenon in that "[a] rejection of pleasure as an end in itself and a stress on rational self-control were adopted by most Christian writers" in the early church (Price, 1996: 22). Price argues in a related manner to Gaca, that this

sexual practices and pleasures were intimately tied to the gods Aphrodite and Eros (*Ibid.*: 303). For Tatian, this fuelled a call to eliminate sexual desire and activity in its entirety, while for Clement this was a key reason for the development of Christian procreationism in which Christians were directed to reproduce but without any desire for the sexual life (*Ibid.*).[32]

Further, the conviction that Christian devotees might gain blissful spiritual existence in eternity by forgoing sexual desire was commonplace.[33] The pronouncement of bodily urges as unholy or ungodly, led to new interdictions about who was considered a good and bad woman in Gentile lands.[34] Over

regulation took on ferocious passion within the early church, in small part due to the wider Greek thought and cultural ethos but more primarily because of the content of the Christian gospels and the pressure for the early Christian church to set itself apart and distinct from the wider society (*Ibid.*: 28-29). Barbara Walker (1983b) provides a compelling examination of marriage, arguing that it was because of the strong link between pagan marriage and the Goddess-Aphrodite-Mari, that early Christian leaders rejected marriage. According to Walker, "[t]he Christian priesthood was fighting ancient traditions in which it was remembered that male spiritual authority was depending on marriage" and therefore the Goddess (Walker, 1983b: 587). In fact, it was not until the 16th century that a Christian marriage sacrament developed in which pagan marriage laws were revised to place a wife's property in the control of her husband (*Ibid.*: 585-591).

32 Although not addressed by Gaca, this type of mindset is also reflected in the work of some latter leaders in the early church such as Augustine who accepted that sexual reproduction and gender differentiation would have taken place in the original Creation (that which existed before the 'fall') but still believed that marital sex was sinful and second rate (Radford Ruether, 2000: 45). According to Augustine, sex was fundamentally flawed by the Fall because sex in Paradise would have taken place without male ejaculation. Augustine also argued that reproduction within marriage could not take place without 'lust' and therefore sin. Women, he argued, were 'deflowered' through vaginal penetration and therefore were to be the victims of labour pains. According to Augustine, in Paradise women would not have menstruated as it was an expression of women's 'fallen' state (*Ibid.*: 46).

33 The second century Christian church held strongly to the notion of the resurrected body – that death would allow for the immortal life of the soul alone –and through the death all of those bodily urges such as sex, food, and sleep the constraints of the mortal world would be wiped away. Christians, therefore, found that the bodily urges needed to be suppressed during life in anticipation of this final goal (Radford Ruether, 2000: 37). It is perhaps not surprising that in light of this, sexual renunciation became intimately tied to spiritual experience. It became the case that in some threads of Christian thought, virginity became tied to "a vision of transcendence and transformation of the limits of the body itself" a way of thinking that has remained in Christianity to this day (*Ibid.*: 40).

34 Before these injunctions from Paul, women who worshiped other gods than the Lord were often the relatives of Christian people and judged according to the merits of their life and work. Paul, however, termed these women as whores, "for they wantonly deviate from his conception and cultural parameters of biblical monotheism through their sexual, reproductive, and other ritual activities" (Gaca, 2003: 294). Barbara Walker, in her discussion of virgin births, points to the pervasiveness of the 'Holy Virgin' in pagan society; this was a title for the harlot-priestesses of Ishtar, Asherah, or Aphrodite and was

time, endogamy took hold among Christians with Paul strictly prohibiting sexual activity between Christians and Gentiles or non-Christians (Gaca, 2003: 295). Paul adapts from the Septuagint, a rule on marriage which explicitly divides Jews and Christians, Greeks and Christians. What emerges is a protectionism forbidding religiously mixed marriages and a declaration of the sexual disobedience of God's historical people, spouses who convert, and their offspring (*Ibid.*).

According to Gaca,

> [i]t would be hard to overstate the impact Paul's marriage rule has had in Western culture and beyond. Every church wedding, baptism, and coming of age or confirmation ceremony re-enacts his retrieval of Gentiles from their fornicating servitude to other gods and their restoration to their one and only master, the Lord through, in, and with Christ. (*Ibid.*)

And so in the writings of early Christians, a clear glorification of celibacy is made, as is the spiritualization of Christian heterosexual marriage, and an emphasis on controlling the satisfaction of sexual desires through a strong emphasis on procreation. These interdictions are related to two broader trends during the time period including a mind and body dualism as well as a push to disassociated with the gods Aphrodite and Eros and the elements of pleasure and sexual practices with which they were associated.

Intense debate revolves around whether there existed status determinative homosexual identities in the ancient world and Christianity's early response to same-sex relationships. Both Foucault and Halperin, argue that in the ancient world, sexual practices were fluid and not imbued with the sense of essentialized identity found in the 'homosexual'. According to the well known historian of sexuality, David Halperin,

> One of the most distinctive features of the current regime under which we live in the prominence of heterosexuality and homosexuality as central, organizing categories of thought, behavior, and erotic subjectivity. The rise to dominance of those categories represents a relatively recent and culturally specific development, yet it has left little trace in our consciousness of its novelty. As a result, not only do we have a hard time understanding the logic at work in other

not about physical virginity but meant unmarried women involved in healing, prophesying, sexual worship, and other important roles. The concept of virginity was adopted by early Christians "out of simple imitativeness" and then fashioned to degrade women's sexuality and suit the patriarchical structures of the church (Walker, 1983a: 1049-1051). "Theologians in effect severed the two halves of the pagan Goddess" so that sexuality and motherhood were rarely considered two parts of the same whole thereby degrading real womanhood, female sexuality and "exalting a never-attainable ideal" (*Ibid.*,: 1050; 1051).

> historical cultures' organizations of sex and gender, but we have an even harder time understanding our own inability to understand them. (Halperin, 2002: 3)

Both Halperin (2002) and Foucault (1978) argue in their work, that homosexuality as a concept of fundamental identity, was simply not present before the 19th century. Foucault and Halperin's work has been vociferously critiqued by feminists, in particular who point out the lack of gender analysis in their work to account for the unique experiences of women in the construction of sexual subjectivity. Amy Richlin, for example, contends that there were sexual minorities in ancient society who did indeed face systemized discrimination and labels which suggested a status determinative identity (Shaw, 2000: 406-416).

Bernadette Brooten (1996), in her provocative work on early Christianity, argues that there was a strong awareness of women to women sexual love and that it received widespread rejection and at times, pathologization. She argues that this was because it involved a transgression of gender norms. These women had 'unnatural' sex in the fact that there was no active or passive partner. Ancient thinkers supposed that a woman experienced pleasure only "under a man" and having pleasure outside of this phallocentric frame, was both against nature and divine will (Brooten, 1997: 359; 361). More than a fear of sex or a concern with procreation, "ancient commentators on sexual love between women were eminently concerned with maintaining a gender-stratified social order" (*Ibid.*: 361). Brooten suggests that this type of thinking is commonly upheld in contemporary Western society and Christianity (*Ibid.*).

John Boswell's prominent and also controversial work, *Christianity, Social Tolerance, and Homosexuality* (1980), provides yet another perspective, arguing that the status determinative identity of homosexual did exist in ancient and medieval societies, but any discrimination or pathologization of these identities did not come forth from Christianity. Rather,

> [r]eligious beliefs may cloak or incorporate intolerance…But careful analysis can almost always differentiate between conscientious application of religious ethics and the use of religious precepts as justification for personal animosity or prejudice. If religious strictures are used to justify oppression by people who regularly disregard precepts of equal gravity from the same moral code, or if prohibitions which restrain a disliked minority are upheld in their most literal sense as absolutely inviolable while comparable precepts affecting the majority are relaxed or reinterpreted, one must suspect something other than religious belief as the motivating cause of the oppression. (Boswell, 1980: 6-7)

Boswell argues that Christianity was born in a Greek and Roman culture which was tolerant of same-sex eroticism, that there was nothing in Christian scripture or early tradition which required a hostile assessment of homosexuality, that medieval Christians had no hostility to same-sex eroticism, and that it was only in the 12th and 13th centuries that Christianity began to be hostile towards homosexuality (Kuefler, 2006: 2). Boswell's investigation has been vociferously critiqued by feminists who decry his lack of gender analysis, gay advocates and scholars who argue that Boswell discounts the very real oppression practiced by the church on LGBTQ people in history, and other scholars who simply contend with the factual base of his argument (*Ibid.*: 7-11).

My own perspective on whether there were or were not pathologized same-sex identities in early or medieval Christianity, tends to lean towards affirming the feminist analysis made by Brooten and Richlin. Regardless, both point to the very socially imbued nature of sexuality norms and the justification for these norms being subject to many different explanations. Whether agreeing with either or neither Boswell, Foucault, Halperin, Brooten, or Richlin points to the fact that Christianity is not an abstract force but rather the institutions of religion, the wider society, and the practices of individual people are all interrelated and responsible for producing and reproducing normative frames on sexuality (Wiesner-Hanks, 2000: 4).

SEXUALITY NORMS AND ANABAPTISM

A quick look at the early Anabaptist predecessors of Mennonites reveals some similar trends in sexuality norms to those found in early and medieval Christianity. Marion Kobelt-Groch's (1988) examination on Anabaptist marriage found that it was the case that certain groups of Anabaptists left marriages when their partner did not convert to Anabaptism, an indication that Anabaptists had adapted Paul's statements against inter-religious marriage to their situation. In the writings of early Anabaptists, the sex act was portrayed as something which was to be focused around procreation and pleasure was generally rejected (*Ibid.*: 32). It was even the case that some Anabaptist groups completely rejected marriage and sexual relations (*Ibid.*: 34).[35] Al-

35 Kobelt-Groch (1988) suggests that marriage took a secondary role among Anabaptists because marriage, and the intensity of that union, may have interfered with the Anabaptist focus on the whole of the community of believers. She also suggests that polygamy or more accurately, polygyny, likely emerged among some Anabaptists because of the strong ethic of sharing among this group. Further, Anabaptist emphasis on individual spiritual experience in guiding life as well as Old Testament passages condoning multiple wives helped to create a climate in which polygamy was accepted (Kobelt-Groch, 1988: 32-34). For the time, such marriage practices were truly blasphemous in light of the Catholic

though it is true that marriage and sexual practices varied among different Anabaptist groups, the diversity of actions reflect the focus among Anabaptists to seek new ways of living spiritual lives and the interweaving of sexual norms with that attempt (*Ibid.*: 35).

John Klassen comes to the similar conclusion that family loyalties and feelings often took a secondary role to faith. There was an emphasis on the spiritual union of the couple in marriage and a union formed not only on the basis of sexual desire (Klassen, 1986: 554-555). Klassen alludes to these standards as reflective of a broader trend in Protestantism while Kobelt-Groch does not place this in context. Similarly, Stephen Boyd suggests that the Anabaptists who entered into new marriages, did so in order to create a new understanding of the relationship between mind and body so that they separated 'the flesh' and 'the will' (Boyd, 1999: 46). Again, many of the Anabaptist ways of conceiving the body and spirit as separate, the disassociation with sexual desire, and emphasis on endogamous marriages is similar to those ideas found in the early Christian church. It is with this historical context, that I seek to comprehend the sexuality norms as prescribed by Mennonite churches and institutions today.

1.4 Patriarchy, Power, & Peaces

The relationship of this work to the field of peace studies may not be readily apparent to all readers. Nor has it always been apparent to me in the course of this writing process; in reality, this project has done nothing but produce more conflict in my life–within myself, with family and friends, and also between me and the upper middle class Canadian society of which I am a part. So what does all of this conflict have to do with peace? I will shine light on this question in the course of this section, both personally and in general.

1.4.1 What are the Connections? Feminism & Peace Studies

The relationship between feminism, gender, Peace Studies has not always been a straightforward one. Although all branches of feminist studies are concerned with questioning the conceptual frameworks and normative standards of our world and in particular, the silencing of women's voices, the

church's strict no divorce policy and opposition to polygamy. Anabaptists gained a reputation for having loose morals in the eyes of many in mainstream society (*Ibid.*: 36).

consequences of this and the proposals for change differ greatly (Weber, 2006: 1). According to peace researcher Annette Weber, it was in fact feminism which was responsible for provoking Peace Studies towards understanding the interconnected nature of all forms of violence and the "continuum of violence running from domestic violence to war" (*Ibid.*: 2). Particularly with the rise of post-colonial feminists, a critique on the uniformity of women's experience was made. Peace scholar Cynthia Cockburn, notes that it became increasingly apparent that any analysis of gender could not be made without considering race, ethnicity, class, religion and other aspects of life which shape the experience of women (Cockburn, 2004: 43). So, here too, Peace Studies became concerned with the multiplicity of peaces and conflicts.

1.4.2 Re-interpreting Patriarchy

In some cases when feminist or gender analysis is applied to peace studies, patriarchy is the basis from which a critique is made on social structures and through which the rights of women are advocated. According to one such scholar, John Brewer, women find themselves suffering structural violence in society because of their socially constructed positions within economic, social, and political contexts (Brewer, 2010: 101). In terms of war, Brewer argues that socially constructed norms on gender speak women as poor combatants and undervalue the political role of women as agents of social change. At other times, social norms construct women as having a more 'natural' ability for peacemaking, thereby reducing public roles to an extension of private roles (*Ibid.*). Indeed, many studies on gender and sex in peace and conflict studies rotate around a discussion of patriarchal and hierarchical oppressions as they relate to peace and conflict in the home, community, and world.

It would be hazardous to ignore the fact that oppression in its physical, cultural, and structural forms is a reality for many people who hold desires, genders, and sexes outside of the hetero/homo, male/female, man/woman binary. It would also be dangerous to ignore the processes by which this violence affects people and the gendered nature of Peace Studies. It is because of the multiplicity of oppressions that I observe, that I believe a more complicated understanding than that of patriarchy is necessary to understand power, violence, and possibilities for peace as it sexuality.

What is commonly termed post-feminist studies or post-structuralist feminist studies sees patriarchy as a limited tool of analysis and instead looks to various, intersecting systems of knowledge and discourse which inform our understanding of the very nature of peace and how it might be achieved. As Nira Yuval-Davis notes, patriarchy is a crude instrument of analysis as in some societies women have power over some men as well as other women. Further, patriarchy fails to consider the multiplicity of oppressions existing in particular, concrete situations (Yuval-Davis, 2004: 7). "Contrary to what the notion of patriarchy suggests," writes Yuval-Davis, "women are not usually just passive recipients and non-participants in the determination of gender relations" (Yuval-Davis, 2004: 8).

In an intersectional approach, the categories of 'have' and 'have not' in power relations are not so clear cut and are, in fact, seen as a false dichotomy (Wochrle, 1999: 42). Further, if holding to the notion that gender is always constructed in relation to 'the other', it would be quite impossible to attain the liberation from patriarchy so often hoped for in some schools of feminist study. As Christine Delphy argues, gender is not static and always defined in relationship so that even if it would be possible to make it so that 'women' gained the same 'rights' as 'men', the meaning of 'men', 'women', and 'rights' would likewise be very different in that process (Delphy, 1996: 39).

1.4.3 Power

Instead of focusing on the unilateral domination of one person or group over another and patriarchy as its most pronounced manifestation, I draw here on the work of Michel Foucault who argues that power exists only in relationship to resistance and through action (Foucault, 2003: 137).[36] Power, writes Foucault, is "the multiplicity of force relations immanent in the sphere in which they operate and which constitute their own organization" (Foucault, 1978: 92). It is formed in relationship between 'the other', constituted as the subject, who is acted upon, and the one who acts. Power acts upon the actions of others where freedom exists. When there is no freedom and where force is applied to physical bodies or things, violence is present (Foucault, 2003: 137).

36 Foucault's work has come under extensive criticism from feminists who argue that his work on sexuality and power fails to account for the divergent experiences of women. Lynn Hunt (1992) argues that Foucault's conception of power is genderless in Volume I of *The History of Sexuality*, yet in Volume 2 and Volume 3 of *The History of Sexuality* he proceeds to offer an exclusive history of the desiring male (Hunt, 1992: 83). Hunt argues that the 'individual' or the subject, used by Foucault to make his arguments on power and the rise of the technologies of the self, are specific to the experience of adult males and that women did not necessarily have the same access to the ownership of the self (*Ibid.*: 84-85).

Foucault lays out his argument, noting that power

> operates on the field of possibilities in which the behavior of active subjects is able to inscribe itself. It is a set of actions on possible actions; it incites, it induces, it seduces, it makes easier or more difficult, it releases or contrives, makes more probable or less…it is always a way of acting upon one or more acting subjects by virtue of their acting or being capable of action. (Foucault, 2003: 138)

In other words, power is a relational, situational, unstable force which both constitutes and is constituted by resistance. And being relational, where there is power there is also resistance; they cannot exist without each other (Foucault, 1978: 93-95). “At the very heart of the power relationship, and constantly provoking it, are the recalcitrance of the will and the intransigence of freedom… [It is] less of a face-to-face confrontation that paralyzes both sides than a permanent provocation” (Foucault, 2003: 139). Relating this notion of power back to my own experience, it is indeed a very healthy thing that I am experiencing such conflict in thinking about sexuality as it shows that neither what I hold dear nor what I feel that I am fighting against is the unilateral, completely violent, dominant force. Rather, inherent in this conflict is also a freedom to think, to challenge, and to transform.

1.4.4 Subjectivity and Identification

It is the very act of living within the constantly provocative power relationship, which helps to constitute the individual/subject. Here, I come back to Stuart Hall’s definition of identity being a process of articulation which can never be won, lost, abandoned or sustained (Hall, 1996: 2). In other words, it is living in a power relationship as Foucault outlines where identification emerges. Power is intimately tied to identity and in fact, the existence of the ‘I’, or the individual person/subject who is aware of their individuality is dependent on the exercise of power and that articulation of identities. Power is not a force which represses “but which positively makes us who we are” (Koppensteiner, 2009: 110). The individual human being is “one of power’s first effects” (Michel Foucault quoted in Koppensteiner, 2009: 110).

The creation of this interiority and sense of inner self is intimately tied to the act of confession. Foucault offers a detailed investigation of confession, as “a ritual that unfolds within a power relationship” (Foucault quoted in Bernstein, 1997: 16-17) and is the process by which a confessor puts into words that which has been previously culturally unspeakable.[37] It is through confession that the subject is produced as holding an interiority full of hidden inclinations. And it is through confession, he argues, that subjects self-regulate and find through the telling, an absolution. And so confession "polices even as it appears to pardon" and becomes instrumental in the process of subject self-creation (*Ibid.*: 18).[38]

Judith Butler also affirms the interconnection between power and identification. She notes that if in fact

> I am someone who cannot be without doing, then the conditions of my doing are, in part, the conditions of my existence. If my doing is dependent on what is done to me, or, rather, the ways in which I am done by norms, then the possibility of my persistence as an 'I' depends upon my being able to do something with what is done with me. (Butler, 2004b: 3)

Butler argues that people find that they are constituted by norms, dependant on them while simultaneously living in ways that "maintain a critical and transformative relation to them" (Butler, 2004b: 3). Foucault's assertion that, "[e]very relationship of power puts into operation differences that are, at the same time, its conditions and its results" (Foucault, 2003: 140) helps to suture together the notion that power is both a necessary force in the process of individualization, division, and also of relationship.

1.4.5 Subjectivity Breaking Down

Butler shows, however, that at some point the subject, the 'I' can break down in the course of the power relationship. This happens, she argues, when a person chooses to incorporate ways of being which do not make the 'I' fully recognizable, such as transgender people who may not identify or fit with the binary sex and gender norms so central in Western society; these people are then denied the existence of the 'I' within the community (Butler, 2004b: 3). For Foucault, this involves a place in which 'the other' has no freedom. This

37 Foucault argues that the act of confession was secularized in the nineteenth century with the emergence of medicine and psychoanalysis, so that confession expanded from what the confessor knew but kept hidden to be about what was hidden from the confessor himself and only became known through the act of confession (Bernstein, 1997: 18).

38 Bernstein argues that Foucault does not consider the gendered implications of confessions. Bernstein points out that these confessional discourses have channelled discussions of sex and gender to affirm that which is gendered masculine and heterosexual (Bernstein, 1997: 18-21). Furthermore, women were never seen as interactive participants in the same way men were with the rise of confessional techniques in medicine and psychology. Rather, women were objects of study, made hysterical in the medical establishment (*Ibid.*: 18-19).

happens when relations between people become inflexible and static; in such cases, power ceases to exist and rather domination takes its place (Koppensteiner, 2009: 111). Domination takes place "each time relations between people are set in a way that they are no longer reversible and any attempt to change is prevented or blocked" (*Ibid.*: 112). Sexuality, in particular, has had a strong connection to subjectivity in the western world so that deviant desires or sexual practices often become a refusal of particular kinds of subjectivity (Dollimore, 1991: 339).

Noted scholar Gayatri Spivak addresses the question of representing oppressed groups of people directly in her polemic essay, *Can the Subaltern Speak?* (2006). She highlights in this work the intersection of class, race, and gender in the way in which the subaltern[39] is represented and treated in Western European society, pointing to the constant failure this representation inevitably brings. Intellectuals, she argues, may claim to speak for subalterns or even that subalterns are speaking for themselves through confessions. But as Spivak points out, any speaking, acting, and knowing is intimately tied to the forces of capitalist financialization (Spivak, 2006: 29).[40] Placed in a different lens, we could view Spivak's critique as another perspective on the breaking down of subjectivity. Subaltern people, without access to power and from cultural, economic, or gender perspectives which violate the dominant frames of reference in the Western world, remain unheard. Either because they never held this internalized, autonomous 'I' implied by subjectivity or because they do not have the access to the means needed to articulate this subjectivity in the world. It follows that people of diverse genders, desires, bodies, and sexual practices could, in particular contexts, also be subaltern.

39 Rosalind Morris explains that the subaltern is not an identity but a predicament. It is being in the "structured place from which the capacity to access power is radically obstructed" (Morris, 2010: 88).

40 Spivak gives the example of an Indian woman who 'speaks' by killing herself as she attempts to avoid betraying the trust of her companions as a member of one of the many groups involved in Indian independence. Before killing herself, however, she waits until she is menstruating so it will be clear to all that she is not killing herself because of an illicit pregnancy, as was practiced in that culture. In this act she was displacing and also denying the cultural inscriptions prescribed on her body and person. Spivak rails that the 'subaltern cannot speak' having found out that the women's suicide is immortalized even among her female relatives as being because she had an illicit love affair (Spivak, 2006: 34). Spivak writes, "[s]he 'spoke,' but women did not, do not 'hear' her" and because she was not heard, she is a subaltern (*Ibid.*: 35).

Specifically, to what degree is it the case for LGBTQ Mennonites that their very subjectivity and membership in the Mennonite community is questioned or not acknowledged? As discussed earlier, the ideal of community as an understandable entity of people sharing certain common beliefs and principles can be a site where subjectivity breaks down. For some, to find a place within the ideal constructs of community, a change of the 'I' is necessary because holding desires or bodies outside of the male/female binary and heteronormative frame means to cease being recognized as a human being, as an ethical person, or belonging to a community (Koppensteiner, 2009: 111). In the Mennonite community, to what extent do idealized discourses enforce a compulsory heterosexuality, by which the position of queer persons is called into question? Is it the case that being bisexual in the Mennonite community at times, in fact, becomes impossible, unless you want to compromise or change the bisexual identification you hold or leave the community? I delve deeper into these questions as I progress through this book asking in what ways LGBTQ people, have or do not have certain forms of subjectivity available to them, particularly that of being Mennonite?

1.4.6 Peaces and the Meaning for a Life Lived

The question of what this understanding of power and subjectivity means for daily life and peaces is a complex one. For me, I think that being aware that 'I' is embedded in relationships of power which both allow me to distinguish myself as separate from –and simultaneously connected to –the 'other' is the first step. It is the first step towards moving to see with many lenses; to see from many perspectives what is going on, who is saying what and to whom, and to feel to what end these things are being said.

For if I can see relationships through many different lenses, recognizing the multiplicity of factors in any one moment and the interrelatedness of 'I' to the 'other', it leads, I believe, to a yielding. As Butler so poignantly writes:

> For if I am confounded by you, then you are already of me, and I am nowhere without you. I cannot muster the 'we' except by finding the way in which I am tied to 'you,' by trying to translate but finding that my own language must break up and yield if I am to know you. You are what I gain through this disorientation and loss. This is how the human comes into being, again and again, as that which we have yet to know. (Butler, 2004a: 49)

In seeing this interrelatedness it is hard not to see myself, as a bisexual Mennonite, deeply and intimately connected to the biblical literalist Mennonite woman who is adamant that same-sex desire is a sin; this is no easy task at all. Imagine, if you will, the impact if such interrelatedness was recognized as inherent not only to our communities, but to life itself. Such interrelatedness supposes vulnerability in that it recognizes that "I cannot be who I am without drawing upon the sociality of norms that precede and exceed me" nor without reference to 'you' (Butler, 2004b: 32). In this way, by exposing the interrelated nature of existence itself and all identities, gender, sex, desire, and sexual practices are placed firmly on the agenda of peace studies.

I choose to conceive of power as something which is multidirectional, and in this way my understanding of peace also sees the nature of peace exercised within power relationships to be multidirectional and relational. An understanding of peace which is multidirectional and relational however, does not see 'equality' in terms of resource distribution or power as it is traditionally understood, and seeks not one equal peace but rather multiple peaces. This gets away from dichotomies of guilty/innocent, bad/good often all too commonly used when dealing with conflictive situations.

Such a unilateral understanding of peace is still quite common and permeates the way in which peace is so often sought on the familial, community, national, and international levels. As peace scholar Wolfgang Dietrich (2006) outlines, contemporary Western society still largely draws on the notion of a Creator God who expels peace to those who have favour, only now this notion is framed in secular terms. In most contemporary contexts, peace remains framed as a universal right for all who are 'worthy' of it by being of 'good will'. Postmodern interpretations of peace have called into question the grand narratives of international relations and understandings of peace and conflict by arguing that there is not one truth and that "what is perceived as true here and now might be wrong and unjust tomorrow and elsewhere" (Dietrich, 2006: 11).

And so it would be a mistake to view the stories of those that I interview as stories of truth that reveal once and for all the hidden reality of being LGBTQ Mennonite. Foucault's critique of the confession points to the interrelated nature of such self pronouncements as does Butler's theory of performativity. We are always existing within relationships of power and discourses that shape us while we are ourselves shaping, transforming, and even rejecting those very pronouncements; and in the telling, we are always changed. In her discussion of Spivak's work, Rosalind Morris explains that even if it is possible for the subaltern to speak, and in that act, cease to be subaltern, the implication of telling the story of once being without access to power, has its implications. Morris asks,

> [w]hat kind of representation becomes available to the one who, having partially escaped the silence of subalternity, is nonetheless possessed by the consciousness of having been obstructed, contained, or simply misread for so much of her life? (Morris, 2010: 8)

So how is being LGBTQ and Mennonite shaped by confessional stories and the knowledge of being an outsider? It is an interesting and important question, the answer to which goes beyond the scope of this particular work but which merits further examination.

The question of focus here is the nature of identity. I believe that in embracing the pluralities of peaces and interrelated nature of personhood, the category of personhood is opened wide. Any such attempt to open the possibilities for multiplicities in actions, thoughts, and physical constitution is fundamentally a project that is going to cause a lot of conflict about the identity groupings of our world which divide one person from another, and keep some out and others in. It challenges notions of a community as constituted on that which is the same. It contends understandings of each person as once and for all time this/that, heterosexual/homosexual, Mennonite/non-Mennonite. This is not to say that identity politics do not have a place. Indeed, they have a very key role to play especially for LGBTQ people who still face so much discrimination. In fact, identities are important for each and every person for they are the means through which we make sense of our world and around which we rally. Yet, I believe the project of peaces extends beyond identity rights.

The call of postmodern peaces is not for 'rights' as they are commonly conceived, but rather for everyone to be counted as human beings, to 'pass' so that one might find a belonging with oneself in relation to others. I appreciate the words of Judith Butler again here, who writes that to work for sexual 'rights' means that:

> we are not simply struggling for rights that attach to my person, but we are struggling *to be conceived as persons* […] If we are struggling for rights that attach, or should attach, to my personhood, then we assume that personhood as already constituted. But if we are struggling not only to be conceived as persons, but to create a social transformation of the very meaning of personhood, then the assertion of rights becomes a way of intervening into the social and political process by which the human is articulated. (Butler, 2004b: 32-33)

Is there no greater base for the creation of peaces, than expanding how we see our personhood and the personhood of others? To expand what might qualify one to belong in a community?

2. IDEALIZED DISCOURSES OF SEXUALITY

> There is no binary division to be made between what one says and what one does not say; we must try to determine the different ways of not saying such things... There is not one but many silences, and they are an integral part of the strategies that underlie and permeate discourses. (Foucault, 1978: 27)

Indeed, there are deafening silences in the actions made, words spoken and statements written in the Mennonite community. I am interested in analyzing the exteriority of the texts, meaning those objectives and explicit constructions in the texts and words of people which form idealized pictures of identity. By paying attention to that which is and is not said, I will show how being intelligible in the Mennonite community necessitates a heterosexual identification. My aim is not to uncover the 'hidden' intentions behind written words but rather to look at the way in which discourses represent LGBTQ Mennonites as well as sex, gender, desire, and sexual practices more generally. How do these discourses distinguish between 'us' and 'them' through sexuality, making divisions which remove the commonality shared between all people? Further, how do these discourses then go on to try and erase the evidence of this division which defines who is inside and who is outside of the fold of Mennonite? I will argue in the course of this chapter that heterosexual identification and curtailed sexual practices are central in order to self-identify and be recognized as persons belonging to Mennonite and that under the cloak of euphemisms, there is a community which celebrates unity rather than diversity; this is a community that continues to perpetrate a great violence upon persons holding diverse sexual and gender identities.

2.1 METHODS IN DISCOURSE ANALYSIS & CONTEXT OF SOURCES

In this chapter, I look at three Mennonite church conferences including Mennonite Church Canada (MC Canada), the Canadian Conference of Mennonite Brethren Churches (CCMBC), and the Evangelical Mennonite Conference (EMC) and their provincial bodies. I also look at two different Mennonite institutions in and around Winnipeg including Canadian Mennonite University (CMU) and Mennonite Central Committee Manitoba (MCC MB), while giving a peripheral account of three other organizations including Mennonite Economic Development Associates (MEDA), Concordia Hospital, and Mennonite Heritage Village. To examine these institutions and church conferences, I looked to official documents, publications, web based information, and, in the case of the five institutions, oral interviews.

I chose these particular sources because they represent the very public and formal discourses in the Mennonite community on sexuality. My particular focus on church documents and specifically religiously oriented organizations and practices may seem confusing to you as a reader who by now is well aware that this work is concerned with discourses of belonging in the Mennonite community at large rather than only that within those facets of the community which are religious. The fact is that discourses on sexuality from the Mennonite church and religiously associated institutions play a persuasive, authoritative role in framing discussions on sexuality within the Mennonite community at large. Although it is true that I still hold to the idea that Mennonite is a performatively constituted identity, this performativity cannot be separated from religious discourses.

My discursive analysis pays attention to four main facets of the texts and narratives. Firstly, I am concerned with the context of the discourses including: the formality of the event; who is speaking, who is listening and their position, social power, as well as status; the relations between participants; and the opinions as well as ideologies of the speakers (van Dijk, 2007). Secondly, I look at the explicit way in which sex, gender, desire, and sexual practices are spoken about and whether they are framed as part of inherent, stable identities coherently flowing from one another.

Thirdly, I look at the style of discourse which is found in the way that 'sounds' are produced both through that which is spoken and written; the sound may be less or more formal in discourse. Special attention too, is given to the choice of words as "word choice is one of the ways people betray their underlying opinions, social attitudes and ideologies" (van Dijk, 2007: 6). I look specifically at the implication of the use of the word 'homosexual' in the context of these discourses as well as the use of the words 'we', 'them', and 'society' which can assist in making or breaking down divisions between sanctioned and non-sanctioned sexualities.

Fourthly, I pay some attention to rhetorical structure including metaphors, comparisons, irony, hyperboles and euphemisms. These rhetorical structures are optional and used in particular to persuade or produce special effects. Through rhetorical structures, meaning may be emphasized or de-emphasized which has a particular effect on the recipients (van Dijk, 2007: 7). I specifically look at the way in which euphemistic statements are made which provide pleasant sounding promises of love and dialogue which fundamentally underemphasize or misrepresent the violent nature of these discourses.

2.2 Mennonite Church Conferences

Why do these national church conferences matter? I believe they matter because these bodies are shaping some of the key discussions in the Mennonite community on sexuality both within churches and more generally in the community. These larger bodies are often looked to when non-Mennonite people hope to understand what it is to be Mennonite, and also when people who are Mennonite seek an answer to this question. These church conferences have a significant influence on the operation and ethos of organizations which because they were either founded by Mennonites or are associated in some way with these national church bodies, continue to follow or be influenced by the formal statements of these conferences on sexuality. Each of these conferences holds a slightly different relationship to its member congregations and individual constituents which I subsequently outline. Also, each utilizes different means through which to communicate their messages on sexuality.

Mennonite Church Canada

Mennonite Church Canada (MC Canada) is a collective body of 221 congregations and 32,000 individual people across Canada made up of the historical descendants of various waves of Mennonite immigrants to North America as well as "brothers and sisters from all parts of the globe and the indigenous people of Canada" (Mennonite Church Canada, 2010). Mennonite Church Canada itself emerged in the early 2000s as a product of the coming together of several Mennonite conferences, the earliest precursor being formed in 1810 (*Ibid.*).

Historically, the Mennonites ancestrally connected to Mennonite Church Canada come from highly diverse historical geographical and cultural groupings. The General Conference Mennonite Church, for example, which became one of the conferences subsumed into MC Canada, included the historical descendants of primarily Swiss-South German and Dutch-North German Mennonites; it was distinguished by its emphasis on faith, freedom for the individual and individual congregational autonomy, open fellowship with all Mennonites and non-Mennonite Christians,[41] the spirit of dynamic or the ability to change, and fulfilling God's mission through everyday and ordinary living (Kaufman and Poettcker: 1990). Also coming together to make up MC Canada was the Mennonite Church, which was the oldest, and at one time also the largest, Mennonite conference in North America. The Mennonite Church was primarily made up of Mennonites from Swiss-South German background with a small number of families from the Lower Rhine and Hamburg-Altona area as well as a smaller number of people from Dutch, Prussian, or Russian backgrounds. Historically, district conferences held general authority over individual congregations and in particular matters of doctrine and practice were the prerogative of district conference (Bender and Stauffer Hostetler, 1989).

The Mennonite Church and General Conference Mennonite Church included congregations in both the United States and Canada, with some congregations holding dual memberships in both groupings. After coming together as one body in the early 2000s, the conference split into two national bodies, Mennonite Church United States of America and MC Canada. Today MC Canada tends to be known as a conference with a concern for social justice, peace activism, and its engagement with and integration into mainstream society which is comparatively greater than many other Mennonite groupings; that being said, there are of course exceptions to that rule.

In terms of the relationship between MC Canada and its constituent churches and members, MC Canada's bylaws state clearly that area churches, which in the case of Manitoba is Mennonite Church Manitoba (MC Manitoba),[42] as well as individual congregations, are expected to "accept the Confession of Faith in a Mennonite Perspective" as well as "uphold statements of Christian faith and life made by MC Canada from time to time" (Mennonite Church Canada, 2007b: Part II, 4b and 4c). Following the principles outlined in the *Confession of Faith* is in fact required for the membership of any area church in MC Canada. Likewise, membership in a congregation which is part of an area church is required to be appointed to any delegate body, elected position, or committees which make decisions regarding the policies and procedures of MC Canada (Mennonite Church Canada, 2007b: Part III, 7; Part IV, 12).

---

41 As practiced with open communion, membership in inter-faith national bodies, and joint cooperation in hospitals, and old people's homes (Kaufman and Poettcker, 1990).

42 MC Manitoba is "a covenant community of 50 congregations with over 10,000 members" (Mennonite Church Manitoba, 2010), meaning that Manitoba holds approximately one-third of all MC Canada members while holding about one-thirtieth of the Canadian population.

MC Manitoba is a direct body of Mennonite Church Canada although it engages in independent projects at a local level. MC Manitoba follows the requirements for membership in MC Canada including holding to the *Confession of Faith in a Mennonite Perspective* and is responsible for the admission or revoking of the membership of individual congregational bodies in MC Manitoba (and thereby the membership of congregations in the national body, MC Canada).

Officially, it is the case that "[i]ndividual congregations shall retain full privileges of self-determination in their own program. However, membership in the Conference implies the responsible support of resolutions and programs developed together" (Mennonite Church Canada, 1998). This phrase is contained in the context of a document specifically concerning homosexuality which outlines the church's stance as believing that same-sex sexual practices are sinful. To me, Mennonite Church Canada is implying that the support of same-sex sexual practices by an area church or church congregation could lead to expulsion from the national or area body.

Indeed, this has been the case for several church bodies in North America including the 1997 expulsion of the Germantown Mennonite Church, the oldest congregation in North America founded in 1683, and in Canada, the Calgary Inter-Mennonite Church. After becoming a fully Welcoming congregation[43] Calgary Inter-Mennonite Church was expelled in 1999 from the provincial and also national bodies of the Canadian Conference of Mennonite Brethren Churches and later gave up member privileges in the Northwest Conference of the Mennonite Church and the Conference of Mennonites in Canada (both of which later became a part of MC Canada) (Johns, 2010; Epp and Steiner, 2009).

On the flip side, many churches against the inclusion of LGBTQ peoples have similarly left the Mennonite church over the last several decades for its perceived laxity on the issue of homosexuality (Johns, 2010; Epp and

43 The expressions 'Welcoming congregation' or 'Affirming congregation' are commonly used to communicate the viewpoints and practices of a church towards LGBTQ persons. A Welcoming congregation is one in which LGBTQ are welcomed to join in the life of the congregation; quite often this is an informal designation rather than a publically declared or officially institutionalized stance. An Affirming congregation is one where a congregation is publically affirmative of LGBTQ people into full membership and leadership in the church. According to the Brethren Mennonite Council for LGBT Interests, being publically Affirming means: it is a safe space for LGBT people and their families; the church has educated itself about sexuality; and that LGBT people will not be the "topic of controversy" or be caused overt harm (Brethren Mennonite Council for Lesbian, Gay, Bisexual, and Transgender Interests, 2012).

Steiner, 2009). In February 2006 it became widely publicized that the Mennonite Church of Vernon in British Colombia, as well as Saskatchewan's two largest MC Canada congregations, Cornerstone Mennonite in Saskatoon and Grace Mennonite in Neuanlage, were leaving the area and national churches due to the lack of discipline on the subject of homosexuality (Braun, 2008).

Of particular note in this regard is a recent controversy in British Columbia, Canada. A perceived laxity on the part of MC Canada regarding same-sex sexual relationships, has led some congregations in British Columbia (BC) to push for the right to be part of Mennonite Church British Columbia (MC British Columbia) without being part of MC Canada. Provisions were made so that congregations could have the option to be an Area Conference Only Member (ACOM).[44] Similarly, there are congregations in BC who are displeased with the more conservative bend of the area church, MC British Columbia, but would like to retain membership in MC Canada. So far, this type of membership has not been addressed (W. Warketin, 2010).

Although the area church officially retains the responsibility to discipline and regulate membership it is nevertheless also subject to the statements made by MC Canada on sexuality. When a member of the pastoral team at Toronto United Mennonite Church came out as lesbian in 2002, heated discussion with the area church, Mennonite Church Eastern Canada (MC Eastern Canada) ended with the revocation of the pastor's license (Farris-Manning, 2005: 3). According to Cheryl Farris-Manning's discussion of the controversy, MC Eastern Canada issued a statement on their intention to not exclude congregations that were unsupportive of the statements of the church on homosexuality; this suggests an interest of this area church in hearing divergent voices and commitment to not removing congregations welcoming lesbian and gay people in the full life of the church (Farris-Manning, 2005; Mennonite Church Eastern Canada, 2004). Farris-Manning argues, however, that because MC Eastern Canada was bound to official MC Canada rhetoric, it was limited in the options for responding to the sexual orientation of the pastor (Farris-Manning, 2005: 3).

MC Canada is clearly the organization among these 221 congregations and 32,000 people which retains a great deal of privilege and authority in speaking and dictating norms, at least on a formal level with the area churches bound in some way to carry out practices in line with MC Canada's

44 The adoption of the Area Conference Only Member (ACOM) option is also related to broader trends in the political style of several of the founding conferences of MC Canada. For more details please see Mennonite Church Canada, 2007c.

core statements. Further, to be involved in decision making bodies of the church which decide policies regarding sexuality requires being a member of a congregation and therefore an area church which concurs with the existing ideas on sexuality –a policy which it and of itself helps to partially block against divergent opinions.

In terms of executive leadership, it can be noted that in 2010, out of the three conferences I examined, MC Canada was the only one which officially supported the full leadership of women in the church; this is reflected rather well at the national board level where women make up almost one-half of all board and committee members. Although the executive of the MC Canada and MC Manitoba boards are primarily men, women make up a significant portion of the general boards of each of these bodies and are at least in theory, able to be involved in speaking on sexuality norms.

In relation to MC Canada, I analyze those key documents from which sexuality ideals are drawn including Article 19- Family, Singleness, and Marriage from the *Confession of Faith in a Mennonite Perspective* (Mennonite Church Canada, 1995a) as well as two other documents that MC Canada self identifies as forming the basis of their stance on sexuality including the *Resolution on Human Sexuality* (Mennonite Church Canada, 1986) and the *Resolution on Homosexuality* (Mennonite Church Canada, 1998). Further, I look at statements released from MC Canada's Faith and Life Committee (Mennonite Church Canada, 1995b), and other official MC Canada statements on sexuality to understand role these documents have in creating norms that permeate into area churches, congregations, individual lives, and the Mennonite community at large.

To understand the specific context of these documents, a brief history of statements on same-sex sexual relationships in the context of MC Canada and its precursors is useful. Homosexuality found its way into the Mennonite church consciousness in the 1970s and in the 1980s, eventually prompting a study commissioned by the General Conference Mennonite Church and the Mennonite Church on the topic of sexuality. The four year study brought together medical doctors, psychologists, biblical scholars, ethicists, and church leaders and cumulated in a study guide for congregations entitled *Human Sexuality and the Christian Life: A Working Document for Study and Dialogue* (General Conference Mennonite Church and Mennonite Church, 1985).

Shortly after the study was completed, it was adopted by the General Conference Mennonite Church Assembly along with the *Resolution on Human Sexuality* (1986); the adoption of the resolution was a move which proved to outrage many persons who argued that the 1986 *Resolution* was not based on the recommendations found in the 1985 study. Subsequently, the Mennonite Church also adopted an almost identical resolution on sexuality. Contention remained over the meaning of the resolution as well as whether these statements were rules or guidelines to be followed. In 1990 both Mennonite bodies appointed a Listening Committee to hear the voices of LGBTQ Mennonites. The recommendations of this Listening Committee (General Conference Mennonite Church and Mennonite Church, 1992) were presented to the executive councils of both conferences. These recommendations included a call to study homosexuality on all levels of church life and provide more staff support for the purposes of these studies. The recommendations were not adopted and the report was ordered to be suppressed from the general membership (Johns, 2010).

As the conferences were moving to join together, they adopted a new *Confession of Faith in a Mennonite Perspective* (Mennonite Church Canada, 1995a) which did not reference same-sex relationships but referred to sexual practices only rightly taking place within heterosexual marriage. At this time, the tension between "the commitment to maintain a clear and biblical ethical teaching that rules out sexual union between gay or lesbian persons on the one hand, and the commitment to live and show compassion to all-especially the marginalized" became pronounced (Johns, 2010). The 1995 statement, Agreeing and Disagreeing in Love (Mennonite Church Canada, 1995c) followed shortly afterward, as an attempt to bridge the gap between an exclusionary policy on sexual practices and the church's commitment to peace and justice (Johns, 2010).

CANADIAN CONFERENCE OF MENNONITE BRETHREN CHURCHES

Today's Canadian Conference of Mennonite Brethren Churches (CCMBC) trace their history to several villages in the Molotschna colony in Ukraine. This is where groups of Mennonites, who called themselves Brethren, began to meet more regularly to celebrate the Lord's Supper and speak out against what they saw as ethical laxity and abuses in practices of baptism, church discipline, and pastoral leadership (Jost and Faber, 2002). Over time, the main distinguishing facets of the Brethren were water baptism by immersion instead of pouring/sprinkling, an emphasis on personal faith experience beginning in a conversion, discipleship, evangelism, and mission (Epp, 2008: 285; Dyck, 1993: 293-297). Many of these Mennonites migrated to the United States Midwest between 1874 and 1880 from which a number of missionaries were sent to Manitoba and Saskatchewan. The very first meeting of the Canadian Conference of Mennonite Brethren Churches (CCMBC) in

1910, included thirteen churches from Saskatchewan and a few years later involved Manitoban congregations (Lohrenz and Janz, 2009).

The arrival of the Russian Mennonites (Russlander) between 1923 and 1930 and again in the 1940s, significantly expanded the membership of the Mennonite Brethren Church. By 1986, Mennonite Brethren churches, almost exclusively urban in their location, could lay claim to some of the largest evangelical church communities in Western Canadian cities and congregations could be found across Canada, the United States, and South America (Lohrenz and Janz, 2009).

The Canadian Conference of Mennonite Brethren Churches (CCMBC) operates in a manner similar to MC Canada in that it is a national body which regulates the membership of area churches, which in this case are known as provincial conferences. The provincial body of the CCMBC in Manitoba is the Mennonite Brethren Church of Manitoba (MBCM). Any individual congregation, under regulation from the MBCM becomes a member church of the MBCM, automatically becomes a member of the CCMBC (Canadian Conference of Mennonite Brethren Churches, 2006: Article 4). In 2010, the CCMBC had over 250 individual congregational members and 7 provincial conferences (Canadian Conference of Mennonite Brethren Churches, 2010a; 2010b) with congregations under the Mennonite Brethren Church of Manitoba, numbering 38 (Mennonite Brethren Church of Manitoba, 2010b).

Here again it is the CCMBC along with its *Confession of Faith* (Canadian Conference of Mennonite Brethren Churches, 2001) which sets the norms on sexuality. The *Confession of Faith*, developed in consultation with the United States Conference of Mennonite Brethren Churches, is the basis for the membership of any provincial conference or individual congregation. If a member congregation "ceases to be substantially in harmony with the Confession of Faith", its membership privileges can be withdrawn by either the MBCM or the CCMBC (Canadian Conference of Mennonite Brethren Churches, 2006). The Mennonite Brethren Church of Manitoba makes it clear that its organizations and values are centered around the *Confession of Faith* of the Canadian Conference of Mennonite Brethren Churches and that neither the MBCM or any of its congregations shall "pass or accept resolutions or practices which are in conflict with this Confession of Faith" (Mennonite Brethren Church of Manitoba, 2010a). In the course of this chapter I examine the *Confession of Faith* (Canadian Conference of Mennonite Brethren Churches, 2001) as well as other official statements from the CCMBC or the MBCM to highlight what this means for LGBTQ Mennonites.

In 2010, the leadership of the Mennonite Brethren Church of Manitoba was predominately male despite the fact that the MBCM is one of the only

CCMBC provincial bodies which has publicly affirmed women's leadership in the church (Mennonite Brethren Church of Manitoba, 2010c).[45] The position of the CCMBC on women's leadership in the church remains mixed and inconclusive, suggesting that the debate over whether gender is constructed or gender is a reflection of biological 'realities' is still very much raging.

All three of the executive staff of the MBCM in 2010, were men with one-third of the leadership board's executive committee being made up of women, and a one-fifth representation of women as general members of the board. Of the 65 positions available on the board and its committees, in 2010, women held only a meager 16 or about 24 percent. Women made up almost the entirety of the committee concerned with the running of a MBCM mental health care centre, over one-half of the Conflict Resolution Committee. Yet, on other committees there were no women holding committee positions, reflecting the gender imbalance evident in the board. Some of the most notable committees with a total absence of women are those concerned with relationships between the MBCM and prominent Mennonite institutions including Canadian Mennonite University, Mennonite Central Committee, and Mennonite Disaster Service (Mennonite Brethren Church of Manitoba, 2010c).

On a national level in 2010, the Executive Leadership Board of the CCMBC was composed of two men and one woman. The remaining Executive Leadership Board, which includes a total of 16 other persons, has only two women. Notably, the Faith and Life Board, which is charged with commenting on issues of contemporary relevance such as homosexuality, abortion and marriage, has a leadership team of three men. In 2010, one man in this leadership team was a visible minority; which is a significant fact given the overwhelmingly white majority of the MBCM and the CCMBC's other leadership positions (Canadian Conference of Mennonite Brethren Churches, 2010c; Lohvinenko, 2010).[46]

Evangelical Mennonite Conference

45 In 2003, the Mennonite Brethren Church of Manitoba submitted a resolution to the CCMBC calling for the full participation of women in ministry leadership. The response of the CCMBC to the issue was mixed and inconclusive (Heidebrecht, 2003).

46 There are also a number of subcommittees of the CCMBC, the gender breakdown in positions being: Finance/Audit (four persons, four men, zero women); Governance (four persons, four men, zero women); Personnel Compensation (four persons, three men, one woman); Binational Board-MBBS (three persons, three men, 0 women); Binational Board-MBMSI (five persons, four men, one woman); Historical Commission (three persons, two men, one woman); Nominating (nine persons, seven men, two women) (Lohvinenko, 2010).

Once known as the Kleine Gemeinde, this subgroup split from the larger Mennonite church in present day Ukraine during the early 19th century; the group then moved to Manitoba and later founded tight knit communities throughout the North American West as well as in South and Central America in the latter half of the 20th century (Loewen, 1993: 2). The Kleine Gemeinde were one of the smallest groups of Mennonites, known for their inwardly contained communities and strict social boundaries and conservatism (*Ibid.*). The Kleine Gemeinde eventually became known as the Evangelical Mennonite Conference (EMC) and were first based in Manitoba and Kansas and then members spread across Central America, Mexico, Canada, and the United States (Epp, 2008: 284). EMC congregations are distinguished today by the pervasive evangelical currents which run through church practices and beliefs including a strong emphasis on a literal reading of the Bible, church community, and evangelism. In 2010, the conference had 7300 members with 61 individual churches across the world and is primarily rural in its composition (Evangelical Mennonite Conference, 2010b).

Interestingly, whereas MC Canada explicitly emphasizes its ability to revoke the membership of area churches and the CCMBC can do so for individual congregations, the EMC has no area or provincial bodies and holds more direct and explicit statements on individual membership in churches. According to the EMC *Constitution* (2007), membership in a church requires an agreement with the Statement of Faith as well as having "a witness of being a new creation in Christ" (Evangelical Mennonite Conference, 2007: Section II, 1b, 1c).

The section on membership goes on to explicitly iterate the responsibilities of members which includes nurturing "strong, wholesome relationships, whether single and married. Celibate life and heterosexual married life are both honorable and high callings from God" (Evangelical Mennonite Conference, 2007: Section II, 3f). The discipline of members for committing sins (implicitly this includes same-sex sexual practices) is laid out in Section II part 4b which states that if the erring person does not repent of their actions, and private efforts fail to restore the individual into full fellowship within the church, "the church is left with no alternative but to acknowledge, sadly and publicly, that the erring person has broken Covenant with God and His church. This includes a dismissal from membership in the church" (*Ibid.*: Section II, 4b).

Those who speak through the constitution and documents of the EMC are primarily males. In fact, the *Constitution* is explicit in stating that pastors and ministers must be males chosen from the church membership. Deacons, responsible for the care giving ministries of individual churches and their communities, may be "married couples or individuals" (Evangelical Mennonite Conference, 2010b). Administrative leaders in individual churches are not explicitly required to be men nor are missionaries. In the conference's words "women serve on national boards, as council delegates, as missionaries, and within local churches; while they can be selected locally as ministers, the conference does not provide for their ordination" (Evangelical Mennonite Conference, 2010b).

2.2.1 An Assumed Coherence?: A Look at the Exteriority of Texts

Are gender, sex, desire, and sexual practice implicitly or explicitly assumed to coherently flow from one another in the context of these Mennonite church conference documents? Such a question is concerned with the very nature of identities themselves, for if sexual identities are stable, fixed, and inherent it most often follows that a female is a woman by designation of her biological sex, she desires men, and her sexual practices are exclusively with men. In such a conception there is no room for intersex persons, contingent identities, or divergent experiences and practices outside of this linear flow. I found in my investigation of Canadian Mennonite church conferences, that the linear relationship between sex, gender, desire and sexual acts is pronounced.

The *Resolution on Human Sexuality* (1986) of MC Canada, affirms that "sexuality is a good and beautiful gift from God, a gift of identity and a way of being in the world as male and female" (Mennonite Church Canada, 1986). From the outset, this resolution positions sex as binary (male and female) and suggests sexuality as the basis of an identity as male or female; this is an identity which is given as a gift by God, implying an unchanging, essentialized, core and divinely instituted binary. Further, sexuality as a way of "being in the world as male and female" is explicit in pronouncing that being (actions, practices, and thoughts) is necessarily male or female and that as such, a continuity will be present between gender, desire, and sexual practices.

Other church conferences such as the CCMBC and the EMC are more explicit than MC Canada in making statements about sex, gender, desire, and sexual practices. The CCMBC states that man and woman were made in the image of God which "is expressed in the maleness of man and the femaleness of woman" and it is in the covenant relationship of marriage "which includes the sexual union of woman and man, that the richness and the complementary nature of the image of God is expressed most fully" (Canadian

Conference of Mennonite Brethren Churches, 2004). Here, gender is taken to the point of erasure in that it becomes intimately and unproblematically linked to a sex duality; the idea that there exists a true 'femaleness' of women, suggests that the gender epitomized in 'femaleness' is necessarily a mirror reflection of innate biological differences which are manifested in very particular physical markers. Further, this male/female duality is tied to proper sexual practices, when the sexual union of the binary sexes is said to be the way in which the image of God is most authentically expressed.

According to the *Constitution* of the Evangelical Mennonite Conference, "God created the human race, male and female, in his own image" (Evangelical Mennonite Conference, 2007: 8). The position of the church is further expanded in a theological journal for conference pastors which states that "men and women are ontological equals" and "gender distinctions are primarily in-born and regulated by Scriptural norms" (Plett, 2007: 16). Such norms dictate that men "are to take primary leadership in the home and in the church" (*Ibid.*).[47] The church adopts such a complementarian[48] position, arguing that "when men and women celebrate their masculinity and femininity, genuine gender harmony can be enjoyed" (*Ibid.*). For "[i]n the home, members are to regard one another as equals before the Lord, while recognizing God-given roles" (Evangelical Mennonite Conference, 2007: 11).

In the EMC, it is clear that gender is not seen as constructed, but a series of God-given behaviours and actions that comes forth from a particular biological sex. In harkening back to the Genesis literality that God intended only two sexes at creation and overtly stating that it is only through the coming together of a woman's femininity and a man's masculinity that harmony can exist, the EMC is clearly positioning gender as that which reflects a suppos-

---

47 Following Plett, this position is justified by the fact that: 1) God create men and women as equals for different roles (Genesis 2:18-25; 1 Corinthians 11: 7-12); 2) church leadership since the time of the apostles has been in the hands of men; 3) Jesus came as a man and affirmed his desire for male leadership by choosing 12 male disciples; 4) passages in the New Testament that affirm that men are to provide leadership in the home and church (Plett, 2007: 16).

48 Complementarian is a word used by the EMC to describe the position of the conference on women leadership in the church. This position is based around the principle that women and men are equal, and both have inherently different genders made for different roles. Men are the ones chosen by God for church and family leadership (Plett, 2007: 16). According to Plett, taking an egalitarian position (including the notion that men and women are equal, gender is constructed, and women can be in leadership roles) has implications for other theological discussions because "the egalitarian position has often served as a catalyst for liberalism and theological drift. Note the consistent progression from acceptance of egalitarianism to some form of acceptance of homosexual behaviour…many of the pro-homosexual arguments mirror the egalitarian arguments" (*Ibid.*: 22).

edly innate, stable sex. Further, life practices are called to reflect this duality and pre-destined union between men and women.

Not only do the discourses of the CCMBC and the EMC assume a predestined union between men and women, they also position this as central to an ethical and spiritual existence. Walter Unger explains in the CCMBC's monthly publication, *Mennonite Brethren Herald*, that in the covenantal relationship between a man and a woman "[t]here is more than a physical, one-flesh complementarily here. There is a deep, spiritual union…akin to the spiritual union of Christ and the church" (Unger, 2010). It is only through the joining of these two sexes that a relationship which is a reflection of God can take place.

Further, all conferences are also clear in their declaration that a Christian should only marry another Christian believer. Article 19 of the Mennonite Church Canada's *Confession of Faith in a Mennonite Perspective* argues that "[t]he oneness between husband and wife is a mystery which reflects the oneness of the Godhead and the oneness between Christ and his church. We affirm that Christians who marry should marry in the Lord, to a Christian spouse" (Mennonite Church Canada, 1995a). So not only are sex, gender, desire, and sexual practice set up to linearly flow from each other but also holding to a male/female binary sex expressed in Christian heterosexual marriage is the path to living ethically and having a complete spiritual experience.

2.2.2 Biological Realities Pre-Determine Desire and Practices

In addition to the way in which gender is erased and sexual practices spiritualized, the right to desire and engage in sexual practices at all is linked to marriage and reproduction. Article 19 of the *Confession of Faith* (Mennonite Church Canada, 1995a) gives hints about the connection assumed between sexual practices and biological sex. The article states that "sexual union is reserved for the marriage bond" and that this union "is for pleasure and closeness and for procreation" (Mennonite Church Canada, 1995a). The Article goes on to state that it is "through procreation, the human family continues from generation to generation" (*Ibid.*). This passage on the purpose of sexual practice follows a lengthy introduction on the importance of family for the raising of children and also for the growth of wholeness of the church more generally (*Ibid.*).

The CCMBC also states that "[a]t creation God designed marriage for companionship, sexual union and the birth and nurture of children" (Canadian Conference of Mennonite Brethren Churches, 2001: Article 11, 9). This is similar to what is found in the Evangelical Mennonite Conference (EMC)

Constitution which explains that "God instituted marriage for the intimate companionship of husband and wife and for the procreation and nurture of children" (Evangelical Mennonite Conference, 2007: 11). Certainly, some heterosexual sexual practices lead to the creation of children and many more heterosexual sexual practices do not. Likewise, some same-gender sexual practices do not lead to procreation. The link made between sex, sexual practices, and procreation is telling in that it is part of a much longer tradition within Christianity of limiting sexual practices and pleasure to procreation.

Notably, the *Resolution on Human Sexuality* (Mennonite Church Canada, 1986) recognizes that sexism is present in the church, "damaging the *self-esteem* of women and hindering their full contribution to personal relationships and to the church, and denying men *a true understanding* of themselves" [my emphasis] (Mennonite Church Canada, 1986). Although the use of the word self-esteem has a parsimonious ring when describing the gendered violence inherent in the church, it is nevertheless important that there is a recognition that some of the gender expectations have perpetrated a violence and that gender is at least to a certain extent, socially constructed.

In each of these three Mennonite church conferences I examined, sex and gender were divided into a man/woman, male/female binary which were recognized as God given, and inherent to identity. The conferences differ in the degree to which they see gender as constructed with MC Canada recognizing the presence of sexism in the church. The CCMBC offers a vague affirmation of the femaleness of women and maleness of men yet continues to take an inconclusive stance on women in church leadership. The EMC meanwhile, makes more explicit statements that men and women were made by God to fulfill different roles, suggesting that gender is inherent to a person and biologically based. Also interesting is that sexual desire and practices which brought together these binary sexes and 'opposite' male/female genders were associated with ethical living and spiritual experience.

2.2.3 Constructing an Ideal Community: Queer Identities as Peripheral

Although in all three Mennonite conferences, a clear linear progression between sex, gender, desire, sexual practices, and spiritual experience are made, most of what is written in these discourses does not directly reference LGBTQ people. As I will demonstrate in this section, even if not explicitly referencing LGBTQ people, these discourses nevertheless construct an ideal Mennonite community which necessitates heterosexual sexual practices and identification. There is an inordinate amount of emphasis on following norms regarding sexual practices in particular. The almost exclusive discussion of 'homosexuality' rather than gay, lesbian, bisexual, or transgender people, for example, is in fact very telling in what it reveals about the position of LGBTQ persons within the Mennonite community as does the way in which sexual practices outside of marriage more generally are spoken about. This section will examine each of these in more detail to understand how these discourses created an 'us' and 'them'.

USING 'HOMOSEXUALITY' AND 'HETEROSEXUALITY'

The word homosexuality is used extensively in the discourses of the church. In fact, except for a few minor exceptions found in the documents of MC Canada,[49] the other two conferences make exclusive use of the word 'homosexual' rather than gay, lesbian, bisexual, or queer. Interestingly, the word heterosexual is never used nor is it ever recognized that people might hold diverse genders nor sexed bodies as transgender or intersex people do. What is the implication of these choices in language?

In the last third of the nineteenth century, homosexuality as a word entered Euro-American discourse even before the word heterosexuality gained popularity. Of course the sexual practices associated with the term and, controversially, the identities imbedded in the word had existed long before this. Yet, it was a new development at this time which saw the division of every person into either the category of homo- or hetero- sexual and the way in which this word coloured perceptions of non-sexual aspects of life and living (Kosofsky Sedgwick, 2008: 2). The use of the word homosexual implies a continuing association with this type of binary categorization and also with the pathological explanations for same-sex attraction once tied to the term. Today, homosexuality as a term is usually not used to self describe within the LGBTQ population, is regarded as a somewhat dated word, and is sometimes accused of having a male bias (*Ibid.*: 17).

The lack of engagement with heterosexuality in these church texts is also notable. As Jonathan Katz explores in his book, *The Invention of Heterosexuality*, "questioning our belief in a universal heterosexuality goes com-

49 For example: "Some congregations understand that God has called them to invite and include gay and lesbian believers into church membership, whereas other congregations understand that God has called them to resist the acceptance of homosexuality within its churches and in society" (Mennonite Church Canada, 1998). Here it is interesting that when referring to inclusion, the words gay and lesbian are used whereas in the case of the non-affirming congregations, the word homosexuality is used as are the words 'in society'.

pletely against today's common sense" because it is usually assumed that heterosexuality is as old as procreation rooted in the fall of Adam and Eve; it is thought to be "as eternal as the sex and gender differences of that first lady and initial gentleman" (Katz, 2007: 13). Katz contends with the heterosexual premise around which our understandings of sexuality are based to show that heterosexuality is a historical construction, ever in flux and subject to change. [50]

The fact that heterosexuality as a term is never defined or mentioned in these documents of the church shows that heterosexuality remains the fundamental, unexamined norm which is grounding discussions on sexuality. The word heterosexual and the concept itself, what it describes, do not exist separately from each other but are intimately connected. Unfortunately, however, the idea that heterosexuality just is and "exists apart from discourse is itself a powerful conceptual ploy that keeps the historical discourse about heterosexuality from being examined closely" (Katz, 2007: 182). In other words, "heterosexuality…is invented in discourse as that which is outside discourse" (*Ibid.*).

The continual use of the word homosexual and lack of engagement with the word heterosexual could be held to mean any number of things. Firstly, that same-sex attraction and sexual relationships are still pathologized. Secondly, that the multiplicity, changing, and sometimes ambiguous nature of sexualities as captured by bisexual, queer, or questioning labels is not recognized. Likewise, that the performative nature of identifications is also not acknowledged and that the dualistic practices and ways of living communicated in hetero/homo- sexual designations are the only sanctioned categories of being. Thirdly, given that gender or bodily diversity is not even recognized, presumably being a transgender or intersex person is subsumed under the highly inadequate label of homosexual; the label of homosexual then becomes a general category for sexual deviants rather than any concrete descriptor of particular persons, desires, or practices. I conclude that the term homosexual and lack of the use of heterosexual is a means through which these church discourses systematically eliminate the plethora of desires, sex-

50 Following Katz, three arguments are commonly at the root of "an age-old heterosexuality" including: 1) the dialectic to perish or procreate, therefore heterosexuality is a necessity 2) all societies distinguish between two sexes and gender and these are part of a fundamental sexuality which is heterosexual 3) that bodily pleasures coming forth from the sexual encounters of male and female sexual organs are that which is 'natural' and therefore pleasure is heterosexually based. Katz deconstructs all of these arguments of fundamental heterosexuality (Katz, 2007: 13-14).

ual practices, bodies, and genders present and thereby pathologize, limit, and 'other' that which contends with the unspoken and unexamined heterosexual norm.

FRAMING CELIBACY AND MARRIAGE: UNDERSTANDING THE PRIMACY OF SEXUAL PRACTICES

Each of the three Mennonite church conferences I examined were clear in affirming single life, with a particular focus on the sexual practices permitted in such living. MC Canada recognizes "both the goodness of singleness and the goodness of marriage and family in the Lord" (Mennonite Church Canada, 1986). It is unfortunate however, that this is only a chaste, celibate single life which is permissible.

The CCMBC states that all same-sex or opposite sex sexual practices outside of marriage are a violation of proper religious practice. According to the CCMBC, "our sexuality should be expressed only within the covenant relationship of marriage" and the scriptures make clear that lifestyle choices, such as choosing to have sexual intercourse outside of marriage "with members of the opposite sex, the same-sex, or animals" is forbidden (Canadian Conference of Mennonite Brethren Churches, 2004). The use of the word 'sexuality' in its entirety suggests that that which is for marriage may include not only sexual intercourse but the expression of other facets of sexuality as well. Very problematic in my view, since to subsume sexuality as a whole, including an awareness of the body, feelings and thoughts about the body, as well as awareness of desires, is stifling to living a whole life. It is also rather telling that sex with animals is compared to human, consensual sexual relationships outside of marriage.

The conference goes on to make it clear that it is not only homosexuality which is an abomination, for

> it may be possible to have a homosexual orientation, but it is also possible to live a chaste and celibate life. To argue that a disposition towards homosexuality gives a person the right to homosexual practice and intercourse is as wrong as to argue that the heterosexual person has the right to be sexually active heterosexually outside of marriage. (Canadian Conference of Mennonite Brethren Churches, 2004)

Why would churches be so obsessively interested with sexual practices in particular, condemning all expressions of sexuality outside of heterosexual marriage? I am reminded of some of the trends found in the early Christian church to separate the mind and body, which regarded sexual practices as inherently sinful or distracting from a full spiritual life.

In Mennonite Church Canada's 1986 *Resolution*, sexual drives are recognized as a real part of people's lives but "the satisfaction of those drives is not the chief good in life" (Mennonite Church Canada, 1986). In the *Mennonite Brethren Herald*, writer Walter Unger, reflects a similar concern with regulating and containing sexual practices arguing that

> [a]n unbridled search for sexual pleasure has distorted the other purposes of sex, such as procreation and intimacy. A sense of proportionality concerning the role of sex in human relationships has been lost. The Bible describes this disproportionate longing as lust. (Unger, 2010)

The vagueness as to what constitutes sexual practices adds to the challenge surrounding these normative interdictions. If sexual intercourse is not directly referred to, sexual practices outside of marriage more generally are condemned. It is important to note that books on sexual practices usually refer to sexual intercourse as being the penetrative act of an object, fingers, or penis into a vagina. So what sexual practices are being given undue priority and distorting the true meaning of sex? What sexual practices are included? What about anal or oral sex? What about dry humping, petting, manual sex, and kissing? What about masturbation? Might 'sexual intercourse' as referred to in these documents be seeking to include any practice which excites desires or feelings or bodily responses?

Here I reflect back to Chapter 1 in which I briefly outlined some of the early Christian concerns with sexual practices and the aim to control desire and sexual feelings; such norms came forth from a mind/body dualism, aim to secure the worship of a monotheistic God, and the attempt to culturally distinguish Christians from the surrounding society. The flurry of norms within Mennonite churches regarding sexual practices is intimately intertwined with wider trends in early Anabaptism and Christianity.

CREATING "US" AND CREATING "THEM"

Although MC Canada at times recognizes homosexual people as being part of the church, it also 'others' those persons engaging in non-marital heterosexual sexual practices by using words which conceive of them as outside of the community. The 1998 *Resolution on the Issue of Homosexuality* states "that we encourage one another to become 'communities of grace, joy and peace, so that God's healing and hope flow *through us to the world*,' not excluding *those whose sexual orientation is homosexual*" [my emphasis] (Mennonite Church Canada, 1998). Here homosexuals are clearly positioned externally to the community, in the world, and in need of the healing hope of the Mennonite community.

The same resolution also suggests an 'us' and 'them' division when it states that "*we* encourage *one another* to uphold the Biblical call to faithfulness, chastity and self-discipline in all sexual relationships; and that *we* encourage *the sexually and relationally broken* to healing and wholeness in Christ" [my emphasis] (Mennonite Church Canada, 1998). The language at the beginning of the passage suggests a strong sense of community and cohesion in encouraging each other when moving towards particular ideals of sexuality with the use of 'we' and 'one another'. However, later in the passage, when acknowledging persons who do not fit into these ideals, it is again 'we' who are encouraging 'the…broken' rather than 'one another who is broken'.

Reading another explanatory document from MC Canada further gives insight to the way in which 'us' and 'them' is produced. Accordingly, to be in dialogue means to be involved in the "sponsorship of ministries that are directed toward calling persons out of homosexual practices and restoration of the body of believers" (Mennonite Church Canada, 1995b). The clear implication is that homosexual practices are somehow destroying the body of believers and that it is necessary to 'fix' homosexual Mennonites so that the church is not contaminated.

The earlier 1986 *Resolution on Human Sexuality* is vague in its framing of same-sex sexual practices and non-marital sexual practices, suggesting inclusiveness at least in its use of 'us'. The resolution reads: we repent of "*our* fear and repent of *our* rejection of *those of us* with a different sexual orientation and of *our* lack of compassion for their struggle to find a place in society and in the church" [my emphasis] (Mennonite Church Canada, 1986). Further, the resolution goes on to□repent of *our* permissiveness which too often leads to premarital and extramarital sexual relationships" [my emphasis] (*Ibid.*). Certainly, I do not agree that there is anything that must be confessed or repented by engaging in non-marital sexual practices or holding a different sexual orientation; in this sense, the *Resolution on Human Sexuality* remains exclusionary. The use of inclusive language to recognize different sexual orientations as inherent to the community, however, is important to note.

The position of the conference is further made clear when it is suggested that the church can be sure that dialogue on this topic and "the need for discerning thought will extend for many years *because of the debates within society around us*. Even if we were to make 'definitive' decisions, the discussion will continue for at least another decade *because of those external pressures*" [my emphasis] (Mennonite Church Canada, 1995b). Here, MC Canada states that homosexuality is on the church's agenda in the first place because of the external Canadian society and will continue because of external pressures without recognizing the many LGBTQ Mennonites and allies who are pushing for a real dialogue on these issues.

Among the CCMBC, same-sex desiring people are also positioned outside of the community by the conference's suggestion that the whole interest in homosexuality in the church is coming out of secular society's push for being politically correct. Homosexuality, they argue, is getting particular attention in churches and often indecisive answers because of the increasing societal pressure "where any discrimination is thought to be wrong" (Canadian Conference of Mennonite Brethren Churches, 2004). Homosexuality, the conference asserts, has always been a contentious issue but "[i]ts volatility has grown in direct proportion to the growing strength of the homosexual movement and lobby" (*Ibid.*). It would be impossible to deny the very intimate interconnection that an interest in LGBTQ inclusion has with wider trends in society, yet the intent is not to point out the interconnection but position homosexuality and the concern for it as arriving from external sources.

The same document also asserts that homosexuality is often adopted through a "fast lane" lifestyle and that bisexual people are really heterosexual people who have "for whatever reasons, become homosexual" (Canadian Conference of Mennonite Brethren Churches, 2004). By offering such a definition of bisexuality and also suggesting in this document that gay and lesbian people can (and should try to) change their desires, the conference is denying the very right to existence of the LGBTQ Mennonites in their midst. This denial of diverse genders, bodies, and desires is perhaps the greatest and most overt violence that can be practiced in a community and the most profound way in which an 'us' and 'them' is created in which 'them' is completely erased.

Further 'othering' takes place in blanket characterizations which make a link between same-sex desire and sexual practices with promiscuity and indiscretion. According to the CCMBC, although some homosexuals might maintain one intimate relationship with a person of the same-sex, homosexuality "has been largely very permissive and characterized by overt promiscuity" (Canadian Conference of Mennonite Brethren Churches, 2004). The pamphlet goes on to suggest that those with "homosexual tastes" can change, especially those who have developed these tastes by "living in the 'fast lane'" rather than having dealt with their orientation since birth (*Ibid.*).

The violence is especially apparent in the way in which discipleship is defined by the CCMBC as being "true to Jesus in everyday life" and to be true to Jesus, disciples are called "to resist worldly values and systems" by maintaining "sexual purity and marital faithfulness and reject immoral premarital and extramarital relationships and all homosexual practices" (Canadian Conference of Mennonite Brethren Churches, 2001: 9, Article 10). Of key importance is that discipleship is also about community (*Ibid.*). For it is

> [i]n community [that] members grow in maturity as they demonstrate the fruit of the Spirit, use their spiritual gifts and practice mutual accountability in the disciplines of the Christian life. Christians confess sin, repent, and experience God's grace in the life of the Christian community. (Canadian Conference of Mennonite Brethren Churches, 2001: 9, Article 10)

God can "free persons from oppressive addictions" and if God does not, the answer for homosexual persons is "abstinence" (Canadian Conference of Mennonite Brethren Churches, 2004). So, if to be part of a community is to be a disciple, and to be a disciple means to reject 'immoral' sexual practices in everyday life it then precludes LGBTQ Mennonites from the community if they do not believe they need to repent or 'be freed' from their diverse genders, bodies, desires, and sexual practices.

Likewise, in the Evangelical Mennonite Conference, those who want to become members must "nurture strong, wholesome relationships, whether single or married. Celibate life and heterosexual married life are both honourable and high callings from God" (Evangelical Mennonite Conference, 2007: 15). Although homosexual, gay, lesbian, bisexual, transgender, queer, or questioning peoples or sexual practices are not directly referenced there is clearly no space out of the male/female heterosexual marriage norm. Sexual practices outside of the heterosexual marriage norm are furthermore, claimed to be "the symptoms of a sexually broken world" (Peters, 2008: 14).

Ed Peter's article on sexuality in the EMC's journal for pastors, begins with a reference to the billion dollar pornography industry (Peters, 2008). Regardless of one's opinion on pornography and its place in sexual desire and practices, it is clear that Peters is looking to link together pornography with all sexual practices and desires outside of "God-given" sexuality as expressed solely within heterosexual marriage. In an indirect way, he suggests that all sexual practices outside of marriage are sins and that such sin is inherently addictive, oriented to materialism, and does not respect the mystical, spiritual nature of sexual practices. Peters's choice to represent consensual sexual practices outside of marriage in such a disparaging tone is indicative of the way in which those sexual practices outside of heterosexual marriage are pessimistically conceived and 'othered'.

Further, the EMC explains that it is in "[a] Christian home…where Christians reside" and a Christian home is one in which "[b]oth celibate single and the heterosexual married life are honourable and respectable in the sight of God" (Evangelical Mennonite Conference, 2007: 11). In other words, those who live outside of this heterosexual familial norm cannot be members of a

Christian home or perhaps even true Christians since their sexual practices exclude them from inclusion into such family structures.

2.2.4 Love the Sinner, Hate the Sin': Identities & Managing Face

Not only does Mennonite Church Canada do a good job of setting the divisions between 'us' and 'them' based around sexual practices, but it also proceeds to try and then erase these very same divisions that it created through rosy coloured language. In the case of MC Canada, the language used is particularly confusing as the church asserts its commitment to pursuing continuing dialogue and discernment on sexuality. The CCMBC and the EMC are more explicit in framing same-sex sexual practices (and sometimes desire) as sin while insisting on loving the sinner. No matter what the words, however, all in all there remains a fundamental push for uniformity and agreement in the sexualities of the Mennonite community.

The introductory gateway to Mennonite Church Canada's documents on sexuality proposes to give "insight into Mennonite perspectives on same-sex relationships" and other sexual activity outside of heterosexual marriage. Although it proposes to offer Mennonite perspectives, these perspectives include only Mennonite Church Canada sanctioned discussions and writings. Contentious issues are not presented in their entirety and the voices of those who might disagree with the official Mennonite Church Canada positions are not found (Mennonite Church Canada, 2007a). This is indicative of most of the documents on homosexuality of MC Canada which although claim an interest in open dialogue and continuing discernment on sexuality, unequivocally position homosexual people outside of the church and as sinners in need of redemption.

The Mennonite Church Canada's *Resolution on Human Sexuality* (1986) states:

> [T]hat we are all sinners in need of God's grace and that the Holy Spirit may lead us to further truth and repentance…we covenant compassion and prayer for each other that distrustful, broken, and sinful relationships may experience God's healing. (Mennonite Church Canada, 1986)

This statement seems at first both totally inclusive ("we are all sinners") and infused with the hope of healing for all. I would not deny that there are distrustful and broken relationships that would benefit from healing. It is problematic, however, that this passage directly follows a statement that sexual practices are reserved for monogamous heterosexual marriage and that any deviation from this norm is a sin. This passage is not there to remind us all about the difficulties we face in life in living with each other in love. It is there to make clear that the people who are engaging in premarital, extramarital, and homosexual practices are sinners in need of healing from the church in their inherently broken sexual relationships.

The church states its position on sexual practices in the *Resolution on Human Sexuality*, stating that:

> we understand the Bible to teach that sexual intercourse is reserved for a man and a woman united in marriage and that violation of this teaching is a sin. It is our understanding that this teaching also precludes premarital, extramarital and homosexual sexual activity. We further understand the Bible to teach the sanctity of the marriage covenant and that any violation of this covenant, including spouse abuse, is sin. (Mennonite Church Canada, 1986)

Following this, the declaration goes on to say that the church is committed to covenant dialogue and to "mutually bear the burden of remaining in loving dialogue with each other in the body of Christ" (*Ibid.*). They propose that they will continue to "covenant with each other to study the Bible together and expand our insight into the biblical teachings relating to sexuality" (*Ibid.*) And also to "to take part in the ongoing search for discernment and for openness to each other" (*Ibid.*). Further, they state that "[a]s a part of the nurture of individuals and congregations we will promote congregational study of the complex issues of sexuality" and that they "covenant with God that as we discern his will for our lives and our fellowship, we will seek to obey it, through his grace and strength" (*Ibid.*).

Sweet sounding words which are unfortunately, lip service as it is a 'dialogue' which is oriented to first condemn homosexuals as sinners, outside of the community, and then for the rest of the presumably uniform heterosexual community of God to bring them healing. It is a dialogue not premised on a real and open discussion on the nature of sex, gender, desire, and sexual practices. Rather, those engaging in sexual practices outside of the monogamous heterosexual marriage norm are framed as sinning alongside those committing spousal abuse.

In the 1998 *Resolution on Homosexuality* (Mennonite Church Canada, 1998), the introduction highlights the fact that sexuality, and particularly homosexuality has been a contentious issue in Mennonite churches and that there are a variety of opinions in how to approach the conflict. It speaks about how Mennonites have at times dealt with conflict in an unhealthy way which has caused a lot of hurt and pain. And so, in the case of homosexuality,

> we desire to learn from both positive and negative experiences of the past. As we discern God's will for the community of faith, we say 'yes' to procedures that promote redemption, restoration and peace, and we say 'no' to procedures that demonstrate condemnation and rejection. Our goal is to work in a context

> of patient discernment, so that the church may be faithful to 'the way, the truth, and the life' revealed in Jesus Christ and the Scriptures. (Mennonite Church Canada, 1998)

These words frame the introduction to the resolution which follows that lists five assumptions upon which the declaration is made including Article 19 of the *Confession of Faith* (1995a) as well as the *Resolution on Human Sexuality* (1986). The particular purpose of the 1998 *Resolution*, seems to be to offer placating remarks on the importance of dialogue and remaining in a loving, respectful discernment process rather than adding any new insights into the church's stance on homosexuality and sexual practices outside of heterosexual marriage.

Yet, in light of the way in which the church itself defines dialogue, a second look at the 1998 resolution is needed. Several explanatory documents make clear exactly what is meant by words like dialogue and discernment. Remaining in dialogue "should not be construed to mean that the homosexual issue is unresolved or that the position of the church is in question" (Mennonite Church Canada, 1995b). Rather, dialogue is about continuing to offer pastoral care to families and individuals touched by the issue and "admonition to those with a homosexual orientation" and engage in the "sponsorship of ministries that are directed toward *calling persons out of homosexual practices* and restoration of the body of believers, dialogue that reflects the love of Jesus" [my emphasis] (Mennonite Church Canada, 1995b).

It could not be clearer to me that homosexual practices are not sanctioned nor is homosexual desire itself. It proposes that such admonishments and reforming efforts are a reflection of the love of Jesus Christ, yet I would argue that there is hardly anything loving about such an encompassing condemnation of not only same-sex sexual practices but also of same-sex desire itself. Nor is there anything which suggests a true concern with dialogue in such an unequivocal labelling of the sinner.

One of the most plentiful statements on how MC Canada deals with dissenting opinion is found in the *commentary Agreeing and Disagreeing in Love* (Mennonite Church Canada, 1995c). In this document, conflict is recognized as a normal part of life as well as the church, and working towards a future that is mutually agreeable to both parties is emphasized. It is under the 'Life' heading on this commentary, however, that we see an approach to conflict which moves away from a transformative frame to draw on arbitration and resolution paradigms.

> [I]f we cannot reach agreement or experience reconciliation, we will turn the decision over to others in the congregation or from the broader church… this may mean allowing others to arbitrate or implementing constitutional decision-

> making processes, insuring that they are done in the spirit of these guidelines, and abiding by whatever decision is made. (Mennonite Church Canada, 1995c)

The implication of such a frame is that community is formed around agreement and thereby exclusion and that in the frame of ‚agreeing and disagreeing in love' it is the former which is preferred over the latter.

The CCMBC is more explicit in its frame, arguing to 'love the sinner, hate the sin'. We must find a place for the homosexual in the community by loving the person "without condoning the practice", outlines a CCMBC pamphlet on homosexuality (Canadian Conference of Mennonite Brethren Churches, 2004). The CCMBC, the pamphlet continues, should not be silenced on its stance on homosexuality "just because promiscuity in the heterosexuality community has increased dramatically in recent decades" (*Ibid.*). The conference goes on to say that "we encourage all homosexuals to give up their lifestyle and find healing in Christ" (*Ibid.*). The church, they propose, should be a place where those who are sexually broken[51] can find healing in Christ.

Quoting a gay person from a CCMBC congregation who states, "Don't love me that much that you condone my sinful lifestyle," the conference argues that it is possible to love people while admonishing same-sex sexual practices (Unger, 2010).

> Are homosexuals to be excluded from the community of faith? Certainly not. But anyone who joins should know that [the church] is a place of transformation, of discipline, or learning, and not merely a place of comfort or indulgence. (Anonymous quote from gay Mennonite person in Unger, 2010)

Is it possible to 'love the sinner, hate the sin?'. I would argue that the question is misleading. Firstly, to have already made the distinction of another as the 'sinner' is to have completed fully the process of 'othering', of dividing oneself from another, judging the other so that their practices do indeed remain unintelligible as does the person themselves. In making the very distinction of a person as a 'sinner', the judging has already taken place and that person is fundamentally not given full account of their personhood. And so the person must be prepared change their gender, sexual practices, or desires or risk being excluded from belonging.

51 According to Unger (2010) the sexually broken may include those who are "struggling with same-sex attraction or homosexual practice, those in illicit or adulterous heterosexual relationships, or those oppressed with guilt and shame through their involvement in pornography".

2.2.5 Summary

In the discourses of these three Mennonite church conferences, there is a clear separation made which divides those adhering to life within the frames of the Mennonite community's heterosexual marriage norm and those who engage in sexual practices outside of this ideal. Such divisions are premised on an understanding of sex, gender, desire, and sexual practices which assumes a continuity and 'natural' flow between all of these; unarticulated yet underpinning these divisions is the assumption of 'natural' heterosexuality and its corresponding two binary sexes and genders. Further, sexual practices are framed as closely connected with spirituality and therefore following idealized norms of sexuality makes existence ethical and recognizable.

An 'othering' takes place through the explicit use of 'us' and 'them' language' and the positioning of homosexuality as an issue imposed from the wider society. The assertion that homosexuals are in need of saving from the rest of the church, and the negative portrayal of sexual practices outside of the heterosexual marriage norm further helps to create division. In the community's most violent cases, the very existence of diverse genders, bodies, and desires is denied through the use of the word 'homosexual' and the lack of recognition on the changing nature of sexualities. These divisions are then brought to the point of erasure through the use of language which asserts an extremely curtailed interest in dialogue or which positions same-sex sexual practices (and sometimes desire) as sinful but the sinner as lovable. Through such means, the heterogeneity of community is denied and the word community become synonymous with sameness. In the words of Anne Breckbill, Mennonite advocate for LGBTQ rights,

> [i]n the Mennonite Church, unfortunately, it would seem the ultimate value is placed on being in agreement…Variance is not pursued and understood. Variance is rooted out, managed, subverted, contained and hidden. (Breckbill, 2003)

As national organizations, these churches are able to project a unity onto a mass of diversity. They are framing the discussion to be one revolving around homosexuality rather than deal with the complexities of bodies, genders, and desires. In such a frame, heterosexuality remains unchallenged as the base of reality from which analysis is made.

Those who are in executive leadership positions, particularly within the CCMBC, MBCM, and the EMC are primarily white, heterosexual males which no doubt influences the way in which topics of sexuality are approached in these organizations. Community, both at the familial and church level, are so intimately intertwined with sexual norms that the very existence of that which is outside these norms all too often becomes unknowable, non-existent, and a perceived threat to faith communities and families.

2.3 Mennonite Institutions

For this project, I interviewed persons from five Mennonite institutions, two of which will be addressed in the course of this book including Mennonite Central Committee Manitoba and Canadian Mennonite University. I also interviewed persons from three other Mennonite organizations including Concordia Hospital, Mennonite Heritage Village, and Mennonite Economic Development Associates. I choose not to include extensive analysis of these organizations because they did not prove to be mentioned by my LGQ interview participants and a detailed profile of these organizations is beyond the scope of this study. Of note, however, is that LGBTQ persons were eligible for employment in each of these three organizations (Dyck and Sawatzky 2010; Pityn, 2010; Tessmann, 2010). Both persons I spoke with from the Mennonite Heritage Village and Concordia Hospital noted that Mennonite sexuality ideals were a factor in the way in which same-sex desiring persons were received as patrons of the institution in the case of the former and in procedures and policies carried out by the hospital in the case of the latter (Dyck and Sawatzky, 2010; Tessmann, 2010).

2.3.1 Mennonite Central Committee Manitoba

The Mennonite Central Committee (MCC) is an organization which was started by Mennonites and continues to be supported and guided in its direction by many different Mennonite, Brethren in Christ, and Amish church conferences and individuals. MCC is not concerned with evangelism per se but rather is focussed on peace, relief and development work for which it has gained international repute. "MCC is rooted in faith in Jesus Christ and the witness of the global church" (Mennonite Central Committee, 2010a) with the goal of sharing God's love and compassion by working for peace and justice and responding to basic human needs (Mennonite Central Committee, 2010b).

Its mission is approached

> by addressing poverty, oppression and injustice – and their systemic causes; accompanying partners and the church in a process of mutual transformation, accountability and capacity building; building bridges to connect people and ideas across cultural, political and economic divides; and caring for creation. (Mennonite Central Committee, 2010b)

MCC states that it is part of the mission of the larger church, adopting a set of shared convictions as agreed upon by the Mennonite World Conference in 2006 (Mennonite Central Committee, 2010c).

The Mennonite World Conference declaration affirms a belief in a Trinitarian Godhead, the holiness of the Bible, the importance of church community, and the commitment of the global church to living life reflective of Jesus through acts of service and peacebuilding. The declaration also states that

> As a world-wide community of faith and life we transcend boundaries of nationality, race, class, gender and language. We seek to live in the world without conforming to the powers of evil, witnessing to God´s grace by serving others, caring for creation, and inviting all people to know Jesus Christ as Saviour and Lord. (Mennonite Central Committee, 2010c)

In North America, MCC is supported by many different Amish, Mennonite, and Brethren in Christ "communities of faith" as well as people who are not Anabaptist. MCC Canada also receives funding from the Canadian government's Canadian International Development Agency (CIDA), other non-government grants, as well as profits from relief sales and thrift stores (Mennonite Central Committee, 2010d).

Much of MCC's mission as the peace, development, and relief organization of Mennonite churches in North America is carried out through international programs. With a major 2011 re-structuring, these programs are now under the direction of a joint program of Mennonite Central Committee Canada (MCC Canada) and Mennonite Central Committee United States of America (MCC USA). An appointment of two directors, representing each of these bodies, ensures that the responsibility for international programs lies jointly between these organizations (Mennonite Central Committee, 2011).

MCC Manitoba (MCC MB), which is the focus of this study, is one of the areas bodies within MCC Canada which has a number of important local programs and which is also the funnel for all Manitoban contributions and personnel to the national body and international programs (Rempel, 2010a). I sat down with Peter Rempel, Executive Director of MCC MB, to better understand the organization's relationship with the Mennonite community at large and its policies, actions, and programs as they relate to sexuality and in particular LGBTQ Mennonites.

MCC MB is formally owned by eight Mennonite conferences in Manitoba ranging from the Somerfelder Mennonites to Mennonite Church Manitoba. These eight different conference bodies appoint representatives to MCC MB's boards. In addition, MCC MB holds an annual meeting, the delegates to which are appointed by these conferences. Furthermore, about one-half of all individual donations going to MCC in Manitoba come from members of these churches as do many of the one thousand volunteers who give their time to MCC projects in Manitoba (Rempel, 2010a).

MCC MB sees itself with a three pronged role in the Manitoba Mennonite community. As alluded to above, MCC MB is the channel in Manitoba for all resources given to MCC at large including cash donations, material resources, and personnel. In addition, MCC MB runs a number of programs in the province including projects in restorative justice, refugee sponsorship, and peace. Thirdly, from time to time MCC is available as a platform for inter-Mennonite dialogue and as a means through which the different Mennonite churches can speak as one voice to an outside body (Rempel, 2010a).

MCC's requirements for service workers and employees include "a commitment to personal Christian faith", an active membership in a Christian church and a commitment "to the teaching of nonviolent biblical peacemaking" (Mennonite Central Committee, 2010e). Further examination of the policies reveals a requirement for service workers and employees to remain sexually celibate "outside of a heterosexual marriage relationship during their terms of service with MCC" (Mennonite Central Committee, 2010f). The organization elaborates that:

> Persons of homosexual orientation who meet MCC personnel criteria as noted above will be considered for MCC service if they are willing to abide by MCC's requirement of celibacy for all outside of a heterosexual marriage and if they will not use MCC as a platform from which to advocate for same-sex sexual relationships. (Mennonite Central Committee, 2010f)

Peter Rempel explained that these particular 'lifestyle requirements', as they are called, come from the *Human Resources Policy Framework*[52] and MCC MB goes by this document as the basis of its practice in hiring personnel. When asked whether the meaning of celibacy has been flushed out, Rempel was not aware that any explicit discussion on what celibacy means has been undertaken on a Manitoban, national, or bi-national[53] MCC level. Similarly, it has not yet been the case that someone of a 'homosexual' orientation has

52 As of April 2012, the *Human Resources Policy Framework* was under review as part of a five year cycle. According to Ilda da Silva Storie, MCC Canada Director of Human Resources, as previously done, every MCC entity has the opportunity to offer feedback on the document. Following this collation of feedback, the document is agreed to by senior staff, which is followed by the approval of each MCC Board; this includes MCC U.S.A, MCC Canada, and their regional/provincial bodies (da Silva Storie, 2012).

53 The 2011 restructuring of the organization meant that MCC bi-national was disbanded and programming and matters decided by that umbrella organizational structure were reassigned to different MCC national or area/provincial bodies (Mennonite Central Committee, 2011).

used MCC as a platform for advocating for same-sex relationships of which Rempel is aware (Rempel, 2010a; 2010b).

The full document outlining MCC's policies on sexuality explains that MCC "attempts to reflect the Mennonite and Brethren in Christ position on sexuality as sensitively as possible" and states that "MCC constituent denominations and conferences (with the exception of some congregations) and many MCC partners understand sexual relationships outside of heterosexual marriage as being contradictory to their biblical understanding of sexuality" (Mennonite Central Committee, 2007). What is of note, I believe, is that there is a clear recognition that some congregations may have a different understanding of sexuality. Furthermore, this document also recognizes the pain experienced by those who cannot serve with MCC because of this policy:

> In recent years, a number of MCC constituent congregations and individuals have urged MCC to accept personnel who are in committed same-sex relationships, rather than excluding them from service with MCC as a result of this policy. While recognizing the deep commitment of these voices to the church and to MCC, as well as the deep pain of those who cannot serve with MCC as a result of this policy, MCC is committed to upholding the confessions of faith of its conferences and denominations. (*Ibid.*)

Here is it specifically the conference confessions of faith which are pointed to as guiding MCC's policies on sexuality a fact which I will show later was reinforced in practice in MCC Manitoba. This particular sexuality policy is up for review every five years, and as of April 2012, it was undergoing this process (*Ibid.*; da Silve Storie, 2012).

Interestingly, in terms of gender equality, MCC does hold a policy which makes clear that discrimination based on gender is not tolerated. In fact, when people are being interviewed for positions with MCC, Rempel notes that they are asked if they have experience with discrimination along racial or gender lines and how they have dealt with that. MCC is of course looking to hear that the interviewee is opposed to such discrimination. When I asked if these gender equality policies extended to transgender individuals, Rempel was not aware of any policy applying to those individuals and was not aware of any conversations about whether there was a need to have such a policy. Rempel said that he knows of no transgender people who are employed with MCC Manitoba (Rempel, 2010a).

There have certainly been calls for changes to MCC's policies regarding sexuality. Several years ago in Manitoba a person applied for a MCC position and in the course of the interview disclosed that they were in a same-sex relationship. At that point, "we had to say sorry you won't be eligible to serve with MCC" (Rempel, 2010a). Subsequently, that person's home church and friends organized a letter writing campaign and MCC MB received fifteen letters from constituents asking for a change in policy. Those who wrote in support of the change included a number of MCC Canada and MCC MB staff. Rempel explains MCC MB's response:

> The response that I worked out at that point which I think was subsequently adopted by other MCCs when the question came up and that was marriage is a matter that's defined in the confessions of faith of the Mennonite churches that own us and it's not MCC's role, MCC's role is to abide by the confessions of faith of our Mennonite churches…it's not our place to change them or to contradict them or to institute policies which are counter to them. (*Ibid.*)

The letters did prompt an early review of the *Human Resources Policy Framework* in 2007, and specifically policy #152 as discussed above, but the policy was not changed as Rempel recalls. The message communicated was that "basically…if you want MCC to change its policy it's the churches who have to change their confessions of faith" (*Ibid.*).

Yet MCC certainly pushes its constituency in other areas which has caused conflict with some churches and individuals. Rempel notes that "there are different perspectives on some things that MCC does" including some groups or individuals wanting MCC to take a greater role with evangelism or not be as political as they are (Rempel, 2010a). In 2010, MCC Manitoba spoke to the provincial government about Northern hydroelectric development projects which has been contentious not only in conservative churches but also more generally (*Ibid.*). Why then, is MCC particularly resistant to engaging with the topic of sexuality?

In Rempel's memory, there has only been one case to date where policy #152 has been explicitly drawn upon to refuse employment to a person holding a same-sex sexual relationship. Rempel reflected that in so far as someone identifying as having same-sex attraction, being in a relationship with a person of the same-sex, but remaining celibate, no cases have emerged. Likewise, there have not been any cases where a staff person was hired and then violated the same-sex relationship celibacy requirement as far as Rempel is aware (Rempel, 2010a).

In terms of the violation of the celibacy requirement for heterosexual persons, Rempel notes that "it's a bit fuzzy there cause we don't make a habit of checking who's living with who, you know, or what people are doing, you know, away from the office so I've never become aware that" (Rempel, 2010a). In short, "[p]eople know what the expectation is and probably know what the consequences would be if it was flagrantly ignored and certainly what the consequences would be if it would be public knowledge and so the situation hasn't come up in Manitoba anyways" (*Ibid.*).

In 2010, MCC organized a conference entitled *Nurturing Healthy Sexuality*, which was hosted by MCC and a number of other Mennonite conferences and organizations.[54] It featured a number of different sessions on healthy sexuality in marriage, singleness, as well as a session on same-sex attraction. The instigation to launch such a discussion was in part brought about by a meeting of MCC MB with a group of people who were asking MCC to change its policy on hiring. Rempel notes that these individuals suggested that if MCC was not able to change its policies it should be open to hear the stories of pain of those LGBTQ persons who have been rejected by the Mennonite church and community. An additional instigator was the fact that MCC MB deals with unhealthy sexuality in a number of its programs[55]. For MCC MB addressing how to nurture healthy sexuality, particularly among its Mennonite constituency is a very obvious complement to the work already being done to foster peace through healthy sexuality (Rempel, 2010a; Mennonite Central Committee Manitoba, 2010).

Officially, "[t]he purpose of the conference was to provide a forum in which the various challenges and perspectives in the Mennonite community on healthy sexuality could be presented and discussed openly" (Mennonite Central Committee Manitoba, 2010). However, there was a lot of backlash for the conference, particularly the same-sex attraction forum which presented the voices of a number of gay men who were LGBTQ affirmative. "We got a lot of flak subsequently," noted Rempel, as it was the perception of some that the workshop only presented the perspective of needing to tolerate and accept same-sex attraction and did not offer a biblically based discussion (Rempel, 2010a). Because MCC MB was the lead organization in terms of registration and publicity the conference was, and continues to be, widely perceived as an MCC conference. "Now we're dealing with rumours that MCC is hiring gays and lesbians and MCC is promoting same-sex marriage," Rempel explains (*Ibid.*).

In response to these rumours, MCC MB issued a statement on June 30, 2010 to the leaders of all Manitoba Mennonite church conferences as well as

---

54 These organizations and conferences included: Canadian Mennonite University, Evangelical Mennonite Conference, Genesis House, Mennonite Brethren Church of Manitoba, Mennonite Church Manitoba, Recovery of Hope, and MCC Manitoba (Terichow, 2009).

55 For example, MCC MB supports sex offenders when they are released from prison so that they do not offend again in their Circles of Accountability program. Furthermore, in its Voices for Non-violence program, MCC MB supports individuals and churches dealing with clergy or domestic abuse and it also works to support Low German Mennonite in southern Manitoba, where anecdotal stories suggest there is incest and rape present in the communities (Rempel, 2010).

all pastors and chairpersons of MCC member congregations, chairpersons of the Thrift Shop Board, Relief Sale and Meet Canning Committee chairpersons, MCC MB Board members and MCC MB staff. The memo clarified a number of topics about which some conferences, churches, or peoples were concerned and quite prominently featured a clarification of MCC MB's position on sexuality. The memo stated that all statements made at the conference and by the presenters were personal opinions and not statements made on behalf of MCC or any sponsoring organizations (Mennonite Central Committee Manitoba, 2010).

Furthermore, the memo acknowledged the critique that only one perspective of same-sex relationships was presented and affirmed that

> MCC, as a ministry of the Mennonite churches, abides by the beliefs of the Mennonite churches regarding sexuality and marriage. They uniformly define marriage as a covenant between one man and one woman and confine sexual relationships to heterosexual marriage. Thus MCC continues to expect its staff and service workers to be celibate other than in a heterosexual marriage. MCC is not calling for or promoting acceptance by churches of same-sex marriage or same-sex relationships. (Mennonite Central Committee Manitoba, 2010)

Of note is that the memo gave the reason for MCC's participation in the conference as emerging in complement to its program work with unhealthy sexuality and did not mention the advocacy and concerns of those LGBTQ Mennonites and allies who approached MCC MB about changes to human resource policies (*Ibid.*).

Even with this clarification, Rempel stated that some people have said that they are withdrawing support from MCC because it is hiring gays and lesbians. In 2010, the Old Colony Mennonite Church, decided not to re-appoint their representative to the MCC MB Board because they understood that MCC was hiring gays and lesbians. Similarly, the long-time Secretary of the Morris Relief Sale has said that he is withdrawing his support. Rempel notes that he has heard that individual volunteers in thrift shops and relief sales are also withdrawing support from MCC. Although the choice to disassociate with MCC is often also related with a number of other issues particular conferences and individuals have, in Peter Rempel's words the *Nurturing Healthy Sexuality Conference*, has "cost us some supporters already" (Rempel, 2010a).

> Some people say this [sexuality] is none of MCC's business, we did not create MCC to be talking about sexuality and so you know regardless of what position they thought came through in February at that conference, they just don't think MCC should be involved in conferences about healthy sexuality in the first place. (*Ibid.*)

Rempel has responded to such statements by pointing to the clear involvement of MCC in programs of unhealthy sexuality. Rempel notes the pastoral concern for the pain LGBTQ people experience at the hands of the Mennonite church and that that is a conference and congregational concern (*Ibid.*).

Yet Rempel suggests that MCC might have a role to play in hearing the stories of LGBTQ Mennonites although not necessarily responding to the needs communicated in those stories.

> We're not here to provide pastoral care for them [LGBTQ Mennonites], not particularly though it did register with me when I heard them say there are some…people who are in a lot of pain about rejection by the Mennonite church and I wouldn't, and I think we [MCC MB] need to, we in so far as we're [MCC MB] part of the church, and instrument of the church we need to hear that too even though it's not as MCC's place to, I don't think it's our role to respond to that particular need that's not what MCCs been set up for, so we haven't gone there. (Rempel, 2010a)

When asked whether MCC Manitoba sees a continuing role in facilitating inter-Mennonite dialogue on topics of sexuality, Rempel stated, "[t]he question hasn't come up. It could be that some people are working at this, maybe a program staff person is working on this in some quiet way that I'm not aware of but we're not taking any initiative at this point" (*Ibid.*). Rempel states that MCC has not "made a conscious decision to do or not do anything at this point. The question hasn't come up" (*Ibid.*).

In 2010, MCC MB underwent a number of administrative changes which allowed a greater degree of flexibility in hiring. These administrative changes include the transferring of two programs into a separate organization, including MCC MB's Fetal Alcohol Spectrum Disorder (FASD) program and El'Dad Ranch as well as two other restorative justice programs for persons previously or currently serving time within the criminal justice system. The organization under which these programs now lie is Initiatives for Just Communities (IJC). IJC is still by in large controlled by MCC; its board is appointed by MCC MB and it cannot change its bylaws or statement of purpose without MCC MB's permission. Furthermore, the majority of funding for IJC comes from MCC (Rempel, 2010a).

Yet, IJC employees are not subject to the hiring requirements found in MCC national or Manitoban bodies. While employees are required to respect the Christian ethos behind IJC programs, Christian faith, active church membership, support of MCC peace stance, nor celibacy outside of heterosexual marriage are required (Rempel, 2010a). This move was made in part so that people could be hired more quickly and easily and to broaden the funding support base that MCC MB receives (*Ibid.*). Furthermore, the formal administrative shift was made in light of MCC's awareness of its vulnerability to a human rights complaint.

Previously, workers within some of the programs now within IJC were sometimes not subject to MCC's hiring requirements; MCC was cognizant of the complaint that could be launched given a hypothetical situation where someone would apply for a job within the main MCC MB office, refused based on the hiring screens but apply for a frontline service position with El'Dad Ranch and not be subject to the application of that screen (Rempel, 2010a).

Rempel also pointed to MCC MB's awareness of the Ontario Human Rights Commission court case against Christian Horizons, an evangelical Christian organization serving adults with developmental disabilities.[56] Rempel notes that could still have serious implications for MCC.

> [W]ell, if that would apply to MCC we'd shut, that's who we basically serve. That's [the general public] 90 percent of our clientele. So if that would be applied to us and then we would be in a real squeeze with our present policy so we're following that in terms of...what the ultimate ruling on that will be and then whether that will, like at this point they're just going on that's an application or interpretation of Ontario's law, will that then become the way that Manitoba law is interpreted? (Rempel, 2010a)

MCC MB has a hiring policy which remains exclusionary and in my opinion, also antithetical to its commitment to work for peace and justice. The fact that securing the values of workers on racial and gender equality takes such a central role in the hiring process whereas concerns about discrimination based on sexual practice or gender identity is not present, is gapingly contradictory. MCC's commitment to reflecting the beliefs of the churches, as articulated in their statements of faith, is problematic because there is of course

---

56 Christian Horizons, a publicly funded organization, required staff to sign a morality statement which barred extra-marital, pre-marital, and same-sex sexual relationships. A May 14, 2010 decision from Ontario's Divisional Court ruled that the organization could maintain a morality statement staff were required to sign but that it had to delete the reference to same-sex relationships in this statement because that was discriminatory. The decision was premised on the fact that Christian Horizons provides support to more than 1,400 Ontarians, regardless of creed, is publicly funded and does not provide religious education or indoctrination. Christian Horizons failed to prove that "avoiding a same-sex relationship was a valid occupational qualification for a support worker" (Ontario Human Rights Commission, 2010). The decision also noted that "'support workers are not hired or expected to bring the residents into the Evangelical Christian religion by having them adopt a certain lifestyle. The fact is that the support workers' employment and the tasks they perform are not intended to infuse the residents of the homes that Christian Horizons serves with the lifestyle morals that Christian Horizons demands of its adherents'" (*Ibid.*).

a great amount of diversity within these different conferences, not only in terms of opinions on the appropriateness of different sexual activities but also in terms of other facets of confessions of faith.

Thankfully, MCC recognizes the diversity in beliefs of sexuality yet remains stuck in its commitment to reflect the values of Mennonite conferences as expressed in confessions of faith. Promisingly, MCC MB has not ruled out the possibility of being involved in discussions surrounding sexuality and it has formally recognized the pain of LGBTQ persons excluded from serving with MCC. Furthermore, its IJC program, although it is controlled by the heterosexual staff and board of MCC MB, may allow limited opportunities for LGBTQ Mennonites to be a part of MCC MB's work. Further legal developments might one day increase opportunities for the involvement of LGBTQ persons with MCC.

2.3.2 Canadian Mennonite University

Canadian Mennonite University (CMU) is a Christian university based in Winnipeg, Manitoba which "through research, teaching, and service…inspires and equips women and men for lives of service, leadership, and reconciliation in church and society" (Canadian Mennonite University, 2010a). CMU is the child of several Mennonite colleges which came together in the late 1990s to form a collective university. CMU has grown over the years and now offers five bachelor programs with several different majors (*Ibid.*). In 2010, there were 500 students in the student body on the Shaftesbury campus in Winnipeg. Of these students, 47.1 percent came from Mennonite churches in Canada or internationally,[57] 39.5 percent came from other Christian denominations, and 13.2 percent came without a disclosed church affiliation (Canadian Mennonite University, 2010b). These numbers do not include Menno Simons College, which is a college of CMU, affiliated with the secular, publicly funded University of Winnipeg offering programs in International Development Studies and Conflict Resolution (Canadian Mennonite University, 2010a).

I sat down with Wesley Toews, Registrar and Assistant Vice President Academic to better understand the operation and ethos of this organization regarding sexuality. CMU is owned by two Mennonite church conferences

---

57 This includes 24.4 percent of the total student body from MC Canada congregations, 12.9 percent from CCMBC congregations, 8.5 percent from other Canadian Mennonite congregations, and 1.3 percent from international Mennonite congregations (Canadian Mennonite University, 2010b).

including the Mennonite Brethren Church of Manitoba (MBCM) and Mennonite Church Canada (MC Canada). The CMU board members "are drawn essentially from these two owning constituencies" and it is the board which approves all program directions, hiring of faculty, new openings for faculty, and any new curriculum (Toews, 2010). To give an indication of the hands on nature of these church bodies at CMU, Wesley Toews explains that the choice to have a curriculum requisite in biblical and theological studies "went so far as to making it onto the conference floor at one point which indicates then that the church had a fairly grassroots involvement in determining what the shape of the curriculum would be at CMU" (*Ibid.*). These two conference bodies also provide a significant amount of financial support in addition to sending students and supporting them in the course of their studies. CMU also gets a significant amount of support from Mennonite Brethren churches and individuals across Canada and other Mennonite individuals and congregations through donations or sending students (*Ibid.*).

The strong relationship of CMU with the church is not a coincidence, "CMU has been very intentional about working to foster and nurture that relationship" (Toews, 2010). For "CMU views itself as a university of the church for the world" and its mission is to equip students to carry out the church's mission, which although can be defined various ways is essentially about seeking God's kingdom and justice "and that also has to do with creating community because the Kingdom of God is a society or a community that gives its allegiance to God and to God's justice on earth" (*Ibid.*). CMU's policies for students, faculty, and staff are created with the aim of fostering such a community, and expressions of sexuality are a component of that concern. Given its strong connection to the church, "appropriately, the confessions that these conferences [MC Canada and MBCM] hold are our confessions and we acknowledge those confessions" (*Ibid.*).

As examined subsequently in this chapter, these confessions both have very particular things to say about sexuality and sexual practices. These confessions remain the basis of CMU's hiring policies for faculty (Canadian Mennonite University, 2007) as well as the official policy for student conduct within the community as reflected in the *Respectful Campus Policy* (Canadian Mennonite University, 2003). A closer examination of each of these policies and specifically practices on these policies, however does suggests that there exists a measure of curtailed openness to LGBTQ persons and that CMU is carrying out the sexuality ideals found in the confessions of faith with a degree of flexibility.

Officially, CMU's hiring policy states that for CMU's Shaftesbury Campus and Outtatown programs,[58] all "faculty members, Outtatown leaders, and senior administrators…are expected to be Christian, and be in sympathy with and have respect for the Mennonite faith perspective" (Canadian Mennonite University, 2007). Employees of CMU are also subject to a number of specific regulations as are faculty which include "self-identification as Christian" as well as "active participation in the life of a Christian congregation" and an "affirmation of the confessional statement of one of the constituent denominations, or, if a member of another denomination or tradition, of the confessional tradition of his or her denomination" (*Ibid.*). This suggests that theoretically, if a person came from a denomination besides the MBCM or MC Canada which explicitly affirmed being LGBTQ, it would be possible to be a gay person and employed at CMU.

Furthermore, it is encouraging that this very same document also clearly states that confessional statements need not be interpreted in their strictest, literalist sense and that offer factors play into the assessment of what constitutes a Christian life.

> The historic Anabaptist emphasis on discipleship means that being Christian entails more than the affirmation of doctrinal statements, valuable as they are, and more than living by a particular ethical code, important as that is. Within this understanding, being Christian is more than a nominal association with the Christian tradition, but implies personal commitment and active involvement in a particular community of faith. (Canadian Mennonite University, 2007)

Moreover, a footnote later in the document explains that the confessions of faith of both the MBCM and MC Canada "point beyond themselves to Scripture and God's self-revelation as the highest authority for the Church and the Christian". For CMU, "[t]o affirm a particular community's confession of faith means to accept it as a helpful and foundational summary of the faith from within which one works, without necessarily accepting every detail of it" (*Ibid.*). And in that vein, long before it became common practice to affirm women's leadership in the MBCM and even MC Canada, CMU's precursors Concord College and Canadian Mennonite Bible College were interpreting

58 The Outtatown Discipleship School "is a unique program for students seeking a life-changing experience of adventure, travel, service and Christian studies" which involves a series of courses, travel, and study around the world (Outtatown Discipleship School, 2010).

church documents on women's leadership very liberally which was reflected in the practices of those institutions in hiring and teaching (Toews, 2010).

Although CMU's hiring policy suggests the possibility of leniency regarding hiring and sexual practices, it has not yet been the case that a faculty, staff, or administrator within CMU from a MC Canada or MBCM background has openly deviated from the sexual practice norms contained in the confessions of faith and it remains to be seen how these hiring policies will be interpreted. Similarly, it has not yet been seen what happens if the confessional tradition of a person from outside MBCM or MC Canada directly contradicts the sexuality ideals in the confessions of the two owning bodies (Toews, 2010).

The hiring policy for Menno Simons College (MSC) is quite a bit different as the college is closely associated with the University of Winnipeg (UW) and receives a significant number of casual students from that secular, public university student body. For Menno Simons College, no explicit Christian identification or church involvement is required for hiring nor is any affirmation of the confessional statements of either MBCM, MC Canada, or another Christian tradition (Canadian Mennonite University, 2007).

There are, however, a number of expectations which were reached by a joined CMU/UW Task Force and approved by both universities which include the expectation that

> [f]aculty members, administrators and staff will commit themselves to a process of careful and deliberate reflection, individually and collectively, on how their faith, values, or worldview interact with curriculum development, teaching, and administration. (Canadian Mennonite University, 2007)

Furthermore, it is expected that all faculty, administrators, and staff "demonstrate or commit to development knowledge of and respect for Anabaptist Christian teachings, tradition, and practice, as well as openness to other traditions" (Canadian Mennonite University, 2007). Also, to "ensure the Mennonite identity of the College" it is expected that

> a significant portion of faculty members, administrators, and staff should be active participants in a Mennonite congregation and/or individuals whose Christian faith is compatible with the Anabaptist/Mennonite understanding of the Christian faith. (*Ibid.*)

Again, the details of how this last policy will be carried out in the years to come remains to be seen.

In terms of expectations of students, while CMU recognizes that they are not the church, they are of the church and the creation of a community honoring the commitment to bringing about God's kingdom on earth remains strong. Wesley Toews suggests that the creation of that kind of community is reflected in particular sexual expressions (Toews, 2010). The CMU Student Handbook outlines a number of rules and guidelines regarding community life which "are informed by our identity as a Christian community and by the Anabaptist-Mennonite tradition that has shaped our understanding of the Christian life" (Canadian Mennonite University, 2010c).

These guidelines include a section which outlines the context in which sexual relationships are acceptable. It reads:

> CMU acknowledges human sexuality as a gift and blessing from God and encourages healthy relationships in both dating and marriage. Students in dating relationships are expected to act with Christian maturity, treating each other with honour and respect and using discretion in public expressions of affection.
>
> Sexual intimacy is recognized as a part of the blessing of human sexuality. In accordance with the Confessions of Faith of both the Mennonite and Mennonite Brethren churches, CMU affirms marriage as the proper context for sexual intimacy. Sexual intimacy in any non-marital relationship is considered unacceptable within the CMU community. (Canadian Mennonite University, 2010c)

Notably, this policy does not specifically mention same-sex sexual relationships although prohibition against this is clearly implied through the referencing of both of MC Canada's and MBCM's confessions of faith.

How are these policies carried out on a day to day basis? The handbook explains the school's 'Philosophy of Discipline' which is that "[o]n certain points we do have clear-cut rules that we expect students to observe (e.g., no alcohol or drugs on campus, see below). In other areas, we expect that students' conduct in specific situations will be guided by more general criteria" including good taste, welfare of the community, and consideration of others and that the community makes "a serious attempt to regulate life through commitment, exhortation and mutual accountability" (Canadian Mennonite University, 2010c). Although sexual relationships are specifically referenced in the section which follows that on alcohol and drugs, it is not altogether clear whether certain types of sexual relationships fall into this category of more strictly enforced norms.

Practice in the CMU community suggests that same-sex desiring students in same-sex relationships are not necessarily subject to disciplinary measures or admonishment of any kind within the community. In fact, LGBTQ persons have found a measure of support on campus both in self organization and also from various faculty and staff members. In particular, Toews reflected on CMQ, the anonymous LGBTQ support group on campus.

> [T]hat group [CMQ] exists not without support from faculty and staff. That is faculty and staff and I'm not going to claim that everyone on faculty and staff would be of this mind but faculty and staff generally don't have any desire, to

> stop conversation, to stop the attempt for self understanding and to stop the supporting and compassionate initiatives that students take. (Toews, 2010)

Toews explains that as individual churches have a diversity of opinions and practices regarding many aspects of the confessions of faith, including sexuality, so does CMU. "[T]hough CMU is a university of the church for the world and though it is owned by these two Mennonite conferences, I will not go so far as to make the claim that this topic [of same-sex relationships] is uncontested at CMU" (Toews, 2010).

When asked how CMU sees the LGBTQ students in their midst, Toews notes

> we are aware of them in as much as they declare themselves and I know that various faculty members have often been in conversation with persons who declared themselves and that the conversations is a reaching out, compassionate response….there's nothing in our policy that we intend to discourage students who are gay or transgender or bisexual, but on the other hand we haven't all either done something positive like saying we invite or welcome, like we haven't done something that has been actively inviting or welcoming to my knowledge. (Toews, 2010)

An important and recent inclusion in policies is within the Sexual Harassment section of the CMU Student Handbook which now states that CMU will not tolerate "any degrading of unwelcome remarks, jokes, innuendos, whistling or catcalls regarding a person's…gender or sexual orientation" (Canadian Mennonite University, 2010). This recent inclusion prompted by the advocacy of Ben Borne, a gay student at CMU (Borne, 2010a) now formalizes the protection of LGBTQ students on campus.

The *Respectful Campus Policy* (Canadian Mennonite University, 2003), which covers the whole of the CMU community including faculty, staff and students lays out the formal procedure for dealing with complaints of discrimination or harassment. This document does not explicitly mention degrading or unwelcome remarks referring to sexual orientation or gender identity (Canadian Mennonite University, 2003). However, given the inclusion of sexual orientation and gender identity in the Student Handbook, theoretically at least students would be eligible to use the *Respectful Campus Policy* and its committee structures for grievances related to harassment because of their sexual and gender identity.

CMU offers a number of classes which address the topic of heterosexual human relationships and inexplicitly same-sex relationships. Furthermore, there are a number of classes in political studies and psychology where Toews said he would not be surprised to know that the topic has been approached. To Wesley Toews's knowledge, there has never been any significant conflict emerging between faculty members teaching something which conflicted with the confessions of faith. From time to time, CMU also invites guest speakers to speak on the topic of sexuality (Toews, 2010).

At CMU there exist formal restrictions on the ways in which students, faculty, and staff can be with a clear pronouncement that same-sex sexual relationships are not accepted both in the CMU Student Handbook and also in the Main Campus Hiring Policy. In fact, both of these policies are based on the confessions of Faith from MC Canada and MBCM, CMU's two owning bodies. There are open spaces within the Main Campus Hiring Policy, which suggest that the confessions of Faith might be interpreted liberally and that people from other Christian denominations can abide by their own confessional traditions which may be affirming of same-sex relationships.

CMU faculty and staff support for LGBTQ students and the affirmation of CMQ are a testament to the measure of openness at CMU. Formally, recent amendments made to the CMU Student Handbook protect LGBTQ students from discrimination on the basis of their sexual or gender identities, theoretically allowing them access the *Respectful Campus Policy*. It remains to be seen what the institutional climate and interpretation of regulations might mean for faculty, staff, or administration in a publicly declared same-sex sexual relationship. Likewise, although Menno Simons College's hiring policy is open, there remains a stipulation that the majority of faculty comes from a Mennonite background and it remains to be seen how that policy will be interpreted and practiced.

3. Re-Imagining Sexualities in Discourse

The idealized discourses laid out in Chapter 2 which proclaim sex, gender, desire, and sexual practices as flowing from one another, inherently binary as male/female, hetero/homosexual, in their composition are not the full story. Nor are the institutional discourses which speak those outside of those binaries unacceptable and ineligible for participation. There are many Mennonites who are interacting in these discursive spaces to re-signify of the sexual ideals inherent within the Mennonite heterosexual marriage frame as laid out in church discourses and institutions. Indeed, as both this chapter and the subsequent one will show, although officially these three Mennonite conferences and several of these Mennonite institutions do not affirm or support same-sex sexual practices nor affirm diverse gender identities, informally there exists supporters and networks of people working to bring about change. In the course of this chapter I will lay out what some groups of Mennonites in Winnipeg are doing to contest idealized discourses through formal and informal advocacy.

3.1 The Pilgrim Group, Bethel Mennonite Church

Any discussion of LGBTQ Mennonites in Manitoba will no doubt lead to someone telling you about Val and Wark Warkentin or the Pilgrim Group at Bethel Mennonite Church in Winnipeg. Val and Wark Warketin have long been concerned with LGBTQ inclusion in the Mennonite church. It was an interest instigated by their own personal connections to the topic, first when a close friend and roommate came out to them as gay and later when their daughter came out as a lesbian in her early 20s. When their daughter came out, Val and Wark found it very challenging to process their daughter's coming out as there were few people to talk to and certainly not many people to share with or gain support from within the Mennonite church. Val reflects on her feelings at the time which included a lot of worry for her daughter's well-being both physically and emotionally. "I mean this is our kid and the Mennonite church is not ready for this, what do we do now? So there was a lot of angst there for her safety and for her well-being" (V. Warketin, 2010).

During that time, Val and Wark found a lot of support in a local Parents and Friends of Lesbians and Gays (PFLAG) support group. Although the group had no specific religious orientation, they found themselves surrounded by people who were also struggling with the pain and rejection of their children by churches. Val and Wark's son and daughter have since both left the church and have challenged their parents about why they continue to be part of a church which does not accept their daughter. It is with the ongoing belief in the possibility of change and in their important role in supporting LGBTQ persons in the Mennonite church, that Val and Wark continue to work as advocates even though they grow weary (V. Warkentin, 2010; W. Warkentin, 2010).

For the last ten years, Val and Wark have involved themselves in various formal and informal efforts to educate, dialogue, and advocate for change within the Mennonite community. These efforts included the creation of the Pilgrim Group within their church, Bethel Mennonite Church in Winnipeg, a MC Canada and MC Manitoba congregation. With the permission of their daughter, in 2000 they began having discussions with their pastor about the need to talk about sexuality in the church. These discussions came after Val and Wark wrote a letter in response to the negativity surrounding Calgary Inter-Mennonite Church's discipline within Mennonite Church Alberta, which had resulted in a series of very ugly discussions at the Mennonite Church Canada Assembly in Lethbridge. Prompted by what they heard and read in conference newsletters, Val and Wark wrote a letter to their church newsletter lamenting "the disintegration of the relationships in Alberta" and asking whether it was possible for the church to have a discussion on sexuality without "sinking or denigrating into that morass?" (W. Warkentin, 2010).

The letter was never published, much to the outrage of Val and Wark. Wark reflects, "here we had written what I thought was a very gentle letter [and] nobody heard it. I was just dumbfounded and…if this is what happens?...we felt violated about not being able to talk about what was important to us" (W. Warkentin, 2010). This is an example of what one gay Mennonite man once said was "the violence of silence" (*Ibid.*). They brought their concern of feeling silenced to their pastor, who helped to organize a steering group within the church which would eventually lead the congregation through a three year process of discussing same-sex attraction (W. Warkentin, 2010; V. Warkentin, 2010).

The first year of the process involved a number of Sunday School classes on homosexuality and its meaning, biblical insights into sexuality, and the invitation to small groups within the church to also study and reflect on the topic. During the second year, there were between two and three Sunday School series held dealing with the topic and a number of gay and lesbian Mennonites were invited to speak as well as parents and friends of lesbian and gay persons. In the third and final year of the process, the church looked at the topic of LGBTQ inclusion in terms of hospitality and other non LGBTQ persons who may have found themselves on the margins of the church. Although the process did not end with the church taking a position, in Val and Wark's perspective, it did open up the possibility to communicate within the church about sexuality which would not have been previously possible. Bethel Mennonite is a big congregation of about 600 people with a variety of opinions on sexuality and Wark and Val find that there are many people who remain strongly convicted that homosexuality is wrong, yet they can still talk to most of those people about sexuality (W. Warkentin, 2010; V. Warketin, 2010).

In the Spring of 2004, at the end of the three year process, the steering group recognized that it wanted to acknowledge in some way what the church had gone through in discussing sexuality. The Pilgrim Group was thereafter formed as a means for continuing dialogue, education, and also offering support to people 'affected' by same-sex attraction. Shortly afterward, the Pilgrim Group went through a formal approval process by which it became a permanent ministry of Bethel Mennonite church, a fact which has positively allowed the group to continue to exist and thrive even in what today is a much more conservative church congregational leadership (W. Warketin, 2010; V. Warkentin, 2010).

Since 2004, the Pilgrim Group has met once monthly and brings together many LGBTQ persons from throughout MC Manitoba and MC Canada churches, other Mennonites from different conference bodies including churches part of the CCMBC or the EMC. Non-Mennonites also attend the Pilgrim Group, many of whom have partners who are from Mennonite backgrounds (W. Warkentin, 2010; V. Warkentin, 2010).

Val hopes that the Pilgrim Group is providing for people what PFLAG did for her and Wark. Val reflects that

> I'm telling you that has been and absolutely amazing experience for me to be part of [supporting LGBTQ people and their families], because, I appreciate so much what PFLAG did for us. I spent…the first year I think going to church sporadically and weeping in church feeling not being a part of things at all, how can I continue to be here? And I remember clearly one Sunday morning going in there and feeling taller and saying 'I don't care anymore. I mean nobody can [make me] reject my daughter, nobody has that power, no person in this church or anywhere else has that power' and that made a difference but…it's a process and it took time to get there. (V. Warkentin, 2010)

Although the Pilgrim Group is an official ministry of Bethel Mennonite Church, it has been subject to a measure of silencing. In particular, it has been a sore spot for pastors that people come to the Pilgrim Group from other churches or communities. In fact, the group is not supposed to advertise outside of Bethel Mennonite Church. Word certainly gets around through informal networks, yet it has been made clear that the Pilgrim Group is not an advocacy group but rather a place for telling stories and "more a low key kind of experience within the church" (W. Warkentin, 2010).

Particular revelation of this silencing is that in 2010, Bethel Mennonite Church had a specific initiative underway in connecting with the community around the church and ministering to those at the margins. The formal initiative, entitled Extending the Table, has not included the Pilgrim Group in its brochure, the public document proclaiming the church's interest in ministering to all people. For Val and Wark, this is a glaring omission given that there are so many LGBTQ people in the community and on the margins of the church (W. Warkentin, 2010; V. Warkentin, 2010).

Val and Wark reflected on the informal support they have received both personally and for their work in the Pilgrim Group from many prominent leaders in MC Canada, MC Manitoba, CMU, MCC, and other major Mennonite conferences. As many senior leadership persons in these organizations are in fact members of Bethel Mennonite Church, whenever the Pilgrim Group makes a presentation or organizes a Sunday School session, key leaders in the Mennonite conferences and institutions are quickly aware. Even so, Val and Wark have not experienced any resistance to the Pilgrim Group from outside of Bethel Mennonite Church (W.Warkentin, 2010; V.Warkentin, 2010).

Wark notes that he has received some private support from some leadership within the Evangelical Mennonite Conference, with a former executive member stating privately that he would support moving towards the inclusion of LGBTQ persons in the church but that his hands were tied. Wark reflects that "they [leadership in the EMC and other conservative Mennonite conferences] are much more supportive than you would think based on their public pronouncements" (W. Warkentin, 2010). Also within the Mennonite Brethren Church of Manitoba, Wark sees some movement in the discussion knowing that some members of the editorial staff of the *Mennonite Brethren Herald* have been personally affected by same-sex attraction in their families which is causing them to sit up and take notice. "The personal stories, the individual experiences all of a sudden take on a much different perspective when they involved your own family and it's not an issue anymore, now it's, now we're dealing with people" (*Ibid.*).

Of course, Val and Wark wonder why it is that informally such support can exist yet it cannot be formalized. Reflecting on how an openly gay friend recently served communion in their church with the full support of the church leadership, Val and Wark wonder why it is that the church will not formalize their position. In particular, over the last four to five years they have been witness to an increasing prominence of discussions on LGBTQ topics. Wark reflects that

> we hear an awful lot in our sermons and in our public presentations about how Bethel [Mennonite Church] needs to be more welcoming, needs to be more open, needs to be more accepting, needs to be more interested in the people at the margins. Val and I have these special…filters…on our ears and we hear what they're talking about. They're talking about gay inclusion but they never say those words and we've challenged them over and over. (W. Warkentin, 2010)

Because of this lack of formal public support, however, many LGBTQ people have left and continue to leave the church.

Val laments on the great number of wonderful young people who are dedicated to their faith, the church, and being Mennonite that are leaving the Mennonite community because of its treatment of LGBTQ people.

> We're losing such great, great youth. And the other thing is we have talked to so many people in their 60s, 70s who were shunned, who were excommunicated, who still long to be part of the Mennonite community, identify as Mennonites but they've had these horrible experiences and that can't continue. (V. Warkentin, 2010)

3.2 The Group With No Name & Harmony

Harmony: Mennonites for LGBT Inclusion (Harmony), formally known as the Group With No Name (GWNN) was born in 2008 out of the inspiration gained when a group of people, returned from a Brethren Mennonite Council for LGBT Interests (BMC) weekend retreat. The retreat on Welcoming[59] churches in the United States brought to the forefront the need for an advocacy body for LGBTQ interests within Manitoba. Harmony is currently in the continuing process of discerning its mission and whether it will become

59 The expressions 'Welcoming congregation' or 'Affirming congregation' are commonly used to communicate the viewpoints and practices of a church towards LGBTQ persons. A Welcoming congregation is one in which LGBTQ are welcomed to join in the life of the congregation; quite often this is an informal designation rather than a publically declared or officially institutionalized stance. An Affirming congregation is one where a congregation is publically affirmative of LGBTQ people into full membership and leadership in the church. According to the Brethren Mennonite Council for LGBT Interests, being publically Affirming means: it is a safe space for LGBT people and their families; the church has educated itself about sexuality; and that LGBT people will not be the "topic of controversy" or be caused overt harm (Brethren Mennonite Council for Lesbian, Gay, Bisexual, and Transgender Interests, 2012).

more formally structured.[60] The initial concept was to act as a group of people from within MC Manitoba churches who were concerned about how LGBTQ topics were being dealt with in individual congregations and in the conference as a whole, as well as work in an advocacy capacity (W. Warkentin, 2010).

In 2010, there were 40 to 45 people on Harmony's mailing list, mostly from within Winnipeg and MC Manitoba churches. The group has had some very good discussions with the executive leadership of MC Canada and board and executive leadership of MC Manitoba, encountering a "significant receptivity within conference leadership" (W. Warkentin, 2010). Unfortunately, this interest has been slow to materialize into any action either in education or dialogue.[61]

Harmony distributes secondary resources to congregations looking for information as well as pastors interested in the subject of LGBTQ inclusion (W. Warkentin, 2010). Other activities linked with Harmony have included the launch of a website, which provides information and analysis of some key church documents on sexuality.[62] In preparation for the MC Canada Assembly held in Winnipeg in February 2008, some people associated with the GWNN also organized the Postcard Project. This project involved sending a letter to every MC Canada church in the country asking people who were concerned with LGBTQ inclusion to take the time to write a postcard and send it to the organizing committee. Over 100 postcards were received and put on display in a school adjacent to where the MC Canada Assembly was being held (Wiebe, 2010).

Matt Wiebe explains that "there's sort of a display booth area at the conference and we were declined space because the powers that be don't want to

---

60 Harmony's Vision and Purpose, has since been fashioned and a full version can be found online at their website (Harmony: Mennonites for LGBT Inclusion, 2012b). In brief, they propose to "engage respectfully with Lesbian, Gay, Bisexual, Transgender, and Questioning persons (LGBTQ), Mennonite Church conference bodies, its institutions, and congregations, and the greater Canadian Mennonite community" (*Ibid.*). This includes providing opportunities for dialogue, educational resources, and personal/institutional supports. They self-identify as a group of LGBTQ people and allies who are either members or active participants in Mennonite congregations, most within MC Canada. They also state that they are fully committed to maintaining close ties with the leadership of Mennonite conferences and congregations (*Ibid.*).

61 For more information about 2011 and 2012 conversations on sexuality in MC Canada, particularly the BFC3 process, please see the Preface.

62 Please see Resources and Information section of Harmony's website (Harmony: Mennonites for LGBT Inclusion, 2012c).

talk about this because it's uncomfortable" (Wiebe, 2010). The postcards were powerful,

> so many of the postcards talked about either the person themselves was lesbian, gay, transgender, bisexual whatever or maybe…they had a parent or a child or a friend, or whatever. And it was good, like it was just a lot of like personal comments about the subject and about how we need to be open to talking about these things because right now in the Mennonite church…we don't talk about sexuality. (*Ibid.*)

Between 2010 and 2011, Harmony drafted a resolution which was presented at the MC Canada Assembly in July 2011 which called for a re-examination of *The Resolution on Human Sexuality* (Mennonite Church Canada, 1986) and to begin conversations in the church on sexuality.

An early draft version of this resolution[63] (Group With No Name, 2010) was sent to MC Canada leadership and the unofficial response suggested that there existed a strong interest in the main direction behind the resolution proposing continued study and dialogue on sexuality. MC Canada made some suggestions for changes to the draft motion to increase the chances of the resolution passing, which Harmony reviewed and took under consideration (W. Warkentin, 2010). Wark reflects that,

> the totality of that statement [*The Resolution on Human Sexuality*] has not been taken seriously and it needs to be. In taking it seriously I suspect parts of it are going to change in particular the negativity towards homosexuality is going to have to change. (*Ibid.*)

In fact, Wark believes that just the act of going into a study process often results in a change and a more welcoming stance on sexuality (*Ibid.*).[64] The final version of the motion (Harmony, 2011a) was presented at the July conference by member Ben Borne, and was thought by Harmony organizers to be well received (W. Warkentin, 2011).

Wark noted his opinion that Harmony functions well because it is part of the church and has not positioned itself as an outside advocacy group like the United States based BMC (W. Warkentin, 2010). Not surprisingly, however, Harmony's insider position means that outside of informal peer and kinship

63 For a full copy of this resolution, please see Appendix D in Volume 2 of this book which is available on the website of the UNESCO Chair for Peace Studies (UNESCO Chair for Peace Studies, 2012).

64 The specific interest of Harmony with the repeal of the 1986 Resolution more than other MC Canada statements on sexuality stems from a belief that this particular resolution is the source of exclusion for LGBTQ Mennonites as articulated in an article from Ted Grimsrud on the topic (W. Warkentin: 2010; Grimsrud, 2010).

networks, knowledge of the organization remains minimal. For within the structures of MC Canada and MC Manitoba, no public space for Harmony has yet been made available (*Ibid.*).

Harmony was denied opportunities to set up an information booth at MC Canada Assemblies and also the opportunity to publish in the conference periodical, the *Canadian Mennonite*; until October 2011 this periodical held an informal moratorium on any publications related to LGBTQ issues. Therefore, Harmony has no official means from within the public structures of MC Canada or Manitoba through which to declare its stance. Hope remains that MC Canada and MC Manitoba might be willing to work more closely with Harmony and include the organization and use is as a resource for discussions on sexuality (W.Warkentin, 2010).Still, Harmony continues to reach out to LGBT Mennonites and allies through its website and various initiatives.[65]

3.3 Hope Mennonite Church Welcoming Committee

Hope Mennonite Church (Hope) is widely known in Winnipeg as the LGBTQ friendly congregation and has been for many years. Hope is a member congregation of Mennonite Church Manitoba and Mennonite Church Canada, has approximately one hundred members, and is located in the urban centre of Winnipeg. Within the last five years, Hope's friendliness to LGBTQ people was formalized with the establishment of a Welcoming Committee. Although not always holding a clear sense of purpose or direction, the Hope Welcoming Committee, has been central to this church's process of moving through different discussions on sexuality and looking at the meaning of welcome for this congregation. Discussions have included inviting guest speakers to address the theological and conference aspects of becoming an Affirming congregation as well as general education and information sessions on the meaning of different terms and sexual identities. The church then adopted a consensus statement which stated that the Welcoming Committee would continue to dialogue with the conference and that the church will continue to discuss internally the next steps towards becoming officially Welcoming or Affirming (Read, 2010a).

---

[65] For a current discussion on the work of Harmony and its relationship with MC Canada, please see the Preface.

Matt Wiebe reflects on Hope Mennonite Church's reputation, noting that people who are not comfortable with LGBTQ inclusion tend not to make Hope their home congregation. "[R]ight now we're sort of unofficially Welcoming. Everybody knows but we're not officially Affirming" (Wiebe, 2010). There are several LGBTQ persons who attend regularly and/or are members of Hope, and who are active participants in the life of the church. For Hope Mennonite Church, being a Welcoming church is intimately connected with social justice concerns which are very important to members of this church many of whom are extensively involved in working or volunteering in the surrounding community (*Ibid.*).

One of the main fears the church has had in moving from a consensus statement to becoming publicly Affirming is how the larger conference bodies, MC Manitoba and MC Canada might react. As conference ties are important to people in the church, there remains some fear about being kicked out of the conference (Wiebe, 2010; Read, 2010a). Furthermore, concerns remain that LGBTQ people might be hurt in the continuing dialogue process in which Hope Mennonite Church is engaging (Read, 2010a). Although the Hope Welcoming Committee has tried to keep in close dialogue with MC Manitoba about their progress, Matt Wiebe, a gay Mennonite man who is part of this committee and a member at Hope, perceives a lack of willingness on the part of MC Manitoba to talk with the committee. Positively, MC Manitoba has said that if Hope did become officially Affirming and another congregation in the conference raised an issue about this, MC Manitoba would be willing to act as an "intermediary and try to bring people to a positive conclusion" and that the congregation would not be kicked out of the conference without a lengthy period of dialogue (Wiebe, 2010).

Jodi Read, a queer Mennonite woman who attends Hope, would like to see the congregation come out publicly with a celebration of some sort to recognize its stance and also to lead the wider church in discussions on affirming LGBTQ people (Read, 2010b). Matt Wiebe predicts that the time will come sometime between 2010-2012 when Hope will accept the risk in loosing conference membership and come out as publicly Affirming.[66]

66 As of February 2012, Hope Mennonite Church was in the process of drafting a formal Statement of Affirmation. Sometime during Spring 2012, the statement will be put before the congregation to approve for distribution and discussion. This will be followed by a period of sharing this statement with affiliated church bodies. Within a period of 12-18 months, it is anticipated that the Statement of Affirmation will be officially adopted and a special worship service of celebration will be held (Hope Mennonite Church, 2012a). For

> [M]y personal opinion is that if we really want to move forward were going to have to be willing to take that risk [of conference expulsion], because…we're never going to be 100 percent sure that nothing bad might…happen in terms of reaction from other congregations.…[M]y thinking is…[that] people are starting to move in that direction as well. And people are thinking 'no, we need to make a stand here because this is something we believe in, this inclusion, this welcome, this affirming thought.' (Wiebe, 2010)

3.4 CMQ, CMQ Open Closet & CMU Open Space

CMQ is an anonymous support group for LGBTQ persons on the Canadian Mennonite University (CMU) campus. The group began in 2009 with the number of people participating varying from nine participants in 2009, three in 2010, and two in 2011 (Borne, 2010a; 2012). Participation in CMQ is completely anonymous and in many cases is attended by people who are not out as LGBTQ to anyone. CMQ organizer Ben Borne explains that it "is for those people who really struggle with their family and their Christian faith, whatever and trying to reconcile it or…whatever issues they have" (Borne, 2010a). Ben reflects that the CMU campus is a more welcoming space since CMQ began, and during the 2011 year there did not seem to be the same need for the group among the LGBTQ student population (Borne, 2012).

In 2009, CMQ hosted a public forum for the broader CMU community called CMQ Open Closet. The organizers expected that about 35 people would come to the forum when in actuality, approximately 90 people attended. The forum covered topics such as stereotypes and appropriate use of language in the LGBTQ context. Particularly striking for Ben Borne was the number of very basic questions which were being asked by students, questions which are not being addressed at CMU or in Mennonite churches.

> a lot of people did have some…questions that could be cleared up very easily cause they…didn't quite understand cause they would ask, 'like is it true that all gay people are promiscuous?' or…, 'when can you have a safe place for us to discuss if we disagree?' and '…what are things we can look for if someone is gay?'.…[T]here were these very good questions, very simple questions that people have.…[A]nd we took from that [that]…a lot of people have a lot of questions in our community that are not being touched and they're not being answered. And so because there are a lot of questions, there's a lot of a misunderstanding and it's just never talked about. (Borne, 2010a)

---

more information on the process of Hope's Welcoming Journey please visit their website (Hope Mennonite Church, 2012b).

In 2010, Ben Borne and another student began CMU Safe Space to pick up where CMQ Open Closet left off and answer those questions; the goal was to create a safe and open forum for discussing LGBTQ topics on campus and also other subjects related to the well-being of the student population such as drinking alcohol (Borne, 2010a). In the 2011-2012 school year, one CMU Safe Space event was held to make the presence of CMQ and LGBTQ supports known. Although about 30 people attended that gathering, organizers did not feel the need to hold another event; students are not necessarily more informed about LGBT topics, Ben reflects, but there does seem to be a more general open mindedness among the student population (Borne, 2012).

3.5 Brethren Mennonite Council for LGBT Interests

The Brethren Mennonite Council for Lesbian, Gay, Bisexual, and Transgender Interests (BMC) was formed in 1976 as an effort to advocate for LGBT people within Mennonite and Brethren in Christ Churches in addition to working more generally for education and dialogue on sexuality within congregations (Braun, 2008). The founding member was an employee of Mennonite Central Committee who was fired from his position because of his sexual orientation (*Ibid.*). The BMC is active primarily in the United States although informal personal connections to Canadian advocates on LGBTQ inclusion in the church remain strong.

BMC was formed with the mission "to cultivate an inclusive church and society and to care for the Mennonite and Brethren lesbian, gay, bisexual, transgender, and allied community" (Brethren Mennonite Council for Lesbian, Gay, Bisexual, and Transgender Interests, 2010b). With that aim, BMC works to provide theological and spiritual resources and opportunities for LGBT persons and allies to gain support from one another. Also, BMC is a strong advocate for LGBT inclusion in conference and congregational structures and is involved in broader social justice movements for lesbian, gay, bisexual, and transgender people (*Ibid.*)

In 2011, a local BMC group started meeting in Winnipeg. Kirsten Freed who helps to organize the group, reflects that the purpose is to "create queer space" which offers the opportunity for Mennonites identifying within the LGBTQ community "to be" (Freed, 2012a). "I want to create a space where queer people with Mennonite connections or histories can, if they choose to, find and create community," Kirsten writes (Freed, 2012b). Since it began, the group has met monthly or every second month in an informal, social gathering hosted at participant's homes. There are 12 to 20 people currently on the group's mailing list. Kirsten hopes that by making more contacts with local congregations, the visibility of the group will increase so that it is a well-known space for LGBT Mennonites. This group is one of many local BMC groups which meet across Canada and the United States, information about which is publicized on the BMC website (Freed, 2012a; 2012b).

The Supportive Communities Network (SCN) is a body of the BMC which is concerned with keeping a network of Mennonite and Church of the Brethren communities that are publicly Affirming of LGBT persons. SCN has the objective of supporting opportunities for dialogue in communities, "encourage meaningful dialogue at the denominational level" and "offer support and resources for individuals who are working toward welcome" (Brethren Mennonite Council for Lesbian, Gay, Bisexual, and Transgender Interests, 2010a). This is achieved through the distribution of resources, organization of conferences, and presence at wider church events. In 2012, there were no congregations in Manitoba part of the SCN and only 3 congregations/communities in Canada (*Ibid.*).

3.6 Summary

Mennonites are working formally and informally in churches and with institutions to contend with idealized sexual norms which continue to pervade the Mennonite community. Through support groups such as the Pilgrim Group and CMQ, as well as social gatherings such as Winnipeg's BMC group, LGBTQ Mennonites are finding spaces to be and gain support. Furthermore, through the advocacy efforts of Harmony, church committees such as the Hope Welcoming Committee, and public forums, these Mennonites are raising awareness that LGBTQ Mennonites exist, must be heard, and need to be included.

4. LESBIAN, GAY, AND QUEER MENNONITE VOICES

I interviewed a number of lesbian, gay, and queer Mennonites to hear their perspectives and experiences in being Mennonite. Using Hall's conception of identification, I looked at the narratives of these Mennonites as attestations on how idealized discourses attempt to hail people into a particular place; in this case, it is a place in which bodies are unproblematically binary, gender aligned with biological sex, and desire and sexual practices flowing from those binaries as unquestionably heterosexual. These are the stories of how individual Mennonites have interacted with these discourses, resisting, investing in, and re-fashioning the very meaning of being Mennonite and all of the sexuality norms entailed in that identification.

4.1 INTRODUCTION

I interviewed a total of nine people, whose stories I draw upon in the course of this chapter. These nine people included four women and five men, two of whom identified as queer women, two as lesbian women, and five as gay men. These participants reflected a diversity of experiences in relation to the Mennonite community, with different relationships to Mennonite organizations, churches, family life, and values. Three of these persons were in their early 20s, two in their late 20s, two in their mid 30s, one in their early 40s, and one person in their mid 40s.

KERRI SMITH[67]

When Kerri Smith and I sat down for an interview, I was immediately struck by the determined passion and forthrightness of this young Mennonite queer woman in her early 20s. Kerri grew up in a small Mennonite town and now attends Red River Valley Mennonite Church, an MC Manitoba and MC Canada church in Winnipeg, Manitoba. Growing up, life was intimately connected to the Mennonite church which meant that every Sunday, baring ill-

---

67 This person requested to remain anonymous and therefore all names and identifying details in her story were altered for the purpose of protecting her identity.

ness, Kerri and her family went to church. A strong community was formed around this church which Kerri found herself at odds with it at times given its exclusivity, especially as a youth. The presence of Mennonite institutions such as Mennonite Central Committee (MCC) was pronounced during her youth and childhood with Kerri participating in various MCC projects and volunteer opportunities (Smith, 2010).

Today Kerri is proud of being Mennonite and many of the cultural elements of growing up in a Mennonite home remain important in her today. Mennonite food, jokes, and sharing with others about the historical, cultural, and religious elements that make Mennonites distinctive is important to Kerri. Particularly, Mennonite pacifism as well as the concern for peace and international development found in the Mennonite community was and continues to be a strong source of pride. "I always kind of took it [being Mennonite] with a responsibility in terms of…when you're looking at like peace and conflict and development…it was always like instilled in my brain…Mennonite Central Committee" (Smith, 2010). Taking a Mennonite perspective on peace and development is important to Kerri; so much so that she hopes to do an internship with MCC in the future as part of her ongoing university studies in International Development (*Ibid.*)

Kerri is currently a Sunday School teacher in her church but she has been told that if she was in a same-sex relationship she could no longer be in that role. Along with the very negative and hurtful comments she has heard about LGBTQ people within her church, Kerri is not sure how long she will stay around. Nevertheless, Kerri knows that she will never cast aside her identity as a Mennonite (Smith, 2010).

> I don't think I see myself staying forever in the Mennonite church, unless things change…but I think that I would still attend like Mennonite events and try to keep my ties with the Mennonite community….I totally don't think I could just be like I'm not going to be Mennonite anymore cause that's not, that's not my thing. (Smith, 2010)

MICHELLE TIPPERT[68]

Michelle Tippert, a lesbian Mennonite woman in her early 40s, exuded an intense and plainspoken account on her experience being Mennonite. "I think I've probably always identified myself as being Mennonite," Michelle re-

68 This person requested to remain anonymous and therefore all names and identifying details in her story were altered for the purpose of protecting her identity.

flects (Tippert, 2010). Michelle grew up in a Mennonite community, home, and church as well as having Mennonite ancestry. She also worked as a volunteer and paid employee with four prominent Mennonite institutions, which means that Michelle has experienced a plethora of different cultural and religious contexts within which being Mennonite is carried out. For Michelle, being Mennonite is multi-faceted and both related to culture, community, and also the church (*Ibid.*).

Michelle found herself being pushed to the margins of the MC Manitoba and MC Canada congregation of which she is a member as a single woman going into her 30s. Oriented as the church was around families and children, there remained hardly any single people left in the church. When Michelle realized in her 30s that she was a lesbian, she had trouble finding a space to express that within the church. Today Michelle and her partner are working to negotiate their space within the Mennonite church and Mennonite community at large, caught in the tension of speaking up and staying quiet (Tippert, 2010.)

Ben Borne

Sitting down with Ben Borne, an energetic and verbose gay man in his early 20s, I could not help but be inspired by his passion. Ben grew up in a Mennonite family and in a Mennonite church in Saskatchewan which was part of Mennonite Church Canada and Mennonite Church Saskatchewan. Therefore, not surprisingly, being Mennonite is very much linked to those two things: faith and family tradition. Family tradition includes Mennonite food, affiliation with various Mennonite organizations, and allegiance to family. "They [my grandparents] are very encouraging people with strong beliefs about family. Very loyal people. They've always taught very important lessons about being loyal to your family and they raised me right, you know?" (Borne, 2010a). Ben has in particular always admired the way in which his grandparents have been involved in the Mennonite community through involvement with Mennonite nursing homes, Mennonite Central Committee, and in church life (*Ibid.*).

Ben was baptized into the Mennonite church and lives his Mennonitism daily as a peacekeeper with a commitment to living differently. As Ben grew up he began to learn about the importance of being part of a community of believers and the church always tried to nurture Ben's ministry skills. Ben took the Explore Program through Associate Mennonite Biblical Seminary and afterward became the interim youth pastor at his church. He preached his first sermon at fourteen and now is involved also in worship leading. "[M]y connection to the church is very deep now and you know especially with the kids and the parents of those kids [that I was a youth pastor for]" (Borne, 2010a). Ben now attends Canadian Mennonite University (CMU) in Winnipeg but nevertheless stays very closely tied to his home church in Saskatchewan. He remains extremely dedicated to being Mennonite, working for LGBTQ awareness within the CMU community, and walking with his church through the process of moving towards welcome (*Ibid.*).

JUSTIN DUECK

Justin Dueck is a gay, Aboriginal, Mennonite man in his late 20s full of smiles, joy, and a disarming honesty. Justin grew up in a small, tight knit Mennonite community in Manitoba's Interlake called Mennville where the local Christian private school, social gatherings, and family life was intimately connected to the Evangelical Mennonite Conference church in the village. Being Mennonite was part of all aspects of life in this village and Justin as both a gay person and someone who accentuated his feminine attributes, often felt ignored and not taken seriously in the context of his community. In his teenage years, Justin left that community to venture to Steinbach, another, albeit larger, Mennonite dominated community and attended Steinbach Christian High School (Dueck, 2010).

For Justin, being Mennonite today does not involve formal connections to Mennonite institutions, churches, nor to particular Mennonite communities, yet being Mennonite continues to be important to Justin in his daily life. One of the primary means through which Justin is Mennonite is in his efforts to form and be accountable to a community of both Mennonite and non-Mennonite friends who are engaging specifically with topics of sexuality and addiction in their lives. Furthermore, what Justin identifies as his Mennonite values of hospitality, genuine conviction, and treating others well, constantly guides his daily living (Dueck, 2010).

SCOTT BERGEN

An intellectual, thoughtful gay man in his early 20s, Scott Bergen is very clear in identifying himself as ethnically Russian Mennonite but not ethnic in the sense of an ethnicity intrinsic to faith. For Scott being in the Mennonite church and coming out as a gay man proved impossible for him, and so he has completely left the Mennonite church and his personal spiritual journey has led him to a place of agnosticism (Bergen, 2010b).

Scott explains where he is at now in his life:

> I'm comfortable with my sexuality. I don't believe that God exists but I don't believe that God doesn't exist, agnostic. Yet, I still resound very strongly with Mennonitism not only because that's where I came from but also because…it has a lot of the same pillars that I hold important now, although in very different ways: justice, social engagement with…larger society for the larger good, a sense of eschatological hope, all these sorts of things. In that sense I'm very Mennonite still, in a religious sense I suppose I'm not. (Bergen, 2010a)

Scott grew up in the Mennonite church and in a Mennonite family. For many years he was actively involved in his church and studied theology at Canadian Mennonite University with the aim of one day becoming a pastor. For Scott, his theological questioning and coming out to himself as gay, led to a place where he realized that he could not be out, gay, and in the Mennonite church (*Ibid.*)

Even though no longer subscribing to those religious aspects of being Mennonite, Scott tries to live the core pillars of what he thinks Mennonitism means everyday through his actions. "I try to embody…those values. I think if you just sort of put me on mute you know,…cut out the narrative and watch my actions I try to live in such a way that I look Mennonite" (Bergen, 2010a) At the same time, embodying these Mennonite ideals is not always respected by religious Mennonites, Scott noting that some Mennonite pastors who have spent energy working against him and his activism. The label Mennonite, he notes, cannot so quickly be linked to holding specific religious beliefs alone (*Ibid.*).

JODI READ

For Jodi Read, being Mennonite is not at all connected with any ethnic or cultural markers. For her the emphasis on peace and justice, priesthood of all believers, and community responsibility and accountability are central to what brought her into the Mennonite fold and what keeps her involved in Mennonite churches. Jodi, a self-assured queer identifying woman in her mid 30s, had her first foray into Mennonitism in an assignment with Mennonite Central Committee. This led to about twelve years of her professional life spent within the organization working in peace and justice initiatives in Chile, Bolivia, and on the US/Mexican border on the topic of immigration. Jodi also obtained her Masters degree in Conflict Transformation and Peacebuilding from Eastern Mennonite University in Virginia, has attended various Mennonite churches, and is now a member of a Mennonite church in Tucson, Arizona. In Winnipeg, she attends Hope Mennonite Church (Read, 2010b).

At times Jodi is challenged in not being ethnically Mennonite which is given away by her non-Mennonite last name. Yet Jodi finds that "I think having been in MCC for so long I kind of have my Mennonite credentials" (Read, 2010b). For Jodi, being Mennonite is an identity that she chooses to draw or not draw on depending on her context.

> I think I grab on to that identity when it's something that I care a lot about and peace and justice concerns would be one....So I can choose to hang on to the beliefs when I want to or connect myself with organizations or institutions but I can also not at times. (*Ibid.*)

MATT WIEBE

Matt Wiebe grew up in a conservative, non-denominational evangelical church and in a Mennonite environment of family cultural traditions and values which were instilled into him deeply. When at 25, Matt became the only openly gay man in his large congregation, he was removed from his position as a Sunday School teacher. After this, he made his church home at Hope Mennonite Church, an MC Manitoba and MC Canada congregation. Today Matt, a friendly and eloquent gay man in his late 20s, believes being Mennonite is intimately tied with a concern for peace, social justice, and serving others. Matt is a member of Hope Mennonite Church because he sees those values as a strong focus of that church and that is also the reason for Matt's activism for LGBTQ rights and also professional work in helping other people.

> [T]hat's why I think...you can have LGBT Mennonites because being Mennonite's such a broad concept and I think sometimes people think it needs to be a very restrictive box but it isn't necessarily...a lot of different types of people can fit into the core value of what it means to be Mennonite in my thinking. (Wiebe, 2010)

MARK BRUBACHER

Mark Brubacher exudes a simultaneously soft spoken and powerful account of being a gay Mennonite man. Now in his mid-late 40s, Mark grew up in a more conservative Mennonite church and Mennonite home in Southern Ontario. For the first years of Mark's life his family attended a Mennonite church where there was no TV or radio permitted and there were strict dress codes. When Mark was five, his family began attending a more liberal Mennonite Church congregation, but his family life remained quite conservative as Mark's father was from an Old Order Mennonite Church background and his mother also from a conservative Mennonite background. For the past eighteen years, Mark has attended Bethel Mennonite Church in Winnipeg, a MC Manitoba and MC Canada church. Mark came out as a gay man just over six years ago in his early 40s, married and a father of four children. Although there are some cultural food ways and family gatherings which Mark relates as part of what it means to be Mennonite, religious expression and personal faith is central to Mark's sense of being Mennonite (Brubacher, 2010).

Mark continues to struggle with whether expressing his faith through the Mennonite church is the best for his life and has tried to leave the Mennonite church several times. Time after time, Mark finds himself back in the Mennonite church, unable to leave the tradition which is so intimately connected to his life and faith. Mark is extensively involved in dialogue and activism for LGBTQ inclusion in the Mennonite church and hopes that his presence proves integral to shifting ideas on homosexuality in his church (Brubacher, 2010).

JULIA ZACHARIAS

Julia Zacharias grew up in a small southern Manitoba Mennonite community where her father was the pastor of the local Evangelical Mennonite Mission Conference church. In this place, all of life including school, family, and community was intimately connected to the church and being Mennonite. Julia, a warm, self-reflective lesbian Mennonite woman in her mid 30s, notes her very close and intimate relationship with the Mennonite church and Mennonite educational institutions which led her towards pursuing a PhD. Julia hoped to one day teach theological studies at a post-secondary Mennonite institution but left behind that dream when she came out as a lesbian, realizing that she would never be able to be at the centre of the Mennonite community as she desired (Zacharias, 2010).

For a time Julia found a place in the Mennonite community at Hope Mennonite Church which she left following her marriage which, painfully, was not sanctioned by the Mennonite church. Being a Mennonite today for Julia is not connected with any formal structures of the Mennonite church or community. Rather, being Mennonite is intimately tied to relationships with Mennonite family and friends as well an appreciation for community, and an interest in social justice issues or international development. Furthermore, Julia's everyday appreciation for life's sacred moments and ethical living is something she sees as being very Mennonite. "That to me feels really Mennonite that ethics is sort of part of everyday, every concern, every moment, that all you do matters I guess" (Zacharias, 2010).

4.2 Hearing the Mennonite Community Speak

Most of the interview participants reflected on the way in which sexuality, gender or LGBTQ persons were spoken about or not spoken about; they also spoke about how LGBTQ people were treated in the Mennonite communities, institutions, and churches of which they were and continue to be a part. Silence was a major theme emerging in the stories of many of these Mennonites. After asking the explicit question of some of the participants, 'what did you hear the Mennonite community saying about LGBTQ people?' it was notable that a common response was that there was nothing explicit ever said to them yet this not preclude a clear message being communicated.

Justin Dueck notes that sexuality was one of those things that "are just not talked about like in the community" (Dueck, 2010). In Mennville, where Justin grew up, he notes that "I think a lot of the people in the community, they were so, there was such a lack of sexuality like that people were so just benignly sexless almost like in the way that you dress and the way that you act" (*Ibid.*). Although there was silence in spoken words, however, community perceptions of certain sexual acts or ways of being was clear to Justin when several young women who were pregnant before they were married or dressed in sexualized ways were excommunicated or negatively spoken about (*Ibid.*). Mark Brubacher does not recall the church explicitly preaching about homosexuality or sexuality, but it was nevertheless always clear to Mark in church, school and just generally in society that being LGBTQ was wrong, particularly evident in the way that children teased each other using words like fag (Brubacher, 2010).

Ben Borne echoes a similar sentiment although he remembered a session his youth group had on discussing sex and homosexuality which was neither affirming nor condemning, but a neutral discussion. Overall, however, Ben indicated that the lack of teaching about sexuality growing up made him feel undereducated and confused (Borne, 2010b).

> I think because I was always taught that sex was private and dirty, and just awkward which in some ways it is…Because of this teaching from my grandparents that my view of sex was really repressed and that any form of outward sexual expression would be considered...not sinful but unsavoury. (Borne 2010b)

Similarly, for Julia Zacharias, sexuality was something which was by and large not spoken about. During Julia's high school years, any talks about sexuality were concerned primarily with whether or not you had sex before marriage rather than same-sex relationships. Besides one particular sermon in Julia's church which condemned homosexuality, there was hardly any conception of being LGBTQ.

> [B]eing queer would have been sort of largely been nonexistent in my experience of being Mennonite. Like I just didn't know what that was or how it would look if it appeared in my life. It wasn't about it being bad or ugly it just wasn't there. (Zacharias, 2010).

Although as Julia grew older she knew that being gay meant two men being together, it was not until Julia knew her first openly gay person when she was 23 that a conception of what being gay really meant developed (*Ibid.*).

Julia explains,

> [L]ike there's a difference between having a real idea of what that is [being gay] when you know a gay couple or play with their kids or something when you're a kid, you know what I mean? There's a shift in just a concept and this is a reality. (Zacharias, 2010)

Matt Wiebe reflects that it is not only sexuality in relation to same-sex practices, but that in his experience Mennonites

> don't like to talk about sex and so, like even heterosexual sex. So when you talk about like being welcoming to LGBT people, that's talking about…two subjects which people…in the Mennonite church, are just not comfortable with: which is sexuality,…sexual acts, and then also gender identity. And gender identity is like sort of the transgender side of things. But people…in the Mennonite church don't like to think about gender identity because there's specific roles for men and women and so you talk about gender identity it sort of starts to muddy the waters, so to speak…I think, it's going into people's comfort zones and trying to push them a little bit. (Wiebe, 2010)

In a grade 5 health, class which outlined the biological differences between boys and girls, Matt realized that he was attracted to the other boys in his class rather than the girls. And so he recognized the difference "but I also knew that I wasn't supposed to talk about [it]. It was like an ingrained thing, you don't talk about those kinds of thing. So I didn't" (*Ibid.*).

Yet others noted more explicit norms communicated about sexuality and LGBTQ people. Kerri Smith reflects on the implicit gender norms in the Mennonite community which were placed on her and also on the more explicit statements made on same-sex relationships. Growing up she heard quite clearly from the church that homosexuality was wrong and "those people were like not proper people" (Smith, 2010). In her church, she remembers very clear messages being communicated about LGBTQ people.

> I remember there was one girl, ironically one of the girls I did not get along with, but one person…in junior youth. Junior youth is grade 7 to 9. And we

> were debating this once and she was trying to say like there's was nothing wrong with…LGBT community and like our youth leader and everyone else in the youth was just tearing her apart like. You know, 'these people are wrong'. Like, 'that is wrong, like you can't do that!' (Smith, 2010)

There was some tolerance, Kerri says, in that it was recognized that same-sex desiring people could be together, but it was clear to Kerri that marriage was off limits and she had the sense there remained a message of "we don't really want them" (Smith, 2010).

Likewise Scott Bergen heard very clear messages communicated from his church regarding same-sex relationships and attraction.

> [S]ame sex marriage was preached against from the pulpit with Power Point slides and everything. I remember that. It was always official, if it's on Power Point, God said it….I remember in Sunday School we're taught…it was wrong and here's a list of you know the couple Bible verses, they're pulled out and preached in the traditional evangelical way. That was the first time I knew it was wrong, right then in my Sunday School class. (Bergen, 2010a)

The most poignant message that being LGBTQ was wrong, however, came for Scott when his pastor, a very large and imposing man, gave a speech from the pulpit urging the congregation to sign a petition; this was a petition that was being circulated by the Canadian Alliance political party in the early 2000s, which called the government not to expand the definition of marriage.

> The symbolism is overwhelming, he put it [the petition] for us to sign afterward on the communion table at the front of the sanctuary beside the big open Bible. The centre of all this most important symbols of the Mennonite faith and then there's this petition there against…equal marriage. And my response to it,…I believed so strongly that he was right that actually I signed that, and believed it to that degree. (*Ibid.*)

Besides the overt statements, Scott also notes that there were always small heterosexual assumptions that reinforced the "pulpit truth statements about being gay", epitomized in questions to Scott such as if he had a girlfriend (*Ibid.*).

Several participants also noted that there was not a lot of room to be different in Mennonite circles. Kerri Smith indicates a very strong affiliation with being Mennonite and vociferous commitment to keeping that identification. And simultaneously, for Kerri being Mennonite has a strong association with being conservative and exclusivity. "There's not a lot of wiggle room for people who are different and for people who are maybe like, newer" (Smith, 2010).

Justin Dueck pointed to the homogeneity demanded in the Mennonite community noting that Mennonites are accepting of people in the secular world and aspects of secular culture as long as one of their own does not take on aspects of being attributed to the wider secular world.

> So there's definitely a lot of…segregation and like just like total being shut out of community cause…Mennonite society is a bit of a conformist society like…you're participating in community so you have to…adhere to…the guidelines of that community. (Dueck, 2010)

Kerri notes that the Mennonite community does not always have the best reputation, particularly in the queer community. Kerri says that when she tells fellow queer people she is Mennonite they ask with incredulity "you're queer and you're a Mennonite? Ooooh, good luck with that!" Kerri notes with a smile, "like I get a lot of hugs. A lot of people feel bad for you" (Smith, 2010).

Michelle Tippert is unique in that she remembers a great deal of openness and communication about sexuality from her parents in particular; she noted that there was also space within the Mennonite congregation, school and community within which she was raised to discuss sexuality. Michelle reflects that

> my parents also were very open minded and we had discussions of sexuality from a fairly young age when it came up. And it was clearly told that you know, people are born certain ways and they are who they are and…they shouldn't be ashamed of that. (Tippert, 2010)

She remembers in particular going to the Saskatoon Conference of the General Conference Mennonite Church in 1986 where her parents as representatives of her home church did not vote with the conference to approve the now notorious *Resolution on Human Sexuality* (Mennonite Church Canada, 1986). "So, I grew up with that experience where just because the greater church was more conservative they [my church and my parents] weren't necessarily following that line" (Tippert, 2010).

As a young girl growing up in a small and tight knit Mennonite community, Michelle had the opportunity to explore the topic of being LGBTQ. In particular, she recalls a German class where a discussion of being lesbian arose and "I remember being one the people who, the only girl who said 'what's the big deal?' or whatever" (Tippert, 2010). Further, at the Mennonite high school Michelle attended, she remembered writing a paper for her Bible class on biblical perspectives on sexuality. "I never felt like I was being told your views are incorrect or it's sin, like that never came up" (*Ibid.*).

At the same time, Michelle does remember being one of the few people who ever did talk about LGBTQ issues, a fact she attributes to her home life and parental guidance on the topic rather than the church or community at large (Tippert, 2010). When Michelle was nine a family trip around North

America brought them to Washington, DC on the eve of a gay rights protest. Michelle remembers many slides of their Washington trip with men holding hands in the background. She explicitly recalls her parents talking about the protest, why there were men holding hands, and what was going on without any judgement or condemnation (*Ibid.*).

Although Jodi Read did not grow up in the Mennonite fold, since she began identifying as Mennonite she has witnessed a lot of interest and passion within the churches she has been a part of in engaging the broader church in dialogue on LGBTQ inclusion and has not "heard as many ways that people have spoken poorly of LGBT folks" (Read, 2010b). Jodi is a member of a Welcoming church in Tucson, Arizona and attends Hope Mennonite Church in Winnipeg, a church moving towards an official Affirming stance. Yet Jodi is also aware of the negative way in which Mennonite Church USA has dealt with Pink Menno, an LGBTQ inclusion advocacy group as well as congregations that are inviting ex-gay ministries into their churches (*Ibid.*).

In particular, Jodi remembers reading a letter written by some leaders of Mennonite churches in Southern California which was very negative in talking about homosexuality. This was particularly striking for Jodi as many of the churches were predominantly attended by immigrants. Furthermore, Jodi had related with several of the signers of that letter in her MCC advocacy work. "I think there's a lot of similarities between those [two issues: immigration and LGBTQ inclusion] cause they're not mainstream, they're not the normal way of thinking" (Read, 2010b).

Clearly, there is a diversity of perspectives among interview participants about what they have heard the Mennonite community saying about LGBTQ people and sexuality both today and in the past. For many, no explicit messages were spoken yet actions and presumptions clearly laid out what was acceptable and within community norms. For others such as Kerri and Scott, more explicitly negative messages were heard whereas both Michelle and Jodi note overall positive experiences in the Mennonite circles of which they have been a part. Justin and Kerri point to the fact that the Mennonite community was and is not a place which celebrates differences, which may account for the confusion within Kerri's queer community in her being both queer and Mennonite.

4.3 Speaking Up and Standing Out

For many of those that I spoke with, interacting with the silence and the overtly negative messages about same-sex desire or relationships meant being active in regularly and intentionally pushing the limits of gender and sexuality norms in the community; this was done either through dress, behaviour, activism, or continuing in individual dialogue with people in the Mennonite community. In this way, these individuals were and are able to stand out and speak up for their Mennonite-ness which does not follow the heterosexual marriage norm and in that process articulate a diversity of sexualized Mennonite identities.

Kerri specifically identifies her own transgression of gender and cultural norms by engaging in typically male assigned activities; this meant that she did not fit in with the Mennonite community:

> When I was a little kid my favorite activities were play wrestling with my dad and my brothers, sports, so ahh, soccer and street hockey. For a brief period of time I loved wearing dresses but I sort of did everything I wasn't supposed to do. I loved to hang out with the guys and you know, get a little messy. I never wore make-up. I used to dance when I was a kid, and again when I was older…I would never, you know want to have my hair done so every Sunday morning my mom would have to fight to get me into a nice, church appropriate outfit….I don't know. I never really fit in. (Smith, 2010)

However, even though some of the activities she engaged in and friends she had may have pushed the limits of what was acceptable, "as long as I wasn't hurting anybody I didn't really care what anyone thought of me" which led to a lot of "making waves" (*Ibid.*).

For Justin Dueck, challenging gender norms in self presentation was an important part of his experience in being Mennonite and expressing himself sexually. Justin explains:

> I was definitely something…my community had never had to deal with before. They were frowning on the way that I looked,… I would wear eye liner, sparkles, and like I would paint my nails. Like everything was tight, very colorful, lots of jewelry….just taking on [a]…more feminine way of dressing. (Dueck, 2010)

One particularly memorable moment was when Justin was nine or ten and painted his nails before going to his grandparent's house. After arriving at his grandparent's house, Justin's mom saw his nails and then "[s]he was like holding my hands and pouring like nail polish remover, over my hands. And it just like, it was very very, very like dramatic reaction from her and I felt really like kind of ashamed of that whole thing" (*Ibid.*).

Justin appreciated the feminine qualities of things as well as within himself. In seeking to accentuate this and other sexual qualities of his physical appearance, however, he was shamed in the community and church. "I think I tended to be more extreme because I was trying to get people to give me answers for these different things" such as why are particular attributes, clothing styles, etc. only assigned to female gender? (Dueck, 2010).

Today, Justin continues to accentuate his feminine attributes in his dress as well as his self presentation and continues to dialogue with Mennonites many of whom Justin says are homophobic and have had little or no interaction with gay people. "I've been lucky to be able to have, be able to get dialogue out of people that wouldn't normally [have that sort of dialogue with anyone]…And have conversations with people [on]…stuff they wouldn't normally say to anybody" (Dueck, 2010). In this way, both Kerri and Justin challenged and continue to challenge gender and sexuality norms and quite literally stand out to provoke dialogue and articulate their subject position as gay and queer Mennonites.

For other Mennonites, being active in their church in working for LGBTQ rights is central to their experience being Mennonite. Matt Wiebe now attends Hope Mennonite Church where he is actively involved in the church's Welcoming Committee and he is also a participant in Harmony and the Pilgrim Group. Furthermore, Matt sits on the board of Winnipeg's Rainbow Resource Centre, the primary organization in Manitoba and Northwestern Ontario for LGBTQ advocacy and community resources (Wiebe, 2010).

Through these different associations, Matt has given a variety of different presentations on LGBTQ topics in government, churches, businesses, and community settings. From Matt's perspective, the biggest barrier faced in the Mennonite community regarding sexuality is education.

> I think as you learn about things you start to break down those fears you might have about a subject. And I think knowledge is power and I think as people learn something then they realize that 'oh, this [talking about sexuality] isn't as scary as I though it would be'. (Wiebe, 2010)

For Matt such activism is at the core of what it means to be Mennonite. "[L]ike to me serving and…activism like volunteering at Rainbow Resource Centre and social justice are all important things for me and those are all very much connected to the Mennonite tradition" (*Ibid.*).

For Mark Brubacher, standing up and speaking about homosexuality to those around him is integral to negotiating his position as a Mennonite. Mark regularly engages in one-to-one conversations with people in his church as well as those in leadership within conference bodies to tell them more about "what homosexuality is and what it isn't" cause he says there is still a lot of confusion and misinformation (Brubacher, 2010). Mark is also active in the Pilgrim Group at Bethel Mennonite Church, Harmony, and was also a panellist at the *Nurturing Healthy Sexuality Conference*. Mark hopes that his continued presence in the church will help to be an example to others that "yes a person can be gay, can still be a good Christian" and that his efforts in education and raising awareness will help lead to the day when being gay in the Mennonite church will no longer be an issue (*Ibid.*).

Ben Borne is active at an institutional level, being the organizer of CMQ, an anonymous LGBTQ support group on CMU's campus. Ben also started CMU Safe Space which creates opportunities for dialogue on LGBTQ topics within the CMU community. When CMQ hosted an information session on LGBTQ topics entitled CMQ Open Closet, Ben was struck by the question and answer session. "[A] lot of people have a lot of questions in our community that are not being touched and they're not being answered. And so because there're a lot of questions, there's a lot of misunderstanding and it's just never talked about" (Borne, 2010a).

On a personal basis, in 2009 Ben successfully petitioned the CMU administration to include a statement that prohibited sexual orientation discrimination in the sexual harassment section of the CMU Student Handbook.

> I'm very pumped...I was like 'yes!' [because now] if someone discriminates against me verbally...they can be taken and held accountable cause before it was like you could say whatever you want and you couldn't really talk about it....I'm sure someone would do something but it was never official. (Borne, 2010a)

Furthermore, in 2012 Ben and a fellow CMU Safe Space organizer, successfully acquired shower partitions and curtains in the men's washrooms to allow the space to be safer for gay and transgender men (Borne, 2012). Like both Matt and Mark, Ben is concerned with spreading knowledge and breaking the silence on sexuality through education and calling public attention to the topic with administrative changes; it is through this process, that he finds and articulates his position as a gay Mennonite man.

Scott Bergen was also involved in institutional activism within CMU, which he identified as a really important part of his process in "trying to reconcile...openly gay Scott with...the, very closed conservative, anti-gay Scott I was before, and the...closed tradition from which I came" (Bergen, 2010a). Scott's involvement included a lecture given as part of a speech contest on embracing queers in the church and queer rights as a peace issue. He also spoke at CMQ Open Closet where he presented a short global history of sexuality. In addition, Speaking at a CMU fundraising dinner, Scott controversially linked together equality and sexual orientation. Scott reflects on his activist sense:

> Sort of interesting, the Mennonite church has taught me to be activist minded, standing up for justice. Now I'm standing up for justice within the Mennonite church and it's sort of a weird turnabout in that sense. But I've definitely learned that [activism] from them as well. (Bergen, 2010a)

For Scott, engaging in public dialogue on LGBTQ topics has helped him personally negotiate being gay and Mennonite; for him, LGBTQ inclusion is a social justice issue and therefore a very Mennonite concern (*Ibid.*).

In 2010 Jodi Read did a project looking at the Welcoming process at Hope Mennonite Church. In that project, Jodi interviewed three people who have been part of the Welcoming Committee at Hope and through that came to a deeper understanding of the meaning of Welcome in this congregation that she attends. Jodi was also involved in an LGBT oral history project; she sees the intersecting relationships of peace and justice inherent in discussions of LGBT rights as well as border and immigration issues. For Jodi, being Mennonite is intimately connected to peace and justice issues (Read, 2010b). In studying these questions, Jodi can be Mennonite and understand her position as a queer woman.

Julia Zacharias was part of an organizing committee for a weekend conference in the early 2000s which focused on bringing together Mennonites from across Winnipeg in affirming that it was possible to be LGBTQ and Mennonite.

> [J]ust being on that committee was this really cool experience for me. Cause it was this experience of having other Mennonites from around the city just be there and be so positive and be 'this [being LGBTQ] is a really good thing and we need to celebrate ourselves'.(Zacharias, 2010)

It was also a transforming experience for Julia's parents who attended the weekend and were asked to serve communion at the final Sunday morning service (*Ibid.*)

Previously, Julia's dad had spoken out against the homophobic hate which had appeared in his church newsletter, after which both he and Julia's mother, were stripped of all their public roles in their Mennonite church and publicly shamed.

> [T]hey were quite traumatized by that experience. And then to come to this event, although it was only a weekend long but it was so gay positive and it was all Mennonite..... And they got asked to serve communion...So they were really, really touched and really changed by that weekend. And my mom went home and told me... She said it like that with strength in her voice, 'Now, I know I'm an ally!' Like it had really changed something for her. (Zacharias, 2010)

For Julia being out, being lesbian, and being active in the Mennonite church was a tension filled relationship, and through participation in organizing such a weekend, Julia found an important source of affirmation in her position as a lesbian Mennonite. Likewise, Julia's parents could find encouragement in being parents of a lesbian Mennonite by participating in this LGBTQ friendly event.

Michelle sees giving back to her community as integral to being Mennonite and reflects on her many years of volunteering in different Mennonite organizations as a witness to that. Now after processing through coming out, both Michelle and her partner are strengthening their connections to their communities in Manitoba through volunteering and advocacy for student rights in the schools where they teach (Tippert, 2010).

For these Mennonites, speaking up in one-on-one conversations and acting out publicly through speeches, panel discussions, committee work, research papers, and participation in LGBTQ friendly events, was and continues to be an important way in which they negotiate their position as LGQ Mennonites. For Ben, Mark, and Scott it was through public action that they came to understand deeper their own sexuality and their position in the Mennonite community. They were also able to share their knowledge and opinions with others with the hope of affecting change. For many, such as Scott, Jodi and Matt, concerning themselves with the justice issues inherent in LGBTQ rights is in itself a very Mennonite act, reflecting wider Mennonite theology and practice. For others like Justin and Kerri, publicly subverting gender norms through their self-presentation and interests was how they declared who they were and sought to provoke dialogue. Giving back more generally with involvement in the community was integral to Michelle's daily act of being a lesbian Mennonite. In Julia's experience, participation in public events helped her to find a space of support and affirmation to relieve some of the tension inherent in being out and being Mennonite.

4.4 The Quiet Queer in the Land

Certainly, speaking up and standing out is an important way for many of the interview participants to better define or affirm their position as queer, lesbian, or gay Mennonites. Such publicity however, comes laden with a great deal of tension. Indeed, when is it time to speak up and what is it time to stay quiet? Several participants reflected on this challenge. Michelle and her partner of several years are now out to their small group at Winnipeg Mennonite Church, an MC Manitoba and MC Canada congregation. And although Michelle supposes that many people outside of her small group are aware that she is a lesbian woman and that Karen is her partner, they have not stated in front of the church the nature of their relationship. In Michelle's words "we're out, but…not so far out that you're saying it in order to make change. Like that's not happening in my life" (Tippert, 2010).

In coming out to her small group, Michelle stated that there was some hesitation due in part to the realization that her involvement in volunteering or work with different Mennonite institutions such as Mennonite Central Committee, Mennonite Voluntary Service, Mennonite Disaster Service, and Manitoba Mennonite Collegiate would be over. When encouraged by a member of her small group to get political and try to work for these organizations even as an out lesbian woman, Michelle determined that she was not interested in pursuing that. "Maybe as a group, as a society…or as a whole church we can [bring about change] but I don't see how my individual pushing will help this situation" (Tippert, 2010). Without any contact with those organizations, Michelle already knew that that was going to be the end of that part of her life. For her, this realization came with some sadness while acknowledging that she had taken the opportunity to work for those organizations and that such work was not in her immediate or current life goals (*Ibid.*).

Michelle reflected at various points in our conversation about the tension between staying quiet and speaking out. One of the members of Michelle's care group, an older gentleman involved in church leadership, told her that she would probably have the most impact in the church by just coming to church. "He said, 'you don't need to stand up and say 'I'm gay'. You don't need to do this. You just need to keep living your life the way you do, people will respect you for that, people will know eventually'" (Tippert, 2010). Michelle and her partner Karen have largely employed this strategy both at church and also in the school where they are both teachers. By and large it has proven very successful in that "nobody has to start making statements of judgements and all of that" (*Ibid.*). "It's safe so we're doing it," states Michelle (*Ibid.*).

Yet, Michelle notes that another part of her feels that her and her partner are ready to come out more strongly and Michelle sees that as important for youth that she teaches and also for young people in the church. "I feel more strongly that it's important to have some role models who are gay or lesbian," she reflects (Tippert, 2010). By

> being told that by coming to church you're making an impact you're also still maybe being told to just keep quiet. Like you aren't completely but there's a bit of that subtle message in there which is fine if you feel safer by being quiet but, I don't know. (*Ibid.*)

Other LGQ Mennonites echoed a similar sentiment of feeling the tension between speaking out and staying quiet. Jodi Read, recently participated in a LGBT oral history project which was an important experience for this Peace and Conflict Studies student who currently is a sessional faculty member at the Canadian Mennonite University and Menno Simons College. I "want to be able to talk about that project with my students because…in terms of building a culture of peace that has a lot to do with it…and it's the research I'm most familiar with lately" (Read, 2010b). Yet, Jodi is hesitant to bring it up in her CMU class because she is aware of some concerns and issues as of late with the topic of LGBTQ rights. "I'm not as willing to go out on a limb….I don't like not being able to talk about it but I feel like I'm also there for a semester and I just need to [be quiet]" (*Ibid.*). Jodi also notes that she is not out in all of the Mennonite settings of which she is a part. "So, do I go under the radar sometimes? Yah! Do I always want to? Not necessarily but I just haven't always found ways to bridge that or communicate that or to see when it is important for people to know or not" (*Ibid.*)

4.5 Sharing Stories and Personal Study

Many of those I interviewed pointed to the importance of sharing their story and hearing those of others in being LGBTQ Mennonite. Of particular note is that most participants mentioned the *Nurturing Healthy Sexuality Conference* at Canadian Mennonite University which took place February 6, 2010. The conference was organized by Mennonite Central Committee and sponsored by a number of different Mennonite institutions and church conferences.[69] The conference had a number of different workshops including being single, sexuality in marriage, and same-sex attraction. Several of those persons who I interviewed were panellists in this session and shared their story of having same-sex attraction.

Although Michelle was not a panellist, this was an important event for her to attend because she felt like before this she had not heard other Mennonites get up and tell their stories about being lesbian or gay. She notes that "it would have made it easier to come out and I think it would be easier for younger people to come out if they heard more stories" (Tippert, 2010). It is not only important to tell stories for the sake of LGBTQ Mennonites but also for the entirety of the Mennonite community. Michelle states that "someone from my church who was attending [the *Nurturing Healthy Sexuality Conference*], it finally hit her….She said, 'we need this people!' Like no kidding!" (Tippert, 2010).

---

69 These organizations and conferences included: Canadian Mennonite University, Evangelical Mennonite Conference, Genesis House, Mennonite Brethren Church of Manitoba, Mennonite Church Manitoba, Recovery of Hope, and MCC Manitoba (Terichow, 2009).

Ben Borne noted that his involvement in CMQ is a source of strength and helped him to negotiate how he was going to come out to his family and church. "I really got, kind of encouraged and a lot of strength from hearing other people's stories and kind of figuring out what I was going to do" (Borne, 2010a). Likewise, Julia Zacharias noted that organizing workshops for the Supportive Communities Network in the early 2000s was a very positive event for her in that it was a place where being LGBTQ was celebrated among all persons (Zacharias, 2010).

Several Mennonites either directly referenced or alluded to the importance of individual study in theology, sociology, or science in their process of affirming their position as gay, queer, lesbian and Mennonite. Mark Brubacher engaged in personal and group studies on different approaches to Biblical hermeneutics; through a re-studying of what are often referred to as the clobber passages, Mark came to be very confident in his faith even if finding himself sometimes at odds what Mennonite religion might say. "It wasn't a choice to be gay and I had to accept who I was regardless of what my Mennonite [religion]…told me….I don't struggle with my faith, I struggle with my religion" (Brubacher, 2010).

For Matt Wiebe, studying before he came out on what it meant to be gay and a Christian was important. He knew that he was not going to try to stop being gay through counselling as his church and parents wanted. "I wasn't going to do that because I already did a lot of research for myself before I came out and knew who I was and I felt a lot better once I came out and once I started being the true me" (Wiebe, 2010).

Likewise, Scott Bergen noted that his personal study of queer theory was important in reconciling being openly gay with the closed, anti-gay tradition from which he had come (Bergen, 2010a). More broadly for Scott, questioning has been a key component of being Mennonite.

> Questions were…an important part of my journey especially teenage years and then on through my first couple years of university which is why I chose to go to CMU and study theology because questions were very important to the faith. But the questions that I asked and the questions I thought to be relevant always had…very profound assumptions behind them such as the belief that God exists and that pacifism is unquestionably the right way to be a Christian and heterosexuality was the only sexuality by which you could live and things like this, were simply unquestionable. (Bergen, 2010a)

In time, Scott began to question some of those fundamental precepts to the point where he not only came to embrace his sexuality as a gay man but also to agnosticism (*Ibid.*).

For others theology has not been at the centre of their process of negotiating their position as queer and Mennonite and do not necessarily see it at the centre of moving the discussion on LGBTQ topics forward. When Ben Borne came out to his grandparents he stated clearly that "I don't want to get down to anything theologically here. I'm not here to argue about theology, this is about us as a family, so theology's off the table, for now. You know this isn't something that we need to wrestle with now" (Borne, 2010a). Growing up Ben always knew that he was gay but never thought that he had to change or heal himself and yet "I had never really reconciled things theologically and maybe to this day I still really haven't; I just try to find a way to make things work" (*Ibid.*). Jodi suggests that it is important to point to the humanity issue of LGBTQ inclusion in moving the discussion forward. "[T]he particular biblical passages that seem to outlaw homosexuality are not important to me. It's not that I totally disregard the Bible, it's just that I don't necessarily find it speaking authoritatively in regards to same-sex relationships," reflects Jodi (Read, 2010c).

Michelle explored the topic of being LGBTQ and Christian in her teen years, writing a paper in Bible class. Rather than theology, for Michelle it was that "I just couldn't imagine a God that wouldn't accept people as they are….Like why would you create people this way if it was sinful? Like it just didn't make sense to me" (Tippert, 2010).

Although Scott's theological questioning was important and he maintains that it is important for the church, he also thinks that theology need not be at the centre of the discussion around LGBTQ inclusion.

> [W]e have not gotten anywhere by re-hashing you know, Leviticus and Paul's words. I still think it's important. I'm not at all suggesting the Mennonite church move forward sort of a-theologically but definitely work through those issues theologically as well but it shouldn't be the focal point of the issue. (Bergen, 2010a)

Being LGQ Mennonite was for many something articulated and supported through community and sharing stories. Furthermore, being LGQ Mennonite for some involved personal study of theology or social sciences whereas others pointed to a greater concern with the relational components of negotiating their subject positions.

4.6 Challenging the Married, Heterosexual Ideal

For many Mennonites being LGQ, being out, and living in the Mennonite community produces many tensions not only around the theme of silence and speaking, but also with different meanings of being Mennonite. Before coming out Ben Borne says that he always felt very repressed because he was holding back his own feelings and who he really was; he thought that being gay and Mennonite was wrong because of the messages he received that being Mennonite was tied to fulfilling heterosexual family traditions. "My grandparents weren't verbally oppressive against gay people but it's just they always had set up this image for me, this need for me to find a woman and to marry" (Borne, 2010a). Indeed, for Ben, being Mennonite is intimately tied with family tradition which in Mennonite circles is centered around heterosexual marriage.

Mark Brubacher alluded to a similar sense of needing to fit the heterosexual marriage norm in order to have kids. "I loved kids so it was just I wanted to have kids and the option or the thought of, being in a same-sex relationship and adopting kids just wasn't even a thought at that point in time" (Brubacher, 2010). So pronounced was this ideal heterosexual marriage norm, that Mark went on to get married and have four children, and it was not until later in his 40s that he was able to come out as a gay man (*Ibid.*).

Likewise, Justin Dueck reflected that he has had to come out to his parents over and over again and that his being gay continues to be

> a huge slap in the face…cause that's such an extreme opposite from the way that…they [my parents] raised me to be, to be Mennonite, to be heterosexual, to…find a wife, have a family, and be happy and contribute to the community by adding more people to the community and to the church. (Dueck, 2010)

For Michelle it was being a single woman in the church for many years which pushed her to the outskirts of belonging. Moving into her thirties as a single woman, Michelle notes, she started to lose her connection to the Mennonite church and community at large, which oriented as it was around families and children, left her on the margins (Tippert, 2010). There were questions from people quite regularly, Michelle explained, such as 'when are you going to settle down?' or 'when are you going to get married?'. Yet, finding a man to settle down with was never one of Michelle's goals. "I didn't fit in in that way and I couldn't figure out why that…never clicked for me….And by the time I realized that 'well, I'm probably not looking for a man, I'm probably looking for a woman,' there was no way of saying that" (*Ibid.*).

For Michelle, saying out loud her desire for women was a great challenge because by the time Michelle came out to herself as a lesbian there was no one left in the church who was a candidate for a relationship, partly because there were just hardly any single people left, male or female. "What would be the point of saying it out loud, that really I'm looking for a woman? So you don't for a long time. That's where if there's any tension between me and the church, even though they might not see it, know it, it is that" (Tippert, 2010).

Justin, Mark, Michelle, and Ben all identified the challenge they faced in being gay, lesbian, and single in the Mennonite community and how not fitting the married, heterosexual ideal led to each one of them negotiating the meaning of Mennonite in their communities and families.

4.7 Out and on the Outside: Life at the Margins

For others, being LGQ Mennonite is a point of tension because of the way in which being out as gay, queer, or lesbian has positioned them at the margins, even when they seek to be at the very centre of churches or institutions. Julia Zacharias saw herself at the centre of the church and Mennonite theological education, pursued that position, and yet eventually was pushed to the margins. Julia undertook theological studies at Canadian Mennonite Bible College (CMBC), CMU's precursor, and then a Masters degree at Associated Mennonite Biblical Seminary (AMBS), and later a PhD in Old Testament in Hebrew Bible. In all of this, Julia notes that she "wanted to ask the questions and kind of push the borders and that kind of stuff but I thought that I belonged in that church, that pushing the borders was fine" (Zacharias, 2010). She reflects, "I wanted to be in the centre [of the church]. That was clearly my goal through a lot of that [Mennonite education]" (*Ibid.*).

During her first year of PhD studies, Julia came out as a lesbian and realized that she could no longer pursue her dream of teaching in a Mennonite institution. So in light of this, and along with a number of other factors, Julia stopped pursuing her PhD and returned to Winnipeg.

> [M]y dream world would have been to finish that degree and teach in a Mennonite institution. That was my world anyway and it was one that suited me fine. And I felt I thrived on that kind of study so it was a good world for me. And, so I did the first semester of that degree and then decided that if I was really going to come out as a lesbian and I really wanted, really, really clearly to just be out, just be myself in all situations, no matter who I was with. And so I decided that if I was going to be an out lesbian in the Mennonite community that I wouldn't be hired by the institutions that I wanted to be. (Zacharias, 2010)

For quite some time, Julia explored the tension of being Mennonite, being lesbian, and being out at Hope Mennonite Church where she found a lot of support in asking questions exploring this tension. There she also met people asking similar questions. As a lesbian woman, Julia and her partner received a lot of affirmation from the pastor and individual members in the church (*Ibid.*).

When Julia and her partner decided to get married, Hope Mennonite Church was not willing to have the marriage as a church event and the pastor of the church was not the officiate, although she did participate. Julia and her partner received a lot of help in the planning and carrying out of that event (Zacharias, 2010).

> All through my story with Hope Mennonite [Church] I would say that like…personally I felt so much affirmation and support from the people there and friendship and at our wedding, people preparing food for us or leading music or helping us organize this or that. Tons of personal support for that event, for us getting married all of what that meant. (*Ibid.*)

Yet the fact that Julia and her partner did not get formal congregational support for their commitment to each other was very painful. "It [the wedding] was lovely and there was that pain about well, I'm not in the centre of the church like I always wanted to be" (*Ibid.*).

For Julia this was the breaking point in her relationship with the Mennonite church.

> And I guess that [the wedding] eventually was what made me tired enough of being at Hope [Mennonite Church] or being in the Mennonite church at all, that tension of well I really want to be at the centre and I think I belong there and I'm tired of not being like that first class citizen who is heteronormative…. (Zacharias, 2010)

So Julia decided to walk away from the church. Although she still feels very connected to many people at Hope and counts them among her friends, she no longer participates in that congregation nor connects herself with the Mennonite church more generally. For Julia being a lesbian Mennonite meant that she could no longer stay in the Mennonite church for the sake of her own personal well-being. Julia still identifies as Mennonite and walks her own spiritual path, taking much of her appreciation for life's everyday sacred moments from her Mennonite experiences and upbringing (*Ibid.*).

Likewise, although Jodi Read has found a church in both Winnipeg and Tucson where she feels included as a queer woman, she notes that it was with some sadness that she realized that she would no longer be eligible to work with Mennonite Central Committee. While listening to a forum about MCC's hiring policies in a legal perspective, Jodi notes that

> I felt kind of [like] an insider and outsider at the same time listening to that conversation. Like I'm no longer in MCC and I'm also never going to work for MCC again which actually when I came to that realization was kind of sad because I spent probably most of my professional life, like twelve years in MCC but I'm also not going to be in a place where I can't be who I am. So…listening to this I was kind of like ahhh…but I can't do anything about it but I'm also the constituency. (Read, 2010b)

Mark Brubacher says he has tried to leave the Mennonite church at least three times. Mark explains:

> if you've got a club, a little clubhouse for boys and…the sign on the outside door says 'no girls allowed'. Then one of the boys says to his little girlfriend,… 'common in, you're allowed to come in the…clubhouse'. And the girl says, 'but the sign says no girls allowed'. When she goes in…she feels sort of nervous about being there and what people will say, what will the other boys say when they see her there. And that's sort of how I feel sometimes. I go [to church] and then I don't feel like I really belong there but I still go. (Brubacher, 2010)

Mark's sense of not belonging has led to him to question whether the Mennonite religion is the means through which he wants to express his faith. However, he notes "it's hard to leave the Mennonite church" (*Ibid.*).

Mark keeps being drawn back to the Mennonite church because of the comfort or familiarity, worship style, emphasis on pacifism, and concern for community. And Mark is hopeful that things will change:

> I think that there's a lot of good people there…People have already said that I don't realize, how much, that my presence in the church how much it's changed some people's minds about homosexuality….[M]aybe I need to continue to be there that people can say, 'yes a person can be gay, can still be a good Christian'. ((Brubacher, 2010)

Recently, Mark was invited to serve communion for the first time in his church which was a very important event, as Mark has been attending Bethel Mennonite Church in Winnipeg for about 18 years (*Ibid.*).

Being present in the church at the margins is a difficult place to be in many respects. Mark believes that he fills an important role by providing education and a positive example of being gay. Mark also sees the positive changes happening in the area of LGBTQ inclusion. Simultaneously, he is aware of how the negativity and non-inclusive stance of the church takes a personal toll on him.

> It's hard though if…for a lifetime you've been taught that you're the worst of all sinners and it's hard to think good of yourself…And whether the church will admit or acknowledge that's what they're saying, that's what they say, so it's tough. (Brubacher, 2010)

Kerri went through a time when she rejected the Mennonite church and community at large. "There's totally a time in my life when I was like 'screw this' and I never went to any church events," Kerri remembers (Smith, 2010).

Kerri notes that "[u]nfortunately, I've seen a lot more of the bad sides of the community than I do the good sides" which is sad because she believes that the Mennonite culture has a lot to offer (Smith, 2010). "I mean like just growing up I had so many problems with people not being inclusive and being very exclusive and close minded and now I see that even more" (*Ibid.*). Kerri notes that she often hears disparaging and homophobic comments from people.

> I always have people being like [mimicking angry, annoyed tone] 'blagh! Same-sex marriage! Blagh! Blagh! Blagh! I don't agree with this, I don't agree with that. Gay people shouldn't have rights, blah, blah, blah, blah, blah, blah, blah, blah, blah'. And totally ignorant and I'm like sitting right there and I'm just like, want to scream at them! (*Ibid.*)

Kerri also sees many good things in the Mennonite church and that is why she continues to attend and be involved in her church (*Ibid.*).

For the last three years Kerri has taught Sunday School which she thoroughly enjoys. "I really want to be more involved with the church but I feel like I'm very excluded in the church and that they don't really want me" (Smith, 2010). Kerri's sense of not being welcome is not without basis. Kerri is not out in her church although her pastor, parents, and some other adults in the church are aware that Kerry is queer. After Kerri came out, she was told that if she had a girlfriend she probably would not be allowed to Sunday School teach anymore. "That made me really angry for a while," Kerry notes (*Ibid.*). Adding to the insult is that Kerri's class is well enjoyed by her pupils and she knows that the church does not have enough Sunday School teachers for all the classes. "It's like, we don't like you that much that we're gonna say that you can't teach even though we're desperate for teachers" (*Ibid.*).

For a while Kerri tried out a United Church but quickly returned to the Mennonite church because she missed "the Mennonite-ness of it all"; in particular she missed her Sunday School class and the worship style (Smith, 2010). Kerri passionately says that "there was a lot of times when I just could not deal but now I'm just kind of like, 'you know what? If you don't want me, that's too bad for you because I've decided I want to be involved in the Mennonite community, so!'" (*Ibid.*).

Kerri does note that slowly people seem to be warming up to her as they begin to see the good work and contribution she is making to the church.

> I've noticed with some people…the change went from like,…, 'you can't teach anymore' to like… 'we appreciate you being around here' and…'we don't want you to get stomped on,' which has a good likelihood of happening [if people in the church know I'm queer]". (Smith, 2010)

She reflects that her coming out was shocking initially because "no one's out in the Mennonite community, it does NOT happen" and so her pastor, parents, and other adults in the church had no experience with LGBTQ persons (*Ibid.*).

Kerri is not sure how long she will stay in the Mennonite church. If her church begins to discuss queer issues, Kerri told her pastor clearly that she will leave within one or two weeks. This is "not because I'm opposed to it [a discussion of queer issues] but because I'm convinced that it will get that bad that in two weeks I will no longer want to show my face there" (Smith, 2010). "I don't want to be the target of two hundred people's crap essentially," Kerri explains (*Ibid.*).

As Scott Bergen was in the process of coming out, he realized that he would have to leave the Mennonite church entirely before he could come out as a gay man. This decision was a difficult one for Scott who had spent many years actively involved in the church and three years studying theology at Canadian Mennonite University with the aim of becoming a pastor. "I viewed my options of maintaining that relationship with the Church and doing what I loved within it, and living as a gay man, as mutually exclusive" (Bergen, 2010b). Just shy of his 23rd birthday Scott realized that "the church wasn't worth staying in the closet for" and resolutely decided to leave (*Ibid.*). Scott explains:

> [E]ngaging in such an emotionally fragile act such as coming out in the context of the Mennonite church, in which I would not find much support, and most certainly condemnation and questioning, I decided that, in the interest of emotional self-preservation, it would be impossible for me to come out as a gay man while simultaneously trying to be part of the religious life of Mennonites. [And so by leaving behind Mennonite religion,] pastors who had condemned homosexuality throughout my adolescence would have no moral authority to condemn me with their theology, I would not have to bare feeling outcast by the community that had once embraced me, I would not have to see myself nor my family excommunicated from their congregation. (*Ibid.*)

When asked if he ever would consider returning to the Mennonite church, Scott noted a number of things that would need to happen for him to consider returning including an end to hetero-centrism, an apology "for the damage done and the lives destroyed" and a deliberate effort by the church to actively work for LGBTQ rights (Bergen, 2010a).

Scott says that he would like to see the church

> working as an activist for that [LGBTQ rights] in the same way that Mennonites work as activists for everything else [like] for…clean drinking water in the small village in Zambia….It needs to be publicly proclaimed, sought after. (Bergen, 2010a.)

For Julia and Scott being out in the Mennonite church proved impossible and to protect their own well-being both decided to leave the church. The point of decision for Julia revolved around the painful way in which she found herself on the margins when her marriage did not receive formal congregational affirmation. Scott, knowing the lack of support and questioning he would be subject to if he came out, made the decision to leave the church. Both Mark and Kerri remain in the church and do so at the margins, with Mark holding a strong desire to be a positive example and Kerri holding an interest in being more involved in congregational life. Yet both of them articulated the challenge of being in the church given the negativity and lack of understanding they find around them.

4.8 Finding a Space: Support and Affirmation at the Back Door

Several of the participants I spoke with had received quite a bit of support in the churches, institutions, and community at large. Even persons in leadership offered their support to these LGQ Mennonites, yet this was not publicly declared. When Ben Borne came out in 2009, he received a lot of support from the pastor of his home church and the Pastoral Team in his church. After coming out his pastor said to him,

> I would be really ok with you worship leading, song leading, preaching, and you know, being a very vital part of our church….You know, I don't want to take your membership out. I don't want you to have to feel like that….You know, we hired you as our youth, interim youth pastor and I would still hire you again and I would still work with you. This doesn't change anything about you because you were gay then and you are now, so it's not that big of a deal. (Borne, 2010a)

Ben continues to be an active part of his home church, leading worship and serving communion. His congregation also gave him a bursary for his continued studies at CMU in 2010 (*Ibid.*).

Particular evidence of support from church leadership for Ben came after his grandparents wrote a letter to the Pastoral Team suggesting that they could reimburse the church for all of the money they invested in building Ben's leadership skills through various conferences and education bursaries. His grandparents, aware that Ben would likely never be able to be a pastor in the Mennonite church, felt "bad that Ben came out of the closet for the church" (Borne, 2010a).

Ben's Pastoral Team unanimously said that they would not accept any money, that their financial support was not dependant on any particular codes of morality, and that they still believe Ben has leadership gifts. "It's very positive. It's very, very it's a happy ending and very unexpected," Ben explains (Borne, 2010a.).

> You know, I was expecting to be kicked out of the house…The church I wasn't too worried about but I was expecting there to be some cold, some bitterness….I'm part of their family, and I grew up…in the congregation. And I guess I shouldn't have been worried because in the end…I'm still a member and I can't…be excommunicated basically. [laughing] You know I'm a very vital part [of the church] I think…and they [the church] treat me like that and I feel like that. (*Ibid.*)

At CMU, Ben is received very positively as a gay man by the community although there are struggles. "I've experienced a lot of acceptance and I've experienced a little bit of trouble because there's also a lot of people who just would rather not talk about it and kind of leave it in the middle" (*Ibid.*). Open and overt homophobia is not plentiful with the exception of one particular student on campus (*Ibid.*).

In the 2011-2012 school year, Ben became the Student Council President and was aware that some CMU faculty and staff were worried about the constituency response to an openly gay student in that role. The school maintained the position that "students will do what they do" and so while Ben did not encounter resistance, he also did not feel particularly supported (Borne, 2012).

There are certainly a number of professors and student life staff with whom Ben feels comfortable discussing how things are going and who provide theological resources.

> I don't want to say that they're [student life staff] Affirming because they'll get their funding pulled from the school….You know, that's a worry that the conferences will take the money away from the school if they become publicly Affirming, so that's why they haven't really done it yet. (Borne, 2010a)

Ben finds both a great deal of support in his home church and at CMU, yet neither of these is publicly Affirming. Ben's dream is that someday his congregation will be publicly Affirming of LGBTQ persons and Ben articulated that he would like to be part of this process. He suspects that many people in his congregation do not know that he is gay and so it will be a process of first coming out to the congregation before movement towards this can begin to be made (*Ibid.*).

Likewise, overtly homophobic encounters with people are not frequent in Justin Dueck's life. One particularly upsetting encounter was when Justin was attending Steinbach Christian High School (SCHS). The Mennonite family he was planning to live with during his studies found out that Justin was gay, went through his unpacked belongings and kicked him out of the house before he had even finished moving in (Dueck, 2010).

> So homosexual also equalled pedophile to them. So they thought they were afraid for their children which was the reason they were getting me to move out which I was…so furious about….I was totally unwanted and was something that they were just disgusted by and afraid of, like super scared of, like that I was a pedophile. (*Ibid.*)

Yet, Justin says his experience has been positive and only negative in the sense of "people sort of trying to just ignore the fact that I'm gay, like within the Mennonite community anyway" (*Ibid.*). Justin credits the respect he receives to his prominent family background and his adherence to Mennonite principles in the way he treats people including an emphasis on generosity, hospitality, and love. "As much as I was pushed sort of to the outer limits of community I was still sort of part of it so I…didn't have a lot of feelings that I was gross. Like I was odd, I was strange" and there "was raised eyebrows," Justin explains (*Ibid.*). As a result, Justin was sometimes not taken very seriously in the community.

Today Justin is no longer involved in the EMC church, nor any other Mennonite church conference and he has moved away from his childhood home of Mennville. Nevertheless, Justin continues to find a place in the wider Mennonite community forming strong connections with other Mennonites on an individual basis. "I always kind of like gravitated towards people…even within the gay community, within anywhere where there's Mennonites" (Dueck, 2010). And Justin continues to feel some sense of connection to Mennville as well.

> [I]t's funny because…as much as I've sort of removed myself from that community [Mennville],…there is still a place for me there….I'd definitely be…accepted as just like a member of the community kind of at large, more than like part of the spiritual community. (*Ibid.*)

The support Justin receives in individual encounters with people from Mennville keeps him feeling joined to another group of Mennonites, albeit he is relegated to the position of being strange (*Ibid.*).

Mark Brubacher notes that he encounters a lot of ignorance, particularly among older people, and also a lot of support from people within his church.. Yet, much of this support has been private. "[T]he pastors said that if I ever want to bring a partner to church that they'll deal with that when it comes, but that they support that. But they're not willing to put that in stone or write that, or commit to that at this point in time" (Brubacher, 2010). Mark relates a conversation that he had with a MC Canada executive member who said that theologically the inclusion of LGBTQ people is not going to be an issue in twenty years. "Well, theologically if it's not going to be an issue in twenty years, then theologically why is it an issue today?" Mark reflects (*Ibid.*). "A lot of them understand but they're afraid [for their job]" (*Ibid.*).

Julia Zacharias knew that when she came out as a lesbian woman she would not be hired by Mennonite educational institutions. She attributes this to the constituencies of these institutions which tend to be "a step or two behind in terms of progressive thinking compared to the school and the students in it and the staff, like the professors" (Zacharias, 2010). Julia sensed she was being groomed for the job of being a Biblical scholar in a Mennonite institution and although she was supported by professors who thought she was a fabulous scholar, Julia knew it would be difficult for them to give her that support if she was out "because their job's on the line. Their funding for their school is on the line and it if they still want their school…there has to be that balance of 'can we be openly supporting them [LGBTQ people]?'" (*Ibid.*).

Scott Bergen also reflected on the support he received at CMU and the simultaneous muzzled nature of that support. During a fundraising concert for CMU, Scott was asked to give a short speech promoting CMU and speaking on his experience volunteering in Paraguay. During his speech he spoke about gender, economic status, and race as well as sexual orientation, all as topics which concern equality. "I got in a little bit of trouble for that…cause I was allowed to talk about gender and equality but not sexual orientation and equality" (Bergen, 2010a).

Yet Scott noted that from what he heard, people in the Winkler church responded very positively to what he said as had most of the people from CMU who attended.

> for the most part in the audience people I heard were very positive, *even if they didn't have language for their enthusiasm* about me approaching the subject they were excited that it was, in Winkler. At CMU people were positive and intrigued I think because I had deliberately tried to frame things in a way different from, I suppose the standards discussion in churches and for them, even if they didn't know what to do with that information they found it intriguing….And I don't know, and just sort of worthy of more questioning. [my emphasis] (Bergen, 2010a)

Matt Wiebe encounters quite a bit of support as a gay man and advocate for LGBTQ people and has "met some really great people but I'm not going to say there's not been challenges" (Wiebe, 2010).

Matt was subject to some homophobic reactions in his advocacy work within the church. He reflects, "if we really want to move forward with these topics [LGBTQ inclusion, sexuality] then I'm willing to take on that kind of possible backlash from a couple people because it's important to talk about these things" (Wiebe, 2010). Matt notes that there is a great diversity in terms of where people are in their thinking on LGBTQ inclusion but unfortunately the wide spectrum of opinions and feelings Matt has witnessed informally tend not to be appreciated in formal structures and institutions such as MC Manitoba or MC Canada; Matt suggests that these institutions are so afraid of the extremes of either affirming or condemning positions that they are not willing to start discussions about sexuality (*Ibid.*).

Similarly, Michelle Tippert experiences quite a bit of informal support in her church. For all this support, however, the church remains slow in moving towards any sort of official position or stance as an Affirming congregation. Michelle notes that discussions about sexuality began in 1997 and she was struck at the time with the openness to those discussions, and that it did not lead to any splits in the church (Tippert, 2010).

Within the last five years, her church once again held a number of Sunday School sessions on LGBTQ sexuality. At that point Michelle

> was ready for them to start making a move towards saying something more supportive at least…and knowing that lots of people are supportive then maybe it's time to say that we're supportive and…as a congregation they weren't at a point to do that. (Tippert, 2010)

Michelle feels passionately that publicly declaring support of LGBTQ persons would make a great difference in allowing LGBTQ people stay in the church. Michelle explains:

> [E]specially as a younger person I wouldn't want to be part of…a controversy which is what you're afraid that you're going to be part of. And especially as you're coming out, you're trying to figure out yourself…never mind trying to let the church figure out themselves. (*Ibid.*)

Right now Michelle's church remains ambiguous, not declaring whether they are or are not supportive of being LGBTQ. "[S]o now you're asking people to come out and they don't know if they're going to be supported or they aren't. And I think that's where I get most frustrated with the church" (*Ibid.*).

Michelle's articulation of frustration is also found in the stories of many other LGQ Mennonites I spoke with who lament the fact that they receive a great amount of informal support yet the formal structures leave them systematically vulnerable and on the outside. Furthermore, many people I spoke with pointed to the fact that the topic of sexuality is largely unaddressed by churches and institutions and that this remains a source of difficulty.

4.9 SUMMARY

Queer, gay, and lesbian Mennonites are present, active, passionate people dedicated to being Mennonite and in communities, churches, or institutions. Many of these Mennonites are involved in advocating for LGBTQ inclusion either through participation in committees, conferences, panel discussions, speeches, or one to one conversations. Some feel the tension of being quiet and speaking up very strongly. For others, they feel a clear tension in being out as lesbian, queer, or gay and being in Mennonite churches and institutions. This has led some people to leave the Mennonite church or disassociate with Mennonite institutions or even the community at large. For others, they have remained connected to formalized Mennonite bodies while simultaneously experiencing significant personal angst as well as a great deal of hope for the future.

Many participants articulated the importance of sharing stories for personal well-being and also for the health of the Mennonite community at large. For some, intellectual discussions and the personal study of theology or social sciences proved important for their own negotiation of being LGQ Mennonite. Yet others said that such studying was not integral to their understanding of being Mennonite. Most participants experienced a degree of openness and private support within the communities, churches, and institutions with which they are or were associated. Nevertheless, the lack of formal support was, and remains for many, a painful source of exclusion and a continuing factor perpetuating the silence on sexuality.

Throughout the narratives of these nine queer, lesbian, and gay Mennonites, it is possible to see that while each person is constituted by sexuality norms inherent in being Mennonite and dependant on these norms, they are simultaneously living in ways that "maintain a critical and transformative relation to them" (Butler, 2004b: 3). LGQ Mennonites live in interaction with these norms, blazing their own definition of what it means to be Mennonite and living it daily quietly, loudly, and in a myriad of different ways. It is the case that for some, the 'I' sometimes becomes unknowable in the Mennonite community when norms are approached in ways that do not make the 'I' fully recognizable (Butler, 2004a: 3); it is in these cases that people feel pushed to the outside of belonging and their Mennonite identity is called into question by these norms. And while we can learn much from these stories of being LGQ Mennonite, we must view these stories, not in terms of revealing a new truth once hidden about the nature of Mennonite identity but as indications of identities and persons in states of flux. And we must remember that in each telling, a person and the stories are changed in some way which is yet another example of the constant and dynamic process of identification.

5. CONCLUSIONS

> It's very important to me that I am still Mennonite. It's very intrinsic to who I am as well. It's like two identities are coming together...So I guess my challenge then is to figure out how…I can be a Mennonite, how I can be gay, I say I'm a Christian gay. But Mennonite?...that's just a whole new thing. (Borne, 2010a)

Like Ben Borne's challenge, the guiding question of how I and others can be LGBTQ Mennonite has permeated the course of this book; the answer to that question is not a simple one. For it is the case that to be other than heterosexual takes me to a place of 'othering'. It is a place where I am made unintelligible and unethical in the discourses of the Mennonite church and ineligible for participation in Mennonite institutions. The heterosexual marriage norm perpetuates an everyday violence, not just on me or other LGBTQ Mennonites, but each and every Mennonite by limiting possibilities for each person and excluding people from the Mennonite community. This is not to say that this is the full story. Indeed, everyday LGBTQ Mennonites are challenging and reconstituting the very discourses which construct them as the 'other' and are negotiating a place in the Mennonite community.

Now I come back to the original research question: what sexual processes of identification are made possible within the discourses of the Mennonite community and how do LGBTQ Mennonites interact with these discourses to articulate identities? Answering the first part of this question, it is clear that being Mennonite is intimately connected with being heterosexual, married, and engaging in sexual practices within this frame. This is clearly reflected in the discourses of the three church conferences examined (Mennonite Church Canada, the Canadian Conference of Mennonite Brethren Churches, and the Evangelical Mennonite Conference) which position sexed bodies as innately and unproblematically binary in their composition and gender as either the cultural inscription upon those stable bodies or a natural extension of sexed biological limitations. Desiring the 'opposite' gender or sex and engaging in sexual practices accordingly flows quite unproblematically within such a frame. Likewise, in Mennonite institutions it is around this base of understanding that policies and practices are carried out.

Specifically, within MC Canada, the CCMBC, and the EMC there is a clear 'othering' of LGBTQ Mennonites which takes place through the explicit use of 'us' and 'them' language and in the most violent cases, ignoring or denying the very existence of diverse genders, bodies, and desires. These divisions are then brought to the point of erasure through the use of euphemistic language which makes hallow promises of acceptance and dialogue. Through such means, the heterogeneity of community is denied and the word community become synonymous with sameness.

At CMU there is a limited space to be an LGBTQ student with informal and even some formal support networks in place. Likewise, in faculty hiring policy some language suggests that the inclusion of LGBTQ people could be possible. Yet, the official support of MC Canada's and the CCMBC's confessions of faith continue to dominate the policies and practices of this organization and its culture. MCC MB maintains a largely exclusionary hiring policy besides its Initiatives for Just Communities programs, which although are open to LGBTQ Mennonites remain controlled by MCC MB. Like CMU, MCC MB points to the confessions of faith of owning church conference bodies as the basis for its hiring policies. Although MCC MB pushes church conferences on other issues and emphasizes a priority for gender and racial equality, they actively refuse participation from LGBTQ persons; this is a strange paradox in many respects.

In this pervasive frame of understanding sexuality, certain sexual identifications are not possible, both practically and also more abstractly. This was reflected in the narratives of several interview participants, one of whom was unable to come out until leaving the church, another person who left the church because of the way she was denied the privileges and rights of passage afforded to heterosexuals, and several others who have dissociated with different Mennonite institutions. Several people that I interviewed remained openly LGQ and involved in the Mennonite community albeit with some limitations on their participation or sense of inclusion. It was clear in the narratives of each person, however, that these individuals were aware that being LGBTQ Mennonite was not an ethical or sanctioned subject position to hold in the Mennonite community. Each person had to negotiate for themselves how to be out and LGBTQ Mennonite, whether that was through activism, speaking up, silence, personal study, sharing stories, leaving the church, staying in the church, living with a concern for peace and justice, community involvement, or participation in institutions.

Although there are the formalized and idealized pronouncements of what it means to be Mennonite, through daily practices LGBTQ Mennonites are interacting with some of these norms. In understanding Mennonite as a performative identity in this way, it is possible to open up a very inclusive and also transformative way to think about the 'I' and the 'we'. Performativity (Butler, 2008) is the process through which something is constituted by that which it purports to describe. In such an understanding, I am always in a process of negotiating who I am in interaction with the discursive idealizations of who I am, which I am also simultaneously producing. It is, however, in the process of re-producing these discourses through my actions that there is a space for re-signification, re-definition, and transformation.

Taking Hall (1996) seriously suggests that it is never possible to fulfill the discursive idealizations which hail me as 'Mennonite' or 'woman' and all the sexual norms inherent in those words. Even if I wanted to be a married, heterosexual Mennonite, it is impossible to completely fulfill the ideals inherent in any identification. Rather, I can always find myself in "a constant, agonistic process of struggling with, resisting, negotiating and accommodating the normative or regulative rules" by which I regulate and confront myself (Hall, 1996: 14). I hold multiple subject positions, changing depending on my context and none of which are ever fully completed. In this way, my identity as 'Mennonite' and 'woman' is never once and for all completed or static but always shifting and changing, both in relation to the idealizations of what it means to be 'Mennonite' or 'woman' and also my position in relation to these discourses. Just as Mennonite Studies literature points to women who have consistently lived in ways which contested with or deviated from the institutional and theological discourses, so to do the lesbian, queer, and gay Mennonites I interviewed; these LGQ Mennonites live in ways that never fully fulfill nor fully abandon the idealizations of sexuality which speak heterosexual marriage as the real and desirable.

I could read the narratives of those people I interviewed as the articulation of their subject position, LGQ Mennonite. The process by which this subjectification took place was and is of course always intimately related to the discourses, or the idealized pictures which are painted of Mennonite, and individual interaction with these pictures. Certainly, the idealized pictures which are painted of Mennonites shift and change over time as they are interacted with and constantly re-produced. Also, in the very process of articulating an identity, that identity is given a meaning which changes depending on the stories and meanings which are prescribed to it. It is in these individual and collective moments of performatively being Mennonite that these LGQ Mennonites constantly re-signify the very meaning of being Mennonite.

In summary, while interacting with these idealized norms on sexuality, Mennonites are working individually and in groups to create new spaces for being. Val Warkentin reflects that she knows that the inclusion of LGBTQ persons into the Mennonite church and community at large is coming:

> Well, I'm completely confident that within, I don't know what time frame, but that gay people will be accepted in the Mennonite community as members, as full standing participants and members. That will happen. And what bugs me is

> why not now? It's gonna happen. Why are we dragging our feet? It will happen. (V. Warketin, 2010)

Indeed, the possibility for change is present and the hope acutely espoused by several interview participants that one day 'we' would include diverse gender and sexual identities.

Rather, than seeing the 'we' through a lens which supposes that there is a 'we' because there is sameness, community can be built around discourses which construct the 'we', and also the 'I' through processes of identification. This is where the 'I' and 'we' are recognized to be in constant flux, creation, and recreation. Conceiving of community as a place of sameness often requires a change of the 'I' because holding desires or bodies outside of the male/female binary and heteronormative frame means to cease being recognized as a human being, or as an ethical person. Some of my interview participants noted exactly that reality: that they were unable to stay in a Mennonite church or Mennonite institution because they had been rendered unintelligible and unethical.

It is however possible to try and build the 'we' around diversity of practice in living. It is imperative for the Mennonite community to first recognize the inevitability of performativity and then celebrate the diversity of possibility that it holds; to create a Mennonite community where not only in practice, but in discourses as well, difference is recognized and celebrated and all identifications, including that of LGBTQ Mennonite are recognized. In recognizing the inevitability of performativity and the diversity it brings, is also the means through which we call attention to the interrelated nature of each and every one of us. That 'I' and 'we' only exist in relation to 'you' and 'one another'.

Such an understanding of identity, places postmodern Peace Studies at the centre. For the concern does not become rights or securing the one true peace, but rather the interest is what does it mean to count as a person and how might the category of personhood be expanded and the parameters of belonging extended to include all? Furthermore, if I am in fact only 'me' in relation to 'you', what does that do to my sense of individuality and sense of self? It certainly suggests a connection between each and all which extends beyond the individual or person.

In the course of this book, I have explored the topics of identity, and being Mennonite while also outlining academic scholarship currently available on LGBTQ Mennonites. There is much more work to be done. Most of the accounts of LGBTQ Mennonites which do exist helpfully tell the stories of individuals. Yet, there remains a great need for placing the story of LGBTQ Mennonites in an academic frame. It is true that there is an increasing number of works in Mennonite Studies on gender. Many of these have pointed to the regulation of women's bodies and the social construction of gender. Simultaneously, there are a number of scholars taking the position of biological determinism which erases the very existence of any social constructed gender.

Importantly, other scholars have pointed to the way in which there have always and continues to be a great diversity in the everyday practices of women in fulfilling gender norms as prescribed by church, family, and community. A further step of analysis is needed to discuss the very performative creation of bodies, sexual practices, and also desire in Mennonite history. It is imperative for scholars to look once again at woman to woman relationships and man to man relationships with a queer lens, seeing the erotic in common, everyday practices and uncovering the untold history of LGBTQ Mennonites and same-sex desire. Such a history is important as the basis from which we can better understand LGBTQ Mennonites today in Mennonite studies and in the community at large. The historical basis is needed to see that these Mennonites are not a contemporary anomaly in the long story of Mennonites, although the open attachment to LGBTQ identities is a relatively new development. Rather, there is a need to see that there have always been a diversity of bodies, genders, desires, and sexual practices in the history of Mennonites.

The question of how to be LGBTQ Mennonite matters a great deal. For most LGBTQ Mennonites, being Mennonite is intimately and intrinsically linked to their sense of self. And why should it not be? Sexuality is an integral aspect of personhood and when it is limited, not recognized or talked about, we not only fail to see the diversity of sexualities present all around us but we also limit each and everyone of our abilities to live whole and full lives as sexual beings. It is imperative to break the 'violence of silence' which keeps the Mennonite community from seeing and talking about diversities in sexualities. The key is not to only talk more for the sake of talking, but as Foucault suggests, to continue to search and understand why it is that we talk about sexuality as we do, who is talking, and who is keeping the silence.

Certainly, the writing of this book has increased conflict in my life –within myself, with friends and family, and with the world at large. With friends and family, I have encountered everything from consternation that I would even want to explore this topic in the first place to open hostility. Through this process, the question of who am I and who do I want to be have become pressing for me. I came to realize through this work that the answer to these questions are infused with particular discourses on gender, sex, desire, and sexual practices which have always, and continue to be present in and around me. Everyday, I have performatively constituted these very discourses about being a woman, being female, being Mennonite, and being heterosexual. As I realized that these ways of being were not the only ways of being, I wrestled with it all, caught between the awareness of possibility and the reality of the way in which I am made intelligible in my family, among friends, and in my community. I knew I could not just choose arbitrarily a new gender or sex or way of desiring. I am intricately tied to the discourses of sexuality around me and in my life and any sort of attempt at separation from those is a long, arduous, and painful process. Yet, I also recognized that I could not continue to assume unquestioning, and invest so blindly in those very pervasive heteronormative discourses which by default speak me as 'woman', 'heterosexual', and 'female'.

Out of most of my friends growing up and in my early adult years, I was often touted as the 'most feminist' but I really had no idea about what that meant besides asserting that women could be doctors and they did not need to quilt blankets if they did not want to. The work of this book opened me up to seeing the everyday world I live in through different eyes. I see the sexism, the cisgenderism, the heteronormativity of television shows, advertisements, interactions between people, and words spoken. It has brought me to a place of anger as I witness the presumptions made about what is normal and what is good. And as I have been brought to the point of anger, I have also found myself at a moment of release. For in seeing these discourses and witnessing their continual creation and normative power to make some people intelligible and others not, I can also imagine my life beyond them; I can be without a man, I can be a woman who resists femininity and I can desire and be in a sexual relationship with a woman.

I am beginning to open myself up to the choice I have in my desires and in my gender and have come out as bisexual. It is a choice for me, in the sense of choosing to be open to the diversity in sexualities. As Adrienne Rich argues so poignantly,

> the absence of choice remains the great unacknowledged reality, and in the absence of choice, women will remain dependent upon the chance or luck of particular relationships and will have no collective power to determine the meaning and place of sexuality in their lives. (Rich, 1996: 141)

The choice to explore my sexuality through this project was very intentional; bisexuality was its unforeseen and rather non-rational conclusion.

The process of exploring my sexuality was entered into in the hopes of learning to love myself more fully including those spiritual, religious, ethnic, sexual elements of my being. This self love is the beginning of a life long process for me. In the words of Judith Daniluk, counsellor and scholar, sexuality is not a noun but a process. She writes that "this process is emergent and transformative, shaped by each woman's unique history but taking on new qualities and meanings in the context of new and varied roles, experiences, and relationships" (Daniluk, 1998: 9). The implication is "that as human beings, we have infinite capacities to express our sexuality" (*Ibid.*: 10). And so I go forth now intentionally engaging myself with this transformation, recognizing that my words, thoughts, and actions are part of a lifelong process of learning and interaction with the discourses performatively constituted in my life.

Works Cited

Written & Web Sources

Bender, Harold S. And Rodney J. Sawatsky (1989): "Mennonite (The Name)," Global Anabaptist Mennonite Encyclopedia Online, available at: http://www.gameo.org/encyclopedia/contents/M4673ME.html, accessed: 26 August 2009.

Bender, Harold S. and Beulah Stauffer Hostetler (1989): "Mennonite Church (MC)," Global Anabaptist Mennonite Encyclopaedia Online, available at: http://www.gameo.org/encyclopedia/contents/M46610ME.html, accessed: 08 October 2010.

Benner, Dick (2011a): "A reasoned discussion," *Canadian Mennonite*, Vol. 15, No. 21, 31 October 2011, available at: http://www.canadianmennonite.org/articles/reasoned-discussion, accessed: 12 February 2012.

----- (2011b): "Sex dominates this week's headlines," *Canadian Mennonite*, web exclusive, 18 May 2011, available at: http://www.canadianmennonite.org/articles/sex-dominates-weeks-headlines, accessed: 09 February 2012.

Berg, Bruce L. (2004): *Qualitative Research Methods for the Social Sciences*, 5th ed. Pearson, Boston.

Bergen, Rachel (2012): "Westgate student wins human rights award," *Young Voices: Canadian Mennonite*, 9 January 2012, available at: http://youngvoices.canadianmennonite.org/articles/westgatestudentwinshumanrightsaward, accessed: 10 February 2012.

----- (2011): "Sexual Inclusivity motion to be presented at national assembly," *Canadian Mennonite*, Vol. 15, No. 11, 29 May 2011, available at: http://www.canadianmennonite.org/articles/sexual-inclusivity-motion-be-presented-national-assembly, accessed: 08 February 2012.

Bernstein, Susan David (1997): *Confessional Subjects: Revelations of Gender and Power in Victorian Literature and Culture*, University of North Carolina Press, Chapel Hill, NC.

Blank, Hanne (2007): *Virgin: The Untouched History*, Bloomsbury, New York.

Boswell, John (1980): Christianity, Social Tolerance, and Homosexuality: Gay People in Western Europe from the Beginning of the Christian Era to the Fourteenth Century, University of Chicago Press, Chicago.

Boyd, Stephen (1999): "Theological Roots of Gender Reconciliation in 16th century Anabaptism: A Prolegomenon," Journal of Mennonite Studies, Vol. 17, pp.34-51.

Braun, Jan (2008): "From Policy to the Personal: One Queer Mennonite's Journey," *Journal of Mennonite Studies*, Vol. 26, pp.69-80.

Breckbill, Anne (2003): "God's Table and Churchland Security: Creating Welcome within a Culture of Fear," Brethren Mennonite Council for LGBT Interests, initially presented at 2003 Mennonite Church USA Assembly, Atlanta, Georgia, available at: http://www.bmclgbt.org/breckbill.shtml, accessed 27 July 2010.

Brethren Mennonite Council for Lesbian, Gay, Bisexual, and Transgender Interests (2012): "Supportive Communities Network- SCN," available at: http://www.bmclgbt.org/scn.shtml#resources, accessed: 16 April 2012.

----- (2010a): "Supportive Communities Network- SCN," available at: http://www.bmclgbt.org/scn.shtml, accessed: 13 November 2010.

----- (2010b): "BMC Mission Statement and Vision Statement," available at: http://www.bmclgbt.org/mission.shtml, accessed: 17 November 2010.

Brewer, John D. (2010): *Peace Processes: A Sociological Approach*, Polity Press, Cambridge.

Brooten, Bernadette (1996): *Love Between Women: Early Christian Responses to Female Homoeroticism*, University of Chicago Press, Chicago, IL.

Butler, Judith (2008): *Gender Trouble*, 2nd ed., Routledge Classics, New York.

----- (2004a): *Precarious Life: The Powers of Mourning and Violence*, Verso, London.

----- (2004b): *Undoing Gender*, Routledge, New York.

----- (1999a): "Bodily Inscriptions, Performative Subversions," in *Feminist Theory and the Body: A Reader*, Janet Price and Margrit Shildrick, Ed., Routledge, New York, pp. 416-422, reprinted from J. Butler (1990): *Gender Trouble*, Routledge, New York.

----- (1999b): "Bodies that Matter," in *Feminist Theory and the Body: A Reader*, Janet Price and Margrit Shildrick, Ed., Routledge, New York, pp. 235-245, reprinted from J. Butler (1993): *Bodies that Matter*, Routledge, New York.

----- (1993): *Bodies that Matter: On the Discursive Limits of 'Sex'*, Routledge, New York.

Canadian Conference of Mennonite Brethren churches (2010a): "About Us," available at: http://www.mbconf.ca/home/about_us/, accessed: 7 October 2010.

----- (2010b): "Provincial Conferences," in *Partners*, available at: http://www.mbconf.ca/home/partners/provincial_conferences/, accessed: 7 October 2010.

----- (2010c): "Contact Us," available at: http://www.mbconf.ca/contact_us/#CatID23, accessed: 28 October 2010.

----- (2006): *General Operating Bylaw (Constitution)*, available at: http://www.mbconf.ca/resource/File/PDFs/General%20Operating%20Bylaws%20(Constitution).pdf, accessed: 7 October 2010.

----- (2004): *Homosexuality: A Compassionate Yet Firm Response*, Faith & Life Pamphlet Series, Canadian Mennonite Brethren Board of Faith and Life, available at: http://www.mbconf.ca/resource/File/PDFs/Homosexuality_A_compassionate_yet_firm_response.pdf, accessed: 13 August 2010, Kindred Productions, Winnipeg, MB.

----- (2001): *Confession of Faith*, available at: http://www.mbconf.ca/resource/File/PDFs/Confession_of_Faith.pdf, accessed: 13 August 2010.

Canadian Mennonite (2011): "For discussion," *Canadian Mennonite*, Vol. 15, No. 21, 31 October 2011, available at: http://www.canadianmennonite.org/articles/discussion-37, accessed: 12 February 2012.

Canadian Mennonite University (2010a): *2010-2011 Academic Calendar*, Winnipeg, MB.

----- (2010b): "Denominational Data pertaining to Shaftesbury Campus and Outtatown," CMU Enrolment Report, October 2010, Winnipeg, MB.

----- (2010c): "II. Guidelines and Rules for Community Life," in *CMU Student Handbook*, Winnipeg, MB.

----- (2008): "Same-sex Attraction Discussed at CMU Forum," in *The Messenger*, Vol. 46, No.4, 20 February 2008, p.15, available at: http://www.advancedministry.com/files/emc440/The%20Messenger/vol46/Messenger-46-04.pdf, accessed: 15 August 2010.

----- (2007): "Employee Policies, A1 Employment Policies, A1.1 Faith & Hiring," CMU Board of Governors, 23 June 2007, Winnipeg, MB.

----- (2003): "A3.2 Respectful Campus," CMU Board of Governors, 25 October 2003, Winnipeg, MB.

Cockburn, Cynthia (2004): "The Continuum of Violence: A Gender Perspective on War and Peace," in *Sites of Violence: Gender and Conflict Zones*, Wenona Giles and Jennifer Hyndman, Ed., University of California Press, Berkeley, pp. 24-44.

Conzen, Kathleen and David Gerber (1992): "The Invention of Ethnicity: A Perspective from the U.S.A," *Journal of American Ethnic History*, Vol. 12, pp. 3-42.

Cummings, Mary Lou, Ed. (1978): *Full Circle: Stories of Mennonite Women*, Faith and Life Press, Scottsdale, PA.

Daniluk, Judith C. (1998): *Women's Sexuality Across the Life Span: Challenging Myths, Creating Meanings*, Guilford Press, New York.

Delphy, Christine (1996): "Rethinking Sex and Gender," in *Sex in Question: French Materialist Feminism*, Diana Leondard and Lisa Adkins, Ed., Taylor and Francis, London, pp. 30-41, reprinted from (1993): *Women's Studies International Forum*, Vol. 16, No. 1, pp. 1-9.

Dietrich, Wolfgang (2006): "A Call for Transrational Peaces," Virtual Peace Library of the UNESCO Chair for Peace Studies, Universität Innsbruck, available at: http://www.uibk.ac.at/peacestudies/downloads/peacelibrary/transrational.pdf, accessed: 29 June 2010.

Derksen Siemens, Ruth (1999): "Quilt as Tcxt and Tcxt as Quilt: Thc Influcncc of Gender in the Mennonite Girls' Home of Vancouver (1930-1960)," *Journal of Mennonite Studies*, Vol. 17, pp. 118-129.

Dollimore, Jonathan (1991): *Sexual Dissidence: Augustine to Wilde, Freude to Foucault*, Oxford University Press, Oxford.

Driedger, Leo (2000): *Mennonites in the Global Village*, University of Toronto Press, Toronto, ON.

Drumm, René (2005): "No Longer an Oxymoron: Integrating Gay and Lesbian Seventh-day Adventist Identities," in *Gay Religion*, Scot Thumma and Edward R. Gray, Ed, AltaMira Press, Walnut Creek, CA, pp. 47-66.

Dyck, Cornelius J. (1993): *An Introduction to Mennonite History*, 3rd ed., Herald Press, Waterloo, ON.

Dyck, Dan (2011a): "Harmony motion referred to General Board," *Epic News*, 8 July 2011, Mennonite Church Canada, Kitchener-Waterloo Assembly 2011, pp. 2,

available at:
http://www.mennonitechurch.ca/files/events/waterloo2011/EpicNewsFri_web.pdf, accessed: 08 February 2012.

----- (2011b): "On using scripture to discern sexual issues," *Canadian Mennonite*, Vol. 15, No. 21, 31 October 2011, available at:
http://www.canadianmennonite.org/articles/using-scripture-discern-sexual-issues, accessed: 12 February 2012.

Epp, Andrea (2010): "Piecing the Mennonite puzzle together one DNA at a time," *Canadian Mennonite*, Vol. 14, No.2, 25 January 2010, p.21.

Epp, Marlene (2008): *Mennonite Women in Canada: A History*, University of Manitoba Press, Winnipeg, MB.

----- (2000): *Women Without Men: Mennonite Refugees of the Second World War*, University of Toronto Press, Toronto, ON.

----- (1987): "Women in Canadian Mennonite History: Uncovering the 'Underside'," *Journal of Mennonite Studies*, Vol. 5, pp.90-107.

Epp, Marlene and Sam Steiner (2009): "Calgary Inter-Mennonite Church (Calgary, Alberta, Canada)," *Global Anabaptist Mennonite Encyclopaedia Online,* available at: http://www.gameo.org/encyclopedia/contents/C245.html, accessed: 07 October 2010.

Eriksen, Thomas Hylland (1993): *Ethnicity & Nationalism: Anthropological Perspectives*, Pluto Press, London.

Evangelical Mennonite Conference (2010a): "National Office Staff," available at: http://www.emconference.ca/index.cfm?i=11528&mid=1000&id=285070, accessed: 13 October 2010.

----- (2010b): "About the Evangelical Mennonite Conference," available at: http://www.emconference.ca/index.cfm?i=11528&mid=2, accessed: 13 October 2010.

----- (2007): *Constitution and Bill of Incorporation of the Evangelical Mennonite Conference*, originally published 1994, Steinbach, MB, available at: http://www.emconference.ca/files/emc440/resources/EMC%20Constitution.pdf, accessed: 13 August 2010.

Farris-Manning, Cheryl (2005): "Towards a Welcoming Church: A Mennonite Case Example," Presentation, 27 May 2005, *Discerning the Spirit: Re-imagined Social Work*, 4th Annual Canadian Conference on Spirituality and Social Work, London, ON, available at : http://w3.stu.ca/stu/sites/spirituality/manning05.pdf, accessed: 27 July 2010.

Fausto-Sterling, Anne (2000a): *Sexing the Body: Gender Politics and the Construction of Sexuality*, Basic Books, New York, NY.

----- (2000b): "The Five Sexes, Revisited," *Sciences*, Vol. 40, No. 4, Jul/Aug, pp. 18-23, available at: http://www.neiu.edu/~lsfuller/5sexesrevisited.htm, accessed: 5 July 2010.

Foucault, Michel (2003): *The Subject and Power*, available at: http://www.ualberta.ca/~rmorrow/Resources/Foucault-Power%20&%20Subject%20co.pdf, accessed: 6 July 2010, reprinted from M. Foucault (2003): *The Essential Foucault: Selections From the Essential Works of Foucault 1954-1984*, Paul Rabinow and Niklas Rose, Ed., New Press, New York, NY, pp.126-144.

----- (1988): *The History of Sexuality, Volume III: The Care of the Self*, Trans. Robert Hurley, Vintage Books, New York, NY.

----- (1985): *The History of Sexuality, Volume II: The Use of Pleasure*, Trans. Robert Hurley, Pantheon Books, New York, NY.

----- (1978): *The History of Sexuality, Volume I: An Introduction*, Trans. Robert Hurley, Vintage Books, New York, NY.

Funk Wiebe, Katie (1999): "Me Tarzan, Son of Menno –You Jane, Mennonite Mama," *Journal of Mennonite Studies*, Vol. 17, pp.9-21.

Gaca, Kathy L. (2003): *The Making of Fornication: Eros, Ethics, and Political Reform in Greek Philosophy and Early Christianity*, University of California Press, Berkeley, CA.

Gans, Herbert J. (1999): *Making Sense of America: Sociological Analyses and Essays*, Rowman and Littefield Publishers, Lanham, MD.

General Conference Mennonite Church and Mennonite Church (1992): "Final Report: Listening Committee for Homosexual Concerns," Joint Listening Committee for Homosexual Concerns, 20 August 1992, available at: http://faculty.mdc.edu/jmcnair/Joe11pages/Final%20Report%20of%20Listening%20Committee%20for%20Homosexual%20Concerns.htm, accessed: 19 November 2010.

----- (1985): *Human Sexuality in the Christian Life: A Working Document for Study and Dialogue*, Faith and Life Press, Newton, KS and Mennonite Publishing House, Scottdale, PA, available at: http://www.ambs.edu/LJohns/HSCL/hscl0.htm, accessed: 13 October 2010.

Goosen, Rachel Waltner (1999): "A Gender Gap Among Mennonite Peacemakers," *The Mennonite Quarterly Review*, Vol.73, No.3, pp.539-545.

----- (1992): "The 'Second Sex' and the 'Second Millers': Mennonite Women and Civilian Public Service," *The Mennonite Quarterly Review*, Vol.66, No.4, pp.525-538.

Graber Miller, Keith (2011): "Unwrapping Sexuality," *Canadian Mennonite*, Vol. 15, No. 21, 32 October 2011, available at: http://www.canadianmennonite.org/articles/unwrapping-sexuality, accessed: 10 February 2012.

Gray, Edward R. and Scott L. Thumma (1997): "The Gospel Hour: Liminality, Identity, and Religion in a Gay Bar," in *Contemporary American Religion: An Ethnographic Reader*, Penny Edgell Becker and Nancy L. Eiesland, Ed., AltaMira Press, Walnut Creek, CA, pp. 79-98.

Group With No Name (2010): *Notice of Motion*, available at: http://www.bmclgbt.org/2011NoticeofMotion.shtml, accessed: 13 December 2010.

Grimsrud, Ted (2010): "Welcoming But Not Affirming: The Logic of MC USA's 'Teaching Position' on Homosexuality," July 2010, *Mennonites and Homosexuality*, Peace Theology, available at: http://peacetheology.net/2010/07/04/mennonites-and-homosexuality/, accessed: 23 November 2010.

Hall, Stuart (1996): "Introduction: Who Needs 'Identity'?," in *Questions of Cultural Identity*, Stuart Hall and Paul duGay, Ed., Sage, London, pp.1-17.

Halperin, David M. (2002): *How to Do the History of Homosexuality*, University of Chicago Press, Chicago, IL.

Harmony: Mennonites for LGBT Inclusion (2012a): General meeting, Canadian Mennonite University Campus, Winnipeg, MB, 4 February 2011.

----- (2012b): "About Harmony," available at: http://mennoharmony.org/, accessed: 1 April 2012.

----- (2012c): "Resources and Information," available at: http://mennoharmony.org/resources/, accessed: 1 April 2012.

----- (2012d): "Resources and Information," available at: http://mennoharmony.org/resources/, accessed: 17 April 2012.

----- (2011a): "The Motion," available at: http://mennoharmony.org/get-involved/the-motion/, accessed: 8 February 2012.

----- (2011b): "Supporters of the Motion," 5 July 2011, available at: http://mennoharmony.org/get-involved/the-motion/supporters-of-the-motion/, accessed: 8 February 2012.

----- (2011c): "Speakers and Workshop Registration," available at: http://mennoharmony.org/resources/speaker/, accessed: 8 February 2012.

Heidebrecht, Doug (2003): "Continuing the Conversation," Canadian Conference of Mennonite Brethren Churches, Women in Ministry Leadership Study Conference, available at: http://www.mbconf.ca/home/events_and_conferences/learning_together/women_in_ministry_leadership/continuing_the_conversation_mennonite_brethren_and_women_in_church_leadership/, accessed: 17 August 2010, reprinted from *The Christian Leader*, Vol. 65, No. 5, May 2003, pp. 12-16.

Henry, Francis and Carol Tator (1999): "State Policy and Practices as Racialized Discourse: Multiculturalism, The Charter, and Employment Equity," in *Race and Ethnic Relations in Canada*, 2nd ed., Peter S. Li, Ed., Oxford University Press, Toronto, ON, pp.88-115.

Hope Mennonite Church (2012a): "Welcome Committee Roadmap," email from Welcome Committee to Hope Mennonite Church Mailing List, 24 February 2012.

----- (2012b): "Welcoming Journey," available at: http://hopemennonite.ca/WelcomingJourney, accessed: 1 April 2012.

Hunt, Lynn (1992): "Foucault's Subject in *The History of Sexuality*," in *Discourses of Sexuality: From Aristotle to AIDS*, Domna C. Stanton, Ed., University of Michigan, Ann Arbor, MI, pp.78-93

Johns, Loren L. (2010): "Homosexuality and the Mennonite Church," forthcoming in *Encyclopaedia of Homosexuality and Religion*, Greenwood Publishing Group, available at: http://www.ambs.edu/LJohns/H&MC.htm, accessed: 16 July 2010.

Jost, Lynn and Connie Faber (2002): "The History of the Mennonite Brethren," reprinted excerpts taken from *Family Matters: Discovering the Mennonite Brethren*, Kindred Publications, Winnipeg, MB, available at: http://www.mbconf.ca/home/about_us/our_story/#TheMennonites, accessed: 8 October 2010.

Kamitsuka, Margaret D. (2007): *Feminist Theology and the Challenge of Difference*, Oxford University Press, Oxford.

Katz, Jonathan (2007): *The Invention of Heterosexuality*, University of Chicago Press, Chicago, IL.

Kaufman, Edmund G. and Henry Poettcker (1990): "General Conference Mennonite Church (GCM)," in *Global Anabaptist Mennonite Encyclopaedia Online*, available at: http://www.gameo.org/encyclopedia/contents/G4647ME.html, accessed: 08 October 2010.

Kauffman, J. Howard (1994): "Power and Authority in Mennonite Families," *The Mennonite Quarterly Review*, Vol.68, No.3, pp.500-523.

Klingelsmith, Sharon (1980): "Women in the Mennonite Church, 1900-1930," *The Mennonite Quarterly Review*, Vol.54, No.3, pp.163-207.

Klassen, Doreen Helen (2008): " 'I wanted a life of my own': Creating a Single-woman Mennonite Identity in Mexico," *Journal of Mennonite Studies*, Vol. 26, pp.49-68.

Klassen, John (1986): "Women and the Family Among Dutch Anabaptist Martyrs," *Mennonite Quarterly Review*, Vol.60, No.4, pp.548-571.

Klassen, Pamela (1998): "Practicing Conflict: Weddings as Sites of Contest and Compromise," *The Mennonite Quarterly Review*, Vol.72, No.2, pp.225-241.

----- (1994): *Going to the Moon and the Stars: Stories of Two Russian Mennonite Women*, Wilfred Laurier University Press, Waterloo, ON.

Kobelt-Groch, Marion (1988): "Why did Petronella Leave Her Husband? Reflections on Marital Avoidance Among the Halberstadt Anabaptists," *The Mennonite Quarterly Review*, Vol.62, No.1, pp. 26-42.

Koppensteiner, Norbert (2009): *The Art of the Transpersonal Self: Transformation as Aesthetic and Energetic Practice*, Atropos, New York, NY.

Kosofsky Sedwick, Eve (2008): *Epistemology of the Closet*, 2nd ed., University of California Press, Berkeley, CA.

Kuefler, Matthew, Ed. (2006): *The Boswell Thesis: Essays on Christianity, Social Tolerance, and Homosexuality*, University of Chicago Press, Chicago, IL.

Li, Peter S. (1999): "Race and Ethnicity," in *Race and Ethnic Relations in Canada*, 2nd ed. Peter S. Li, Ed., Oxford University Press, Toronto, ON, pp.3-20.

Linton, Faith Elaine and Joyce Gladwell (2011a): "Letters to my sister," 1st instalment, *Canadian Mennonite*, Vol.15, No.21, 31 October 2011, available at: http://www.canadianmennonite.org/articles/letters-my-sister, accessed: 16 February 2012.

----- (2011b): "Letters to my sister," 2nd instalment, *Canadian Mennonite*, Vol.15, No.22, 14 November 2011, available at: http://www.canadianmennonite.org/articles/letters-my-sister-0, accessed: 16 February 2012.

----- (2011c): "Letters to my sister," 3rd instalment, *Canadian Mennonite*,

Vol.15, No.23, 28 November 2011, available at: http://www.canadianmennonite.org/articles/letters-my-sister-1, accessed: 16 February 2012.

Loewen, Royden (2008): "The Poetics of Peoplehood: Ethnicity and Religion among Canada's Mennonites," in *Christianity and Ethnicity in Canada*, Paul Bramadat and David Seljak, Ed., University of Toronto, Toronto, ON, pp. 330-364.

----- (2006): *Diaspora in the Countryside: Two Mennonite Communities in Mid-Twentieth Century Rural Disjuncture*, University of Toronto Press, Toronto, ON.

----- (1993): *Family, Church, and Market: A Mennonite Community in the Old and New Worlds, 1850-1930*, University of Toronto Press, Toronto, ON.

Lohrenz, J. H. and Harold Janz (2009): "Canadian Conference of Mennonite Brethren Churches," *Global Anabaptist Mennonite Encyclopaedia Online,* available at: http://www.gameo.org/encyclopedia/contents/C363ME.html, accessed: 08 October 2010.

McClintock Fulkerson, Mary (1997): "Gender-Being It or Doing it? The Church, Homosexuality, and the Politics of Identity," in *Que(e)rying Religion: A Critical Anthology*, Gary David Comstock and Susan E. Henking, Ed., The Continuum Publishing Company, New York, NY, pp.188-201.

McWhorter, Ladelle (2004): "Practicing Practicing," in *Feminism and the Final Foucault*, Dianna Taylor and Karen Vintges, Ed., University of Illinois Press, Urbana, IL, pp.143-162.

Mennonite Brethren Church of Manitoba (2010a): *Constitution of the Mennonite Brethren Church of Manitoba*, revised March 2010, available at: http://www.mbcm.ca/about/About%20MBCM%20-%20Constitution.pdf, accessed: 7 October 2010.

----- (2010b): *MBCM Assembly 2010*, available at: http://www.mbcm.ca/about/documents/AboutMBCM-Assembly2010Book_000.pdf, accessed: 7 October 2010.

----- (2010c): "Staff and Boards," available at: http://www.mbcm.ca/staff/directory.htm, accessed: 7 October 2010.

Mennonite Central Committee (2011): "MCC names directors of joint international program," News release, 18 July 2011, available at: http://www.mcc.org/stories/news/mcc-names-directors-joint-international-program, accessed: 16 April 2012.

----- (2010a): "Welcome," in *About MCC*, available at: http://mcc.org/about/welcome, accessed 23 August 2010.

----- (2010b): “Purpose and Vision Statements,” in *About MCC*, available at: http://mcc.org/purpose-vision-statements, accessed: 23 August 2010.

----- (2010c): “Leadership and Board,” in *About MCC*, available at: http://mcc.org/about/leadership, accessed: 23 August 2010.

----- (2010d): “Funding and Tax Exemption,” in *About MCC*, available at: http://mcc.org/about/funding, accessed: 23 August 2010.

----- (2010e): “Application Process,” in *Work and Serve with MCC*, available at: http://mcc.org/serve/apply, accessed: 23 August 2010.

----- (2010f): “Requirements,” in *Work and Serve with MCC/Application Process*, available at: http://mcc.org/serve/apply/requirements#expectations, accessed: 23 August 2010.

----- (2007): “Sexuality and Celibacy, Policy #152,” Human Resources/Binational, 12 April 2007.

Mennonite Central Committee Manitoba (2010): Memo Re: Update on MCC, from Peter Rempel MCC Manitoba Executive Director, 30 June 2010.

Mennonite Church Canada (2011a): *Being a Faithful Church 3: Summary Report*, September 2011, available at: http://www.mennonitechurch.ca/resourcecentre/FileDownload/14787/BFC_3_SummaryReportWeb.pdf, accessed: 15 February 2012.

----- (2010): “About Mennonite Church Canada Origins,” in *About Us*, available at: http://www.mennonitechurch.ca/about/origins.htm, accessed: 6 October 2010.

----- (2009): “Being a Faithful Church: Testing the Spirits in the Midst of Hermeneutical Ferment,” Mennonite Church Canada Assembly, 5-7 June 2009, available at: http://www.mennonitechurch.ca/resourcecentre/FileDownload/11298/Being_a_Faithful_Church_final_document_assembly_09_FINAL_as_of_March_20-to_pdf_.pdf, accessed: 16 February 2012.

----- (2007a): “Same Sex Unions and MC Canada,” News release, 23 May 2007, available at: http://www.mennonitechurch.ca/news/statements/ssm/, accessed: 6 August 2010.

----- (2007b): *Mennonite Church Canada Bylaws*, July 2007, available at: http://www.mennoniteechurch.ca/files/about/MCCanadaBylaws.pdf, accessed: 6 October 2010.

----- (2007c): “ACOM Discernment 1. Polity in Mennonite Church Canada, How did we get to where we are?,” Faith and Life Committee, available at:

http://www.mennonitechurch.ca/files/events/edmonton/6-DISCERNMENT.pdf, accessed: 19 November 2010, pp.68.

----- (1998): *Resolution on the Issue of Homosexuality*, Mennonite Church Assembly, Stratford, ON, available at: http://www.mennonitechurch.ca/news/statements/ssm/resolution98.htm, accessed: 4 August 2010.

----- (1995a): *Confession of Faith in a Mennonite Perspective- Article 19: Family, Singleness, and Marriage*, available at: http://www.mennonitechurch.ca/about/cof/art.19.htm, accessed: 9 August 2010.

----- (1995b): "Mennonite Church Council on Faith, Life and Strategy Statement Meaning of "Dialogue"", in *What Do We Mean By "Dialogue"*, Council of Faith, Life, and Strategy, November 1995, available at: http://www.mennonitechurch.ca/news/statements/ssm/dialogue.htm, accessed: 10 August 2010.

----- (1995c): "Agreeing and Disagreeing in Love: Commitments for Mennonites in Times of Disagreement," in *What Do We Mean By "Dialogue"*, March-April 1995, available at: http://www.mennonitechurch.ca/news/statements/ssm/dialogue.htm, accessed: 10 August 2010.

----- (1986): *Resolution on Human Sexuality*, General Conference Annual Sessions, 21-27 July 1986, Saskatoon, SK, available at: http://www.mennonitechurch.ca/news/statements/ssm/resolution86.htm, accessed: 4 August 2010.

Mennonite Church Eastern Canada (2004): "Pointing a Direction on Homosexuality," Executive Board, 25 February 2004, available at: http://www.ambs.edu/LJohns/MCECPointing.pdf, accessed: 19 November 2010.

Mennonite Church Manitoba (2010): "MCM Info," available at: http://www.mennonitchurch.mb.ca/mcm/index.htm, accessed: 7 October 2010.

Mennonite DNA Project, the (2010): "Purpose of the Project," available at: http://www.mennonitedna.com/, accessed: 24 May 2010.

Metcalfe, Dave (2010): "Faith, not DNA, at the heart of being Mennonite," in Viewpoints, *Canadian Mennonite*, Vol. 14, No.5, 8 March 2010.

Miller, Joseph S. (2000): "Appendix A: Who Are the Mennonites?," in *Mennonite Contributions to International Peacebuilding*, Cynthia Sampson and John Paul Lederach, Ed., Oxford University Press, Oxford, pp.275-280.

Miner, Jeff and John tyler Connoley (2002): *The Children are Free: Reexamining the Biblical Evidence on Same-Sex Relationships*, Jesus Metropolitan Community Church, Indianapolis, IN.

Moore, Gareth (2003): *A Question of Truth: Christianity and Homosexuality*, Continuum, London.

Morris, Rosalind (2010): "Introduction," in *Can the Subaltern Speak: Reflections on the History of an Idea*, Rosalind Morris, Ed., Columbia University Press, New York, NY, pp.1-20.

Morton, Mark (2010): "DNA does not a Mennonite make," in Viewpoints, *Canadian Mennonite*, Vol. 14, No.5, 8 March 2010.

Nagel, Joane (2003): *Race, Ethnicity, and Sexuality: Intimate Intersections, Forbidden Frontiers*, Oxford University Press, New York, NY.

Neitz, Mary Jo (2004): "Gender and Culture: Challenges to the Sociology of Religion," *Sociology of Religion*, Vol.65, No.4, Winter, pp.391-402

Nietzsche, Friedrich (2003): *The Genealogy of Morals*, Paul Negri, Ed.(series), and T.N.R. Rogers, Ed.(volume), Dover Publications, Mineola, NY.

Ontario Human Rights Commission (2010): *Ontario Human Rights Commission v. Christian Horizons*, News release, available at: http://www.ohrc.on.ca/en/resources/news/christianhorizons, accessed: 13 November 2010.

Outtatown Discipleship School (2010): "Outtatown Discipleship School," available at: http://outtatown.com/, accessed: 23 November 2010.

Pederson, Jane Marie (2002): "'She May Be Amish Now, But She Won't Be Amish Long': Anabaptist Women and Antimodernism" in *Strangers at Home: Amish and Mennonite Women in History*, Kimberly D. Schmidt *et al.*, Ed., John Hopkins University Press, Baltimore, MD, pp.339-363.

Penner, Carol (1992): "Content to Suffer: An Exploration of Mennonite Theology from the Context of Violence Against Women," in *Peace Theology and Violence Against Women*, Elizabeth G. Yoder, Ed., Occasional Papers No.16, Institute of Mennonite Studies, Elkhart, IN, pp.99-111.

----- (1991): "Mennonite Women's History: A Survey," *Journal of Mennonite Studies*, Vol.9, pp.122-135.

Peters, Ed (2008): "Sex: Pastoring on Dangerous Ground," in *Theodidaktos: Journal for EMC Theology and Education*, Vol. 3, No. 1, February 2008, pp.14-17, available at: http://www.emconference.ca/files/emc440/resources/theodidaktos-03-01.pdf, accessed: 13 August 2010.

Plett, Matthew F. (2007): "Complementarianism: The Biblical Middle," in *Theodidaktos: Journal for EMC Theology and Education*, Vol. 2, No. 1, June 2007, pp.16-22, available at: http://www.emconference.ca/files/emc440/resources/theodidaktos-02-01.pdf, accessed: 15 August 2010.

Price, Richard M. (1996): "The Distinctiveness of Early Christian Sexual Ethics," in *Christian Perspectives on Sexuality and Gender*, Elizabeth Stuart and Adrian Thatcher, Ed., Gracewing, Leominster, Herefordshire, pp.14-32.

Puri, Jyoti (1999): *Woman, Body, Desire in Post-Colonial India: Narratives of Gender and Sexuality*, Routledge, New York, NY.

Radford Ruether, Rosemary (2000): *Christianity and the Making of the Modern Family*, Beacon Press, Boston, MA.

Read, Jodi (2010a): *Affirming Mennonites: The Story of a Church*, private manuscript, University of Manitoba, Winnipeg, Canada.

Rich, Adrienne (1996): "Compulsory Heterosexuality and Lesbian Experience," in *Feminism and Sexuality: A Reader*, Stevi Jackson and Sue Scott, Ed., Columbia University Press, New York, NY, pp.130-143, originally published as A. Rich (1978): *Blood, Bread and Poetry*, Virago, London.

Regehr, T.D. (1996): *Mennonites in Canada 1939-1970: A People Transformed*, University of Toronto Press, Toronto, ON.

Schmidt, Kimberley D. (2001): "'Sacred Farming' or 'Working Out': The Negotiated Lives of Conservative Mennonite Farm Women," *Frontiers: A Journal of Women Studies*, Vol.22, No.1, pp.79-102.

Schmidt, Kimberly D. and Steven D. Reschly (2000): "A Women's History for Anabaptist Traditions: A Framework of Possibilities Possibly Changing the Framework," *Journal of Mennonite Studies*, Vol.18, pp.29-46.

Shaw, Teresa M. (2000): "Sex and Sexual Renunciation," in *The Early Christian World, Volumes 1-2*, Philip Francis Ester, Ed., Routledge, London, pp.401-421.

Showalter Kreider, Roberta (Ed) (2004): *The Cost of Truth: Faith Stories of Mennonite and Brethren Leaders and Those Who Might Have Been*, Strategic Press, Kulpsville, PA

----- (2003): *From Wounded Hearts: Faith Stories of Lesbian, Gay, Bisexual, and Transgender People and Those Who Love Them*, 2nd ed., Strategic Press, Kulpsville, PA.

----- (2002): *Together in Love: Faith Stories of Gay, Lesbian, Bisexual, and Transgender Couples*, Strategic Press, Kulpsville, PA.

Snyder, Arnold C. and Linda A. Huebert Hecht, Ed. (1996): *Profiles of Anabaptist Women: Sixteenth-Century Reforming Pioneers*, Volume 3: Studies of Women and Religion, Wilfred Laurier University Press, Waterloo, ON.

Spivak, Gayati Chakravorty (2006): "Can the Subaltern Speak?," in *The Post-Colonial Studies Reader*, 2nd ed., Bill Ashcroft, Gareth Griffiths and Helen Tiffin, Ed., Routledge, New York, NY, pp.28-37.

Stanton, Domna C. (1992): "Introduction: The Subject of Sexuality," in *Discourses of Sexuality: From Aristotle to AIDS*, Domna C. Stanton, Ed. University of Michigan, Ann Arbor, MI, pp.1-47.

Stern, Maria (2005): *Naming Security- Constructing Identity*, Manchester University Press, Manchester.

Stuart, Elizabeth (2003): *Gay and Lesbian Theologies: Repetitions with Critical Difference*, Ashgate Publishing Co, Hampshire, England.

Sullivan, Nikki (2003): *A Critical Introduction to Queer Theory*, New York University Press, New York, NY.

Swartley, Mary and Rhoda Keener, Ed. (1999): *She Has Done a Good Thing: Mennonite Women Leaders Tell Their Stories*, Herald Press, Scottsdale, PA.

Terichow, Gladys (2009): "Equipping Churches to Nurture Healthy Sexuality," *News*, Mennonite Central Committee, 9 December 2009, available at: http://mcc.org/stories/news/equipping-churches-nurture-healthy-sexuality, accessed: 28 October 2010.

UNESCO Chair for Peace Studies (2012): "Publications of the Chair," available at: http://www.uibk.ac.at/peacestudies/chair/publications.html, accessed: 21 March 2012.

Unger, Walter (2010): "Homosexuality: Blending Understanding, Compassion, and Conviction," *Mennonite Brethren Herald*, Vol. 49, No.6, June 2010, p.11.

Unrau, Ruth (2008): *Encircled: Stories of Mennonite Women*, orig. print 1986, Wipf & Stock Publishers, Eugene, OR.

Urry, James (2006): *Mennonites, Politics, and Peoplehood*, University of Manitoba Press, Winnipeg, MB.

----- (1999): "Gender, Generation and Social Identity in Russian Mennonite Society," *Journal of Mennonite Studies*, Vol.17, pp.95-106.

Valenti, Jessica (2009): *The Purity Myth: How America's Obsession with Virginity is Hurting Young American Women*, Seal Press, Berkeley, CA.

van Dijk, Teun A. Ed. (2007): "Editor's Introduction: The Study of Discourse: An Introduction: The Emergence of a New Cross-Discipline," in *Discourse Studies,* 5 vols, Sage Benchmarks in Discourse Studies, Sage, London, pp.xix-xlii, available at: http://www.discourses.org/OldArticles/The%20study%20of%20discourse.pdf, accessed: 5 August 2010.

Walker, Barbara G., Ed. (1983a): "Virgin Birth," in *The Women's Encyclopedia of Myths and Secrets*, HarperOne, New York, NY, pp.1048-1051.

----- (1983b): "Marriage," in *The Women's Encyclopedia of Myths and Secrets*, HarperOne, New York, NY, pp.585-597.

Weber, Annette (2006): "Feminist Peace and Conflict Theory," Virtual Peace Library of the UNESCO Chair for Peace Studies, Universität Innsbruck, available at: http://www.uibk.ac.at/peacestudies/downloads/peacelibrary/feministpeace.pdf, accessed: 29 June 2010.

Werner, Hans (2008): "'A Mild Form of Deviancy': Premarital Sex Among Early Manitoba Mennonites," *Journal of Mennonite Studies*, Vol.26, pp.143-159.

Wiesner-Hanks, Merry E. (2000): *Christianity and Sexuality in the Early Modern World: Regulating Desire, Reforming Practice*, Routledge, London.

Wilcox, Melissa M. (2003): *Coming Out in Christianity: Religion, Identity, and Community*, Indiana University Press, Bloomington, IN.

Wochrle, Lynne (1999): "Gender Studies," in *Encyclopaedia of Violence, Peace, & Conflict*, Vol.2, F-PE, Lester R. Kurtz and Jennifer Turpin, Ed., Academic Press, pp.41-51.

Yuval-Davis, Nira (2004): *Gender & Nation*, Sage Publications, London.

Interviews & Personal Correspondences

Bergen, Scott (2010a): Interview with the author, 17 October, Winnipeg, MB.

----- (2010b): Personal correspondence with the author, 28/31 October, Winnipeg, MB.

Borne, Ben (2012): Interview with the author, 5 April, Winnipeg, MB.

----- (2010a): Interview with the author, 15 October, Winnipeg, MB.

----- (2010b): Personal correspondence with the author, 21 October, Winnipeg, MB.

Brubacher, Mark (2010): Interview with the author, 6 October, Winnipeg, MB

da Silva Storie, Ilda (2012): Personal correspondence with the author, 18/19 April, Winnipeg, MB.

Dueck, Justin (2010): Interview with the author, 22 October, Winnipeg, MB.

Dyck, Barry and Roland Sawatsky (2010): Interview with the author, 27 October, Steinbach, MB.

Freed, Kirsten (2012a): Interview with the author, 13 April, Winnipeg, MB.

----- (2012b): Personal correspondence with the author, 14 April, Winnipeg, MB.

Lohvinenko, Ruth (2010): Personal correspondence with the author, 20 October, Winnipeg, MB.

Pityn, Kim (2010): Interview with the author, 30 September, Winnipeg, MB.

Read, Jodi (2010b): Interview with the author, 6 October, Winnipeg, MB.

----- (2010c): Personal correspondence with the author, 21/24 November, Winnipeg, MB.

Rempel, Peter (2010a): Interview with the author, 26 October, Winnipeg, MB.

----- (2010b): Personal correspondence with the author, 13/15 November, Winnipeg, MB.

Smith, Kerri (2010): Interview with the author, 13 October, Winnipeg, MB.

Tessmann, Henry (2010): Interview with author, 27 October, Winnipeg, MB.

Tippert, Michelle (2010): Interview with the author, 22 October, Winnipeg, MB.

Toews, Wesley (2010): Interview with the author, 4 October, Winnipeg, MB.

Warkentin, Val (2010): Interview with the author, 16 October, Winnipeg, MB.

Warkentin, Wark (2010): Interview with the author, 16 October, Winnipeg, MB.

----- (2011): Correspondence with Harmony: Mennonites for LGBT Inclusion mailing list, 13 July 2011, Winnipeg, MB.

Wiebe, Matt (2010): Interview with the author, 3 October, Winnipeg, MB.

Zacharias, Julia (2010): Interview with the author, 28 October, Winnipeg, MB.

Masters of Peace

edited by Prof. Dr. Wolfgang Dietrich (UNESCO Chair for Peace Studies)

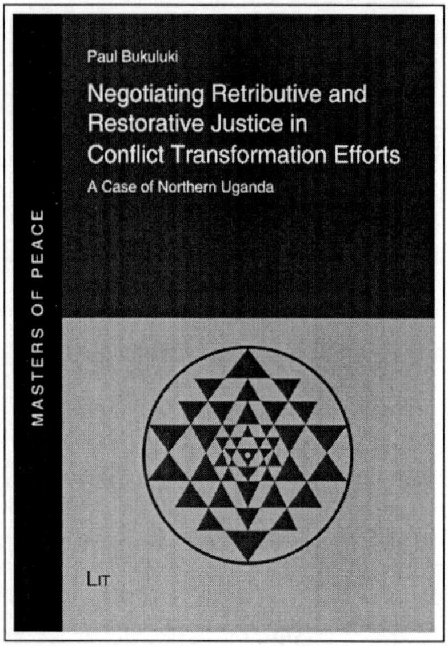

Paul Bukuluki
Negotiating Retributive and Restorative Justice in Conflict Transformation Efforts
A Case of Northern Uganda
This book is based on research carried out in Northern Uganda on the how people in post conflict negotiate between retributive and restorative justice in their quest for peace and justice. In their daily lives, restorative and retributive justices are constantly negotiated and interdependent. People pragmatically choose to apply aspects of each system to serve their goals. An ingenious hybrid of retributive and restorative justice is creatively used to facilitate the achievement of peace and justice. This accentuates the need for a pluralistic system of justice that combines legal and non-legal elements. Institutions like ICC need to adopt a pragmatic approach that works in a particular context.
Bd. 4, 2011, 144 S., 19,90 €, br., ISBN 978-3-643-90093-7

Natalia Lozano
Playing Music, Performing Resistance
The Dynamics of Resistance through Music in the Colombian South Pacific Coast
Could it be that playing marimba music is an act of resistance? Could it be a peace practice? Are musicians from the South Colombian Pacific coast performing peace by playing their vernacular music? These pages are concerned with those questions, and also with the reflections about the concept of peace that they trigger. Through an ethnographical research, this book attempts to grasp peace as an active practice of self-assertion exercised in the daily life of the musicians from a traditionally alienated region in Colombia.
Bd. 5, 2012, 136 S., 19,90 €, br., ISBN 978-3-643-90188-0

LIT Verlag Berlin – Münster – Wien – Zürich – London
Auslieferung Deutschland / Österreich / Schweiz: siehe Impressumsseite